MW00785685

Return to Kahiki

Between 1850 and 1907, Native Hawaiians sought to develop relationships with other Pacific Islanders, reflecting how they viewed not only
themselves as a people but their wider connections to Oceania and the
globe. Kealani Cook analyzes the relatively little known experiences
of Native Hawaiian missionaries, diplomats, and travelers, shedding
valuable light on the rich but understudied accounts of Hawaiians outside of Hawai'i. Native Hawaiian views of other islanders typically
corresponded with their particular views and experiences of the Native
Hawaiian past. The more positive their outlook, the more likely they
were to seek cross-cultural connections. This is an important intervention in the growing field of Pacific and Oceanic history and the study of
native peoples of the Americas, where books on indigenous Hawaiians
are few and far between. Cook returns the study of Hawai'i to a central
place in the history of cultural change in the Pacific.

Kealani Cook is Assistant Professor at the University of Hawai'i, West
O'ahu. He is a Kanaka Maoli/Native Hawaiian raised in Waimea,
Hawai'i Island.

Studies in North American Indian History

Editors

Frederick Hoxie, *University of Illinois, Urbana-Champaign*
Neal Salisbury, *Smith College*
Tiya Miles, *University of Michigan, Ann Arbor*
Ned Blackhawk, *Yale University*

This series is designed to exemplify new approaches to the Native American past. In recent years scholars have begun to appreciate the extent to which Indians, whose cultural roots extended back for thousands of years, shaped the North American landscape as encountered by successive waves of immigrants. In addition, because Native Americans continually adapted their cultural traditions to the realities of the Euro-American presence, their history adds a thread of non-Western experience to the tapestry of American culture. Cambridge Studies in North American Indian History brings outstanding examples of this new scholarship to a broad audience. Books in the series link Native Americans to broad themes in American history and place the Indian experience in the context of social and economic change over time.

Return to Kahiki

Native Hawaiians in Oceania

KEALANI COOK

University of Hawai'i, West O'ahu

CAMBRIDGE
UNIVERSITY PRESS

University Printing House, Cambridge CB2 8BS, United Kingdom

One Liberty Plaza, 20th Floor, New York, NY 10006, USA

477 Williamstown Road, Port Melbourne, VIC 3207, Australia

314-321, 3rd Floor, Plot 3, Splendor Forum, Jasola District Centre, New Delhi - 110025, India

79 Anson Road, #06-04/06, Singapore 079906

Cambridge University Press is part of the University of Cambridge.

It furthers the University's mission by disseminating knowledge in the pursuit of education, learning and research at the highest international levels of excellence.

www.cambridge.org
Information on this title: www.cambridge.org/9781316646991
DOI: 10.1017/ 9781108164436

© Kealani Cook 2018

This publication is in copyright. Subject to statutory exception and to the provisions of relevant collective licensing agreements, no reproduction of any part may take place without the written permission of Cambridge University Press.

First published 2018
First paperback edition 2019

A catalogue record for this publication is available from the British Library

Library of Congress Cataloging in Publication data
Names: Cook, Kealani, 1976– author.
Title: Return to Kahiki : Native Hawaiians in Oceania / Kealani Cook,
University of Hawai'i, West O'ahu.
Other titles: Native Hawaiians in Oceania
Description: Cambridge, United Kingdom; New York, NY: Cambridge University
Press, [2018] | Includes bibliographical references and index.
Identifiers: LCCN 2017043998 | ISBN 9781107195899 (hardback) |
ISBN 9781316646991 (paperback)
Subjects: LCSH: Hawaiians – Ethnic relations. | Hawaiians – Oceania – History. |
Missionaries – Hawaii – History. | Hawaii – History – 19th century. |
Hawaii – Foreign relations.
Classification: LCC DU624.65.C67 2017 | DDC 303.48/296909509034–dc23
LC record available at https://lccn.loc.gov/2017043998

ISBN 978-1-107-19589-9 Hardback
ISBN 978-1-316-64699-1 Paperback

Cambridge University Press has no responsibility for the persistence or accuracy of URLs for external or third-party internet websites referred to in this publication, and does not guarantee that any content on such websites is, or will remain, accurate or appropriate.

Contents

Acknowledgments

I want to thank all the people who made this work possible, but that would probably not be possible. So, I'll thank as many people as I can and hope that will suffice.

This past year the fields of Pacific history and Pacific studies lost Teresia Teaiwa. In addition to being an incredible scholar, she was also a passionate advocate for the importance of Pacific academics, a kind and supportive voice for graduate students and younger academics, and someone willing to speak truths, including uncomfortable ones, whenever it needed to be spoken. I, like many academics of my generation, owe her an incredible debt of gratitude for her contributions and for the example she set. I hope that we may live up to that example.

I want to thank my parents, Frank and Eluwene, who continued to love and support me even when I left a much more reasonable career as an engineer to go to school for ten more years. Thank you, Mom and Dad. I also want to thank my in-laws, Evelyn and Gilbert Tasaka, for all their kindness and support when I was writing the dissertation that eventually became this book.

I also want to thank my dissertation committee at the University of Michigan, Damon Salesa, Vince Diaz, Amy Stillman, and Sue Juster, who helped me not just to shape the dissertation this book is based on, but also for being kind, sane, and having a sense of humor through the process. I've heard enough horror stories to know I was very fortunate to have you four.

I also owe a debt to the various people who helped me locate resources for this work, including Iokepa Salazar, Luʻukia Archer, David Forbes, and Lorenz Gonshor. I would also like to thank the staff at the

Hawaiian Historical Society Archives, the Hawaiian Mission Children's Society Archive, the Hawai'i State Archives, and the Bishop Museum for their considerable aid. I especially wish to thank Kamaoli Kuwada and Paul Meredith, whose discussion on *Maoliworld.com* about John T. Baker's letters led to the research that informed the final third of this book. Paul also graciously shared with me his translations of Baker's interview in *Te Pipiwharauroa*. Finally, I would like to thank Puakea Nogelmeier for allowing me to use the transcribed and translated version of James Kekela's letters, that he, Kamaoli Kuwada, and Nakila Steele put together for *Awaiaulu.org*.

In addition, I would like to thank several people who listened to me ramble on about this over the past ten years and at some point provided support, direction, and the occasional confused looks that told me I needed to rethink things. In addition to those listed above, this includes David Chang, Ty Tengan, Noelani Arista, Noenoe Silva, Ron Williams, Nancy Morris, Rochelle Fonoti, Anna Christianson, Alice Te Punga Sommerville, Aroha Harris, Jessica Kanoa, Keith Camacho, Kehaulani Kauanui, Kerri Inglis, Kamana Beamer, Glenn Petersen, and Joel Tannenbaum. One of these people is not real. A dollar to whoever figures out who that is.

I would also like to thank Aroha Harris, Ngarino Ellis, and Melissa Williams for bringing me to Auckland for a talk on James Tamatoa Baker and for all their hospitality while there. I would also like to thank Arini Loader and Jamee Maaka for their hospitality in Wellington. I hope I can return the favor one day.

Several people have read drafts of this book during my attempts to transform it from a dissertation into a book, and I would like to thank them for their insights and patience: Fred Hoxie, Sara Lee, David Chang, Kiri Sailiata, Dean Saranillo, Lani Teves, and Rebecca Karol. I would also like to thank the anonymous reviewers of the manuscript, who had several comments and pieces of advice that were incredibly helpful.

I also want to thank anyone who is still reading this even though I started every paragraph with some variation of "I also want to thank ..." Thanks for sticking around, I promise the writing gets a touch better once the actual book starts. Not that much better, but better nonetheless.

I also want to thank Louise McReynolds, who convinced me that I should go for my PhD and suggested applying to Michigan. Without her I never would have gone through with any of this. She also once told me my writing was as wooden as the ships I wrote about (it was 2003, pirates were in that year). I hope she sees some improvement.

I need to thank all the people at Mad Tiger Jiujitsu on Oʻahu and Tsugiashi Do Jiujitsu on Maui, who helped keep me sane during the process of writing this. When you're exhausted and someone is putting you in a triangle choke, you feel far less stressed about the organization of whatever chapter you are working on.

I would also like to thank each generation of scholars who fought for the space for indigenous histories to be told and for the generations following who will expand and improve upon that foundation. I hope that my work lives up to the expectations set by those who came before and that future generations might find something within it worth building upon.

Most importantly, I would like to thank Robyn Tasaka. Her love and advice helped me push through the tough spots. She was always there to talk over a problem, reassure me when I had writing paralysis, tell me to stop being crazy when I was scared to read people's comments, or to go for coffee when I needed to get out of the house. I would also like to apologize to my children, Olive Keala and Frances Hoʻopili, from whom I stole many weekend afternoons in 2017 to run off and work on this book.

Abbreviations Used in Footnotes

ABCFM   *American Board of Commissioners for Foreign Missions*
BMA   *The Bishop Museum Library and Archives*
CCM   *Cabinet Council Minutes*
CPIPR   *US Senate, Committee on Pacific Islands and Porto Rico*
ECO   *Executive Correspondence, Outgoing*
FDC   *Fornander Davis Collection*
FOEX   *Foreign Office and Executive Collection*
GRCC   *The George Robert Carter Collection*
HBCFM   *Hawaiian Board of Commissioners for Foreign Missions*
HEA   *Hawaiian Evangelical Association Archives*
HHS   *Hawaiian Historical Society*
HMCS   *Hawaiian Mission Children's Society*
HSA   *Hawai'i State Archive*
JLA   *Journal of Legislative Assembly*
JSE   *Journal of the Samoan Embassy*
OHA   *Office of Hawaiian Affairs*
RJKC   *Reverend James Kekela Correspondence and Articles*

Introduction

Mai Kahiki Mai: Out from Kahiki

They came from the south. We do not know exactly when they came, why they came, or how many of them there were, but we know they came from the south. We know they came from a millennia-old tradition of Austronesian voyaging, discovery, and settlement that had colonized all the inhabitable lands of Oceania. They brought with them a set of agricultural practices and knowledge, developed over thousands of miles and hundreds of generations of voyaging into a transportable agricultural toolkit that would allow them to survive in a wide range of island ecosystems. They brought, either on the initial voyage or later ones, the plants and animals that provided not just their food, but their containers, medicine, and cloth. They brought kukui to fuel their lamps and ʻawa,[1] to ease the weariness and pains of daily life.

They brought with them their gods, genealogies, and heroes; their arts and sciences; their knowledge of the seas and the skies; their dances, chants, feather work, and carving. They brought their language, the Eastern Polynesian line of the broader Austronesian language group, which stretches from Madagascar to Rapa Nui. They brought with them all the things that would one day define so much of Native Hawaiian culture, and of Native Hawaiians as a people, but they were not Native

---

[1] Following on the work of other historians working on Oceanic and indigenous topics, I have opted not to italicize terms from Oceanic and indigenous languages, as these are not foreign languages but rather indigenous languages of Oceania. When the terms are italicized it is only when specifically discussing a word or term as a word or term. For instance, ʻawa is not capitalized in the preceding text, but it would be capitalized in a discussion of the difference between the Hawaiian word *ʻawa* and the Tahitian term *kava*.

Hawaiians. The history of Hawai'i starts not with Native Hawaiians, but with islanders from distant parts of Oceania.

Over the ensuing centuries, however, their descendants would become what we now call Native Hawaiians, Kānaka Maoli, Kānaka 'Ōiwi, Kānaka Hawai'i, or more simply just Kānaka.[2] Cultural and social innovations, variations in ritual and worship and language, and most importantly a strong cultural connection to the land and seas of their new home would define them as a separate people from their migratory ancestors. They would become the Lāhui Hawai'i, the Hawaiian people. New variations of agricultural practices adapted to the lands and waters of their new homes allowed them to first survive and then thrive. They developed vast networks of loko i'a (fishponds), lo'i kalo (taro paddies), and dryland 'uala (sweet potato) farming that allowed them to feed a population that eventually surpassed that of many of the other islands their ancestors had settled.

The great distances involved and the lack of need for persistent travel meant that voyaging to the south eventually either ceased completely or became so rare as to take on an almost mythic quality.[3] As David Chang has argued, however, the lack of direct communication should not be mistaken for a lack of understanding that other lands and other peoples existed beyond the horizon. The people of Hawai'i would maintain numerous mo'olelo (oral histories and legends) regarding voyages to and from Hawai'i. These mo'olelo and other forms of oral culture often retained the names of important places from the south, such as references

---

[2] The terms *Native Hawaiian*, *Kanaka Hawai'i*, *Kanaka Māoli* (true/real person), and *Kanaka 'Ōiwi* (native person) are all in common usage to refer specifically to the indigenous people of Hawai'i. Except in specific cases when Kanaka (singular) or Kānaka (plural) might need to be clarified, I have chosen to primarily but not exclusively use the term *Kanaka/Kānaka* or *Kānaka Hawai'i* throughout this text. I have also chosen to use *Hawaiian* as an adjective to describe things explicitly tied to Hawai'i as a whole, rather than just *Kānaka*, such as Hawaiian history or Hawaiian politics. I have used *Kanaka* as an adjective to describe things related to Kānaka Maoli as a people, such as Kanaka missionaries being specifically missionaries who are Kānaka. Finally, I have chosen to use *'Ōiwi* to modify things specifically tied to or stemming from Ka Wā 'Ōiwi Wale, the time before Cook's arrival that was exclusively shaped and directed by Kānaka, such as 'Ōiwi value systems or 'Ōiwi agricultural methods.

[3] Hard archeological evidence of such voyages is scarce, but by its nature archeology is much better suited to tracing broad shifts in a society rather than specific isolated journeys. There is some hard evidence of such journeys, however, most notably Petroglyph-styles specific to Hawai'i that have been found in Tonga. Shane Egan and David V. Burley, "Triangular Men on One Very Long Voyage: The Context and Implications of a Hawaiian-Style Petroglyph Site in the Polynesian Kingdom of Tonga," *The Journal of the Polynesian Society* 118, no. 3 (2009): 209–232.

to Bora Bora as the original home of Pele and her family. As time passed however, the specific details of these stories sometimes faded into obscurity, and Kahiki (Tahiti) soon dominated Kanaka collective memories of the South. In addition to specifically signifying Tahiti, the term *Kahiki* became a catchall term for all foreign lands. The kolea, or golden plover, for instance, frequently wintered in Hawai'i but laid its eggs elsewhere. Not knowing where exactly that elsewhere was, Kānaka described its homeland simply as Kahiki, somewhere beyond the waters of Hawai'i.[4]

In these mo'olelo, Kahiki remained a place of significant mana, the term used in Hawai'i and other parts of Oceania for a mix of power, authority, and prestige. Indeed, the lack of regular contact may have even inflated the sense of Kahiki as a place of mana. Stories of the arrival of the priest Pa'ao and his chief Pili, for instance, remained prominent on Hawai'i Island, as did the story of the arrival of the female god/chief Pele and her relatives. These mo'olelo and the genealogies related to them explicitly connected the people of Hawai'i to their ancestral homelands, granting the descendants of these lines tremendous mana within the islands. The ruling chiefs of Hawai'i Island and the later monarchs of the Hawaiian kingdom based their authority in part on genealogies that traced their ancestry to Pili, while powerful kāhuna traced their own lines back to Pa'ao. Similarly, O'ahu chiefly lines traced themselves to La'amaikahiki (La'a from Kahiki), another chief from the south. Families in Puna and Ka'u still trace their lineages, familial responsibilities, and mana back to Pele, whose epic story includes her family's migration from Bora Bora.

This period of isolation, which historians and others often define as "Pre-Contact Hawai'i," might also be referred to as *Ka Wā 'Ōiwi Wale*, the time that is exclusively 'Ōiwi, following the practice of the late Kanalu Young. Young developed the term *'Ōiwi Wale*, as a way of defining this period not by the lack of contact with foreigners but rather by recognizing, "the foundational nature of seventeen centuries of settlement and societal development by Native Hawaiian kūpuna [ancestors] before foreign arrival."[5] While some may assume that such a period of isolation would result in a static and potentially moribund civilization, Ka Wā

---

[4] See David Chang, "Looking Out from Hawai'i's Shore: The Exploration of the World Is the Inheritance of Native Hawaiians," *The World and All the Things upon It: Native Hawaiian Geographies of Exploration* (Minneapolis: University of Minnesota Press, 2016), 13–20.

[5] Kanalu G. Terry Young, *Rethinking the Native Hawaiian Past* (New York: Garland Publishing, 1998), 20.

'Ōiwi Wale was still an era of social, cultural, and environmental changes in Hawai'i, albeit changes exclusively developed without outside foreign interference or contributions.

In 1778, Ka Wā 'Ōiwi Wale came to an end when the people of Kaua'i spotted an unusual pair of ships approaching the island, ships arriving not from another island in the chain, but from foreign shores. The men aboard those ships must have struck the Kaua'i people as incredibly strange, in both behavior and appearance. Their speech no doubt struck the Kaua'i people as unusual as well. At times, it would have been absolutely unintelligible, yet at other times the strangers spoke words and phrases in a language quite similar to their own, Tahitian to be exact. These men and their ship had not only come from Kahiki in the generic sense of coming from a foreign place, but they had also spent time on this journey and others in Tahiti. Indeed, Tahiti had been their last stop before Kaua'i. Among this group of partial Tahitian speakers was the expedition's leader, Captain James Cook, whose arrival in Hawai'i launched the islands into an era of rapid demographic, political, social, and cultural change.

RELATIONSHIPS WITH KAHIKI, RELATIONS WITH THE PAST

While Cook's arrival opened the way for a flood of ideas, people, and objects into Hawai'i, it also opened paths for ideas, people, and objects to flow out of Hawai'i. As David Chang has explored in *The World and All the Things upon It,* Kānaka Maoli, like other Oceanic peoples, eagerly explored the world opened by interactions with European and American shipping. Within a generation, Kānaka Maoli had traveled to Europe, the Americas, Asia, and, of course, to other parts of Oceania.

This book examines how Kānaka Maoli understood and developed relationships with other Oceanic peoples as a part of a broader effort to ensure the survival and success of the lāhui in the face of social, political, and cultural changes. These relationships with other Oceanic peoples were inherently colored by Kanaka understandings of their connections to Ka Wā 'Ōiwi Wale. More specifically, Kānaka often viewed their relationships with other Oceanic peoples through the same set of lenses – positive, negative, or somewhere in between – that they viewed their own past.

Nineteenth-century Hawai'i was the site of a prolonged cultural and social conflict over the proper role of Ka Wa 'Ōiwi Wale in shaping the

Hawaiian present and future. A simplified version of this conflict might be posited as being between two extreme visions, a future Hawaiian culture and society that in all possible ways reflected Hawaiʻi during Ka Wā ʻŌiwi Wale versus a future completely free of all traces of Ka Wā ʻŌiwi Wale. In reality, few Kānaka held either extreme view, as neither could be mistaken as a practical option by the mid-nineteenth century. Disagreements over historical memory tended to revolve around the degree to which ʻŌiwi Wale culture might/should remain relevant in Hawaiʻi and what types of culture and knowledge should be practiced or preserved.

Those who leaned toward distancing themselves and the Hawaiian future from the Hawaiian past also tended to follow the teachings and the rhetoric of the American Congregationalist missionaries who arrived in 1821. These missionaries deemed anything from Ka Wa ʻŌiwi Wale, and indeed anything outside of their rigid worldview, to be full of naʻaupō (ignorance and inner-darkness). Such individuals, and their Kanaka followers, typically looked to Congregational religion and an idealized version of American culture to define the Hawaiian future, a future bathed in foreign naʻauao (inner light or enlightenment). To further complicate things, even those Kānaka who sought to retain connections to Ka Wā ʻŌiwi Wale tended to adopt the term *na ʻauao* with respect to the mastery of foreign knowledge and often shared with their more rigid Congregationalist brethren a sense of pride in their shared mastery of foreign naʻauao.

In terms of broader understandings of time, another way of positioning these debates may be through two opposing visions of humanity's position relative to time. In the common European perspective of time, humanity stood with its back to the past, looking forward to the future. In the traditional Hawaiian view, and in much of Oceania, humanity stood with its face to the past, which they described as the time *ma mua*, in front of them. Through tracing the past and understanding it, one could then chart the path of the future, which sat unknown and unpredictable ma hope, or behind one's back. While either perspective can be used to either embrace or deny the past, the European/American "face the future" perspective certainly worked better for those who understood Ka Wā ʻŌiwi Wale as Ka Wā Naʻaupō, the time of ignorance. Coming from such a perspective, they would also be inclined to create a Hawaiian future as far from that past as possible. For those who wished to design a Hawaiian future guided by values, practices, and knowledge rooted in Ka Wā ʻŌiwi Wale, the "face to the past" perspective had far greater resonance. While such a perspective could easily incorporate foreign influences as part of the global past, the Hawaiian past remained the foundation for the Hawaiian present and future.

On a practical basis, nineteenth-century Kanaka views of their past not only differed from individual to individual but also from situation to situation. As Marie Alohalani Brown has shown in her work on John Papa Iʻi, Iʻi's Congregationalist beliefs led him to often portray the sexual and religious culture of the pre-Christian past as inherently naʻaupō. Yet when it came to his understanding of his personal role in the world, he strongly maintained an ʻŌiwi Wale-derived sense of personal duty to the royal family as a kahu or caretaker.[6] John Tamatoa Baker,[7] the Kanaka/Tahitian/British businessman and politician whose story forms the final chapters of this book, was part of King David Kalākaua's Hale Nauā, an organization dedicated in large part to pursuing the wisdom of ʻŌiwi Wale culture. At the same time, he was an agricultural entrepreneur constantly deriding other Kānaka for failing to move from subsistence-plus farming into cash cropping and a full-throated embrace of capitalist ethics. Class, religion, education, gender, nationalism, and politics all played their role in shaping how individual Kānaka might understand and value the ʻŌiwi Wale past in any situation.

Nineteenth-century Kānaka's conflicted and conflicting views of Ka Wā ʻŌiwi Wale are especially important in understanding their relationships to other Oceanic peoples because, then and now, many Kānaka tend to understand other islanders through the lens of the Hawaiian past. The Hawaiian past, after all, is rooted in and built on a broader Oceanic past, leading to a logical association between other Oceanians and the Hawaiian past. Furthermore, by the mid-nineteenth century most Kānaka, saw themselves as more advanced than their fellow Oceanic peoples in terms of their collective naʻauao, defined as the acquisition and mastery of European/American knowledge and material wealth. Between this sense of Hawaiian exceptionalism and their southern roots, many Kānaka developed an understanding of other islanders as being even closer to Ka Wā ʻŌiwi Wale than Kānaka were.

Thus Kānaka perspectives on their own past heavily influenced their understanding and relationships with other Oceanic peoples. Those most eager to turn their back on Ka Wā ʻŌiwi Wale were also the most likely to dismiss, condemn, and separate themselves from other islanders as

---

[6] Marie Alohalani Brown, *Facing the Spears of Change* (Honolulu: University of Hawaiʻi Press, 2016).

[7] Some sources also refer to him as John Timoteo Baker.

part of that past. Those who were most likely to embrace Ka Wā ʻŌiwi Wale as an essential component of the Hawaiian future were also the most likely to embrace other islanders and their collective origins. While still frequently espousing Hawaiian exceptionalism based in a sense of a superior Hawaiian mastery of the naʻauao, they also frequently promoted relationships based on kinship and a shared Oceanic past. In an age where people across Oceania faced common threats from foreign empires as well as common opportunities stemming from easier access to a rapidly changing nineteenth-century world, such relationships would be vital to the futures of all the peoples of Oceania.

HAWAIIAN HISTORIOGRAPHY AND KA WĀ ʻŌIWI WALE

These arguments over the meaning of the Hawaiian past and relationships to other islanders are rooted in two separate but intertwined bodies of academic literature, namely Kanaka-centered histories of nineteenth-century Hawaiʻi and the work loosely connected under the umbrella of Native Pacific cultural studies. In terms of Hawaiian historiography, the arguments presented in this book build upon a larger body of work examining nineteenth-century Kānaka's negotiations between ʻŌiwi Wale ideas, institutions, and values and those coming from abroad. Such work has largely been undertaken as a way of correcting a historiography that for nearly a century had served up little more than apologetics for American imperial expansion into and rule over the islands.

While thorough and professional in their own way, many of these older historians such as Ralph Kuykendall and Gavan Daws relied largely on English-language sources and a set of cultural and disciplinary biases that favored the perspectives of European/American empires over those of Native peoples.[8] The more recent wave of Kanaka-focused histories, however, have employed Hawaiian-language sources as well as Kanaka-centered analytical frameworks to reexamine Kānaka and foreign motivations for implementing nineteenth-century changes; the methods Kānaka and foreigners used to institute such changes; and the results of these changes upon the Lāhui Hawaiʻi. One of the central currents running through such work has been the degree to which such changes

---

[8] See Ralph S. Kuykendall, *The Hawaiian Kingdom*, 3 vols. (Honolulu: University of Hawaii Press, 1938–1967); Gavan Daws, *Shoal of Time: A History of the Hawaiian Islands* (New York: MacMillan, 1968).

were either adapted and adopted by Kānaka versus being implemented upon Kānaka through coercion and trickery. By no coincidence this often corresponds to how individual historians also portray the results of such changes.

Looking specifically at monographs on Hawaiian history, the start of this historiographic period can be traced to 1992 and Lilikala Kameʻeleihiwa's *Native Land and Foreign Desires: Pehea Lā e Pono Ai?*, which examines the disastrous effects of European/American diseases, cultural beliefs, and land tenure in eroding many of the foundational values/metaphors that undergirded much of ʻŌiwi Wale culture. Though by no means dismissive of Kanaka agency, Kameʻeleihiwa's work underscores how foreign interlopers actively sought to undermine the relationships that informed Kanaka society, such as that between the makaʻāinana (the people of the land), the aliʻi (the chiefs), and the ʻāina (land). Jon Osorio's *Dismembering Lāhui* presents a similar argument regarding the Hawaiian kingdom's adoption of European political practices. Osorio, however, also examines Kanaka adoption of and adaptation to the system and their success in employing parliamentary democracy and party politics in the 1870s and 1880s. Other scholars have focused more on Kanaka efforts to meld together ʻŌiwi and foreign practices and ideas in ways that allowed for the preservation of ʻŌiwi ideas, culture, and independence. Noenoe Silva's *Aloha Betrayed* and Kamana Beamer's *No Mākou Ka Mana*, for instance, examine Kanaka cultural and political efforts to preserve and act upon ʻŌiwi logics and values while employing foreign systems and technologies.[9]

While these changes have been the primary focus of these works, one of the underlying issues that these monographs have addressed, either explicitly or implicitly, has been the ongoing conflict throughout the nineteenth century over the value of the Hawaiian past, and particularly the proper role of Ka Wā ʻŌiwi Wale in determining the Hawaiian future. The cultural, political, and social norms and institutions being replaced, after all, were rooted in Ka Wā ʻŌiwi Wale. Changes in Hawaiian culture, for instance, required those carrying out and negotiating those changes to determine what elements of Ka Wā ʻŌiwi Wale should remain, a

---

[9] Lilikala Kameʻeleihiwa, *Native Land and Foreign Desires: Pehea Lā e Pono Ai?* (Honolulu, HI: Bishop Museum Press, 1992); Jon K. K. Osorio, *Dismembering Lāhui: A History of the Hawaiian Nation to 1887* (Honolulu: University of Hawaiʻi Press, 2002); Noenoe Silva, *Aloha Betrayed: Native Hawaiian Resistance to American Colonialism* (Durham, NC: Duke University Press, 2004); Kamana Beamer, *No Mākou ka Mana: Liberating the Nation* (Honolulu, HI: Kamehameha Publishing, 2014).

determination often informed by the general positive and negative associations one had with that past.

Because of the centrality of the Hawaiian past in defining the institutions and norms being challenged, altered, and often attacked in the nineteenth century, one can even map out many of the key moments and trends of the conflict over the Hawaiian past through the existing historiography. One of the earliest and most significant changes, for instance, came in 1819 when Liholiho, Kamehameha II, ended the kapu system under considerable pressure from Kaʻahumanu and Keōpūolani, the most influential of Kamehameha the Great's queens. Due to her genealogy, Keōpūolani was one of the most sacred persons in the islands as well as being Liholiho's birth mother. Kaʻahumanu, though of lower genealogy, was one of the most politically powerful figures in the kingdom based both on her familial connections and her considerable political skill. Kameʻeleihiwa presents this event as a result of a loss of religious faith brought about by sustained foreign contact, particularly depopulation from introduced diseases.[10]

The turning point in *Native Lands* comes less than a year after the end of the kapu system with the arrival of Congregationalist missionaries from the American Board of Commissioners for Foreign Missions (ABCFM), a group whose religious and nationalist devotion led to a tremendous distaste for anything remotely related to the pre-Christian Hawaiian past. Lead missionary Hiram Bingham, recalling his first memories of Hawaiʻi in 1820, wrote, "Some of our number, with gushing tears, turned away from the spectacle. Others, with a firmer nerve, continued their gaze, but were ready to exclaim, 'Can these be human beings?'" Though Bingham would go on to answer in the affirmative, it was only in stripping away all vestiges of their nativeness that such humanity might be revealed.[11] Already introduced to the Hawaiian language by Kanaka converts living in New England, the missionaries soon began to use the Hawaiian language to try and create a wedge between Kānaka and their past.[12] As noted earlier they made frequent use of the terms *na ʻauao* and *na ʻaupō* to refer to enlightenment and ignorance, respectively. The former was associated entirely with New England Congregationalist values and ideas while anything remotely connected to the Ka Wā ʻŌiwi Wale

[10] Kameʻeleihiwa, *Native Land and Foreign Desires*, 74–81.
[11] Hiram Bingham, *A Residence of Twenty-One Years in the Sandwich Islands* (Canandaigua, NY: H. D. Goodwin, 1855), 81.
[12] Kameʻeleihiwa, *Native Land and Foreign Desires*, 137–142.

they decried as naʻaupō. These concepts of naʻaupō and naʻauao would remain relevant to Hawaiian discussions of the proper role of Ka Wā ʻŌiwi Wale throughout the nineteenth century and efforts to define, redefine, and control those terms were among some of the hardest fought rhetorical battles of the nineteenth century.

Despite tense relations with the mission initially, first Keōpūolani and then Kaʻahumanu converted, in no small part due to the largely unrecognized work of Tahitian missionaries Auna and Taua. After conversion Kaʻahumanu used New England–style Congregationalism to create a state religion that filled the religious and legal void left by the end of the kapu system, strengthening her social and cultural position over a kingdom she already exercised effective political control over. Kameʻeleihiwa has shown how the death toll and the desire for a new state religion soon led to rapid conversions to a religion that promised eternal life in exchange for denying and deriding the Native past. According to both Kameʻeleihiwa in *Native Land* and Osorio in *Dismembering Lāhui*, the perceived naʻauao of Western political and diplomatic traditions and the growing mission-promoted portrayal of Native traditions and the Native past as naʻaupō led many Kanaka elites to follow the lead of Haole advisors in creating new political, legal, and economic systems.[13]

By no coincidence these systems also favored the interests of Europeans and Americans in Hawaiʻi. Kameʻeleihiwa examines the way that foreign advisors under Kamehameha III broke land-based reciprocal relationships between the aliʻi and the makaʻāinana through the "Great Māhele" in 1848, which created private property. This, by design, removed the incentives of the makaʻāinana and the aliʻi to support one another economically, a problem further exacerbated by allowing foreign investors to buy land in 1850. Osorio argues that governments set up under the constitutions of 1840 and 1852 came about as a direct result of Haole discourses that "continually subjected [Kānaka] to the pronouncements of their difference and inferiority, which both enabled and validated their dispossession." These pronouncements of inferiority relied heavily on dismissals and condemnations of the Hawaiian past and, by extension, traces of that past among contemporary Kānaka. The governments set up under these constitutions, as well as the decision to allow foreigners to vote and hold office in Hawaiʻi through a conveniently rigorless

[13] H. E. Maude, "The Raiatean Chief Auna and the Conversion of Hawaii," *The Journal of Pacific History* 8 (1973), 188–191; Kameʻeleihiwa, *Native Land and Foreign Desires*, 152–164, 174–192.

naturalization process, provided the relatively small Haole population with a significantly outsized political voice, which they used primarily to benefit their economic, social, and political interests.[14]

Alohalani Brown and Kanalu Young have examined more specifically how tensions over the role of Ka Wā 'Ōiwi Wale affected the kaukau ali'i, a lower order of chiefs who served the ali'i nui as personal caretakers, guardians, advisors, and resource managers. Young's *Rethinking the Hawaiian Past* follows changes in the lives of the kaukau ali'i, starting with the era of the kapu system, through the immediate years after the end of the system, and into the political world of the kingdom under a constitutional monarchy. Brown's *Facing the Spears of Change*, follows a relatively similar path but does so through the life of prominent kaukau ali'i statesman John Papa 'Ī'ī. In both cases the authors argue that despite massive changes such as those described by Osorio and Kame'eleihiwa, the underlying cultural role of the kaukau ali'i, to act as servants and advisors of the ali'i nui, remained intact. The details of such service differed tremendously of course, as seen in 'Ī'ī's changing role from guardian of Liholiho's spittoon to a member of the House of Nobles under King Kauikeaouli. The underlying role of the kaukau ali'i, however, the ethic of their class, remained unchanged, reflecting the ethics and values of the Hawaiian past while their specific services reflected a changing time.

Other relationships, however, changed far more drastically. Sally Engle Merry's *Colonizing Hawai'i* provides a number of examples of how an American-style legal system radically reconfigured society and culture in nineteenth-century Hilo, including a particularly relevant discussion of sexual norms and gender roles. In part these changes were brought on by a privileging of foreign visions of law, sex, and gender rather than understandings rooted in Ka Wā 'Ōiwi Wale. Their adoption and enforcement, meanwhile, also acted to further dismiss the values of Ka Wā 'Ōiwi Wale. The imposition of Western law brought with it an imposition of foreign understandings of sex, essentially outlawing any sex outside of state- or church-sanctioned heterosexual marriage. Laws defining the legitimacy of children and parentage provided a legal assault on more inclusive 'Ōiwi conceptions of parentage, while Western-style marriage gave men legal control over their wives' independence, labor, property, and sexuality. Where once men and women could decide to create or dissolve sexual and romantic partnerships at will, they now found

---

[14] Kame'eleihiwa, *Native Land and Foreign Desires*, 298–305; Osorio, *Dismembering Lāhui*, 252.

themselves, particularly the women, locked into relationships sanctioned and enforced by the state. As shown through the sheer number of people arrested for and found guilty of "crimes" such as adultery, bigamy, and abandonment, many Kānaka rejected such ideas, preferring to maintain individual control over their sexual and romantic activities rather than surrender them to the state. Nevertheless, enforcement of such laws reinforced the missionaries' insistence that Kanaka sexual practices and relationships were proof of a lingering naʻaupō that needed to be extinguished, equating nonconformity with the supposed evils of Ka Wā ʻŌiwi Wale.[15]

Many Kānaka challenged such changes, often explicitly or implicitly rooting their challenges in the authority of the Hawaiian past. In 1819, for instance, Liholiho's cousin Kekuaokalani declared the end of the kapu system as an unacceptable rejection of the Hawaiian past, and specifically of the religious legacy of King Kamehameha the Great. He led an army to battle against Kaʻahumanu's supporters despite overwhelming odds, choosing to die in battle rather than abandon the old system.[16] Kameʻeleihiwa and Osorio have both shown how Kanaka petitioners expressed their dissent against a number of foreign-driven changes during the reign of Kamehameha III, citing their well-grounded fears that such changes threatened the historical relationships that formed the basis for the lāhui. Repeated explanations by the king's representatives failed to quell the fears of the petitioners, leading them to respond with point-by-point rebuttals in later petitions. The use of written petitions and literacy in general showed a population that was by no means reluctant to adopt and utilize foreign innovations, but was eager to preserve elements of Ka Wā ʻŌiwi Wale still vital to their contemporary lives.[17]

On a more general note, during the period between 1820 and 1850 many Kānaka pushed back against mission-led efforts to reject Hawaiian culture and practices simply by defining them as relevant parts of modern Hawaiʻi rather than shameful remnants of a sinful past. Kamehameha III, for instance, spent the first years of his adult reign celebrating elements of Hawaiian culture decried as satanic by the missionaries. During the earliest years of his reign, his stepmother Kaʻahumanu had acted as his regent, instituting strict laws promoting Christian marriage, Sabbath observance,

---

[15] Sally Engle Merry, *Colonizing Hawaiʻi: The Cultural Power of Law* (Princeton, NJ: Princeton University Press, 2000), 250–252.

[16] Kameʻeleihiwa, *Native Land and Foreign Desires*, 78.

[17] Ibid., 193–198; Osorio, *Dismembering Lāhui*, 30–33.

and banning practices associated with Ka Wā ʻŌiwi Wale, including hula, gambling, and even kite flying. Under Kamehameha III's adult rule such practices returned with a vengeance. As Kanalu Young has written, the king's court renormalized practices such as hula and same-sex sexual practices. When one of his aliʻi was seen flying a kite, a brief explosion of kite flying occurred among the nearby population as people signaled, quite visibly, their refusal to deny such pastimes when released from the threat of persecution. Soon, however, the pressure of the Christian aliʻi and sorrow over the death of his sister and lover Nahiʻenaʻena pushed the king, and with him the kingdom, back into the mission fold. Those foreigners most eager to denounce Kānaka ʻŌiwi and their past as inherently inferior returned to their positions of influence.[18]

The year 1855 marked the ascension of another youthful king eager to push back against the social, cultural, and political power of the mission faction, Alexander Liholiho, Kamehameha IV. He was educated at the mission-run Chiefs' Children's School with many of the other aliʻi children, including future monarchs Lot Kapuāiwa, David Kalākaua, Lydia Liliʻuokalani, and William Lunalilo. Due to a mix of his treatment at the hands of mission educators, his visits to America and Europe in his late teens, and the increasingly strong hold of the American mission faction over the kingdom, Alexander's reign was marked by a strong push against the influence of the American mission faction. A cadre of young Kanaka nationalists aided him in these efforts, including other aliʻi nui such as his brother Lot and then Prince David Kalākaua. As Beamer and others have noted, Alexander and Lot removed many missionaries and mission allies from government posts, replacing them with Kānaka and Haole who were hostile to the mission faction's political and cultural agendas. The mission faction was less than pleased by these events, expressing particular anger when Lot handed control of the kingdom's schools over to Abraham Fornander, a naturalized Swede known for his respect for and research into the culture of ʻŌiwi Wale Hawaiʻi.[19]

Alexander and Lot also used their reigns to create multiple avenues for Hawaiian culture to be celebrated publically, something Noenoe Silva has written about in *Aloha Betrayed* and elsewhere. Alexander's introduction and patronage of the Anglican church created not only a

---

[18] Young, *Rethinking the Native Past*, 157.
[19] Beamer, *No Mākou ka Mana*, 172–173; HEA, "Sandwich Islands," *The Missionary Herald*, 61 (1865): 364; Ralph Kuykendall, *The Hawaiian Kingdom: Twenty Critical Years* (Honolulu: University of Hawaiʻi Press, 1966), 108.

Protestant competitor for Congregationalism, it also introduced a creed almost as eager to excuse practices such as hula as the Congregationalists were eager to condemn them. Kanaka missionary James Kekela, returning home from the Marquesas in 1859, was appalled to see the revival of hula, noting that even church members had joined in the dancing.[20] Silva has also written about mission- and planter-driven efforts to stem the growing hula renaissance, efforts stymied through the work of Alexander, Lot, and hula-friendly legislators who managed to water down the resulting hula "ban" to the point where it was effectively toothless. The royal brothers also oversaw the adoption of a licensing system that gave government sanction to Kanaka medical practices, something the missionaries had sought to stamp out for its spiritual dimensions. As seen with the licensing system and hula, the brothers quite eagerly sought to show their people that not only was Ka Wā ʻŌiwi Wale not forgotten, but it lived on in the present and future of the kingdom.[21]

Furthermore, Alexander helped to bring about perhaps one of the most important tools for preserving a place for the Hawaiian past within the Hawaiian future, independent Hawaiian-language newspapers. In 1861, a small ʻahahui (association), of Kanaka writers and nationalists published *Ka Hoku o Ka Pakipika*, the first Hawaiian-language newspaper outside of missionary supervision. As Silva has shown, *Ka Hoku* was printed on the government press, which the ʻahahui had leased from the government alongside an agreement to publish government documents. From the start, *Ka Hoku*'s publishers stated a desire to serve the broader Hawaiian community, not just the Congregationalists, as well as printing Hawaiian cultural texts such as oli (chants) and moʻolelo that often dealt tangentially or directly with spiritual and religious content rooted in Ka Wā ʻŌiwi Wale.[22]

The mission community and the more doctrinaire among the Native Congregationalist population responded with absolute horror and hatred, both at their loss of a print monopoly and at the use of a newspaper to promote and even celebrate Ka Wā ʻŌiwi Wale. They attacked the newspaper from the pulpit and sought to undercut it by subsidizing *Ka Nupepa Kuokoa* (The Independent Newspaper), which was published

[20] James Kekela, "Ko J. Kekela Palapala Aloha Hope in na Ekalesia a pau ma Hawaiʻi nei," January 19, 1859, RJKC, Awaiaulu.
[21] Silva, *Aloha Betrayed*, 48; Noenoe Silva, "He Kanawai E Hoopau i na Hula Kuolo Hawaiʻi: The Political Economy of Banning the Hula," *Hawaiian Journal of History* 34 (2000): 29–49.
[22] Silva, *Aloha Betrayed*, 63–68.

by a missionary descendent and featured angry attacks on *Ka Hoku*, its publishers, and its readers. The mission faction's primary argument was that the newspaper was a tool of the na'auao and to use it for na'aupō purposes such as oli and mo'olelo was to use it for Satan. The publishers of *Ka Hoku* replied by turning the missionary faction's rhetoric against them. If newspapers were a sign of the na'auao, then clearly the Hawaiian people were na'auao for they now had an independent press. By extension their cultural texts must also be na'auao if they were published in a newspaper. The real na'aupō, they continued, came from those who sought to contain and limit the expansion of knowledge, such as those who attacked the publication of *Ka Hoku*.[23]

Abraham Fornander, himself no fan of the mission faction, wrote a short congratulatory note to the king about the willingness of the 'ahahui to fight back against the mission on their own turf, noting that the mission's "unceasing interference will be severely rebuked this time, not by 'licentious and malignant foreigners' but by their own well sheared lambs." Though *Ka Hoku* eventually folded, a series of other independent papers would rise to take its place, filling the lāhui's desire for news, an independent editorial voice, and Kanaka cultural texts. Even the *Kuokoa* would soon begin publishing mo'olelo and other cultural texts in an attempt to maintain their readership.[24]

With the exception of the brief reign of William Lunalilo, the monarchy remained quite firmly behind the development of a national culture rooted both in Ka Wā 'Ōiwi Wale and the adaptation of foreign innovations. When David Kalākaua was elected king by the legislature in 1874, he did so by winning a hotly contested election against Queen Emma Rooke, the widow of Alexander Liholiho. The lack of support from Emma's backers and others among the Kanaka 'Ōiwi population left Kalākaua as the first Hawaiian monarch since Kamehameha I with a true need to shore up his support among the population.[25] In addition to economic, diplomatic, and political projects intended to strengthen both his position and the kingdom, Kalākaua also set about on the most ambitious set of cultural initiatives of any of Hawai'i's monarchs.

Perhaps more than any other monarch, Kalākaua sought to combine foreign and 'Ōiwi elements into a national culture as in touch with its own

---

[23] Ibid., 68, 71.
[24] Abraham Fornander to Kamehameha IV, September 17, 1861, FDC, BMA; Silva, *Aloha Betrayed*, 82–86.
[25] Osorio, *Dismembering Lāhui*, 151–159.

past as it was with the world beyond its borders. Silva's *Aloha Betrayed* examines how a number of Kalākaua's cultural projects did exactly that, including the king's coronation in 1883 and his 1886 jubilee, massive public events that included hula, formal balls, public Hawaiian-style feasts, and state dinners. The king's celebration of hula at these events promoted them as a key component of national culture, part of a broader effort to rejuvenate the national culture through ʻŌiwi Wale culture. By publicizing and including a variety of hula performances at his coronation, the king forced a confrontation with the mission faction over the future of ʻŌiwi Wale culture in the kingdom. Despite a successful indecency case against the printers who published the coronation programs, popular opinion lay solidly behind the king and the hula, preserving and strengthening that essential link to Ka Wā ʻŌiwi Wale. By the king's jubilee a few years later, even the mission-friendly press was more interested in gossiping about specific hula being performed rather than condemning the art as a whole.[26]

In *The Arts of Kingship*, Stacy Kamehiro examines these same events as well as other Kalākaua projects through the lens of nationalist art. In addition to hula, Kalākaua also used architecture, public art projects, and other forms of material culture to promote his vision of a Hawaiian future informed by Ka Wā ʻŌiwi Wale. With an art historian's eye, Kamehiro examines the finer details of well-known landmarks such as the Kamehameha statue and ʻIolani Palace, as well as lesser-known projects such as the national museum, many of whose holdings eventually found their way into the Bishop Museum. In some cases, Kalākaua's role in these nationalist art projects took the form of the preservation and display of items directly from Ka Wā ʻŌiwi Wale, such as the malo of Liloa, a wide feather belt associated with Hawaiʻi Island royalty. In other cases, however, Kalākaua purposefully employed European styles of art alongside subject matters or symbols important to the Hawaiian nation and the monarchy, such as the Kamehameha statue.[27]

Silva has also written about the cultural work of two of Kalākaua's most innovative projects, the Board of Genealogy and its successor the Hale Nauā. These two groups, packed with prominent Kānaka, served as the king's think tanks, seeking out and examining authorities, sources, and artifacts of ʻŌiwi Wale culture and knowledge and applying them

---

[26] Silva, *Aloha Betrayed*, 108–120.
[27] Stacey Kamehiro, *The Arts of Kingship: Hawaiian Art and National Culture of the Kalākaua Era* (Honolulu: University of Hawaiʻi Press, 2009).

to modern political, cultural, and scientific projects.[28] The Hale Nauā also worked to develop the kingdom's image abroad, including planning for the kingdom's exhibit at the 1893 Columbian Exhibition. The exhibit would have combined opera, hula, high diving, marksmanship, and displays of artifacts, clearly intended to proclaim Hawai'i as part of a cosmopolitan global culture yet distinct from the European/American empires that dominated that culture. The overthrow of the monarchy by the mission faction and a deployment of US Marines in January 1893 upset those plans. Mission scion and overthrow mastermind Lorrin Thurston used the exhibition to promote tourism and the Kilauea volcano instead.[29]

Between the overthrow and annexation, the vast majority of Kānaka gathered behind the deposed queen, Lili'uokalani, and against the coup leaders and their plans of annexing Hawai'i to the United States. A combination of Grover Cleveland's anti-imperialism, massive petition drives in the islands, and the queen's personal lobbying of the US Senate defeated the first two attempts at annexation. A third attempt, approved through the questionable means of a joint session of the US Congress, led to what some consider the annexation of Hawai'i and others argue to be the start of the US occupation of the islands. Either way, American imperial control led to a process of Americanization that aimed to strip Kānaka, particularly young Kānaka, of any form of identity that might challenge their loyalty to the empire. Kanaka 'Ōiwi culture came under immediate attack, particularly the Hawaiian language, which the territory banned in schools and in official business. In addition, the mixture of sugar barons and missionary scions who pushed through the overthrow and annexation developed an informal oligarchy that controlled the economy and the ruling Republican Party. Through their control of the territorial governor's office, the oligarchy continued the process of land alienation that had begun under the Māhele. The loss of the language and of connections to the land worked together to squeeze the life from the Hawaiian culture, replacing it with a version of American culture suitable for life as a territorial subject.[30]

---

[28] Silva, *Aloha Betrayed*, 94–109.

[29] Hale Naua Society, 1886–1891: Translation of Documents at the Hawai'i State Archives and Hawaiian Mission Children's Society Library, introduction by Frank J. Karpiel, trans. Carol L. Silva (Honolulu, HI: HSA, 1999), 83–84, 120.

[30] Maenette Kape'ahiokalani Padeken Benham, "The Voice 'less' Hawaiian: An Analysis of Educational Policymaking, 1820–1960," *Hawaiian Journal of History* 32 (1998): 128–129.

Kānaka did what they could to preserve the culture, with older generations attempting to put as much as they could through the newspapers. Stephen Desha's series of articles on Kamehameha I and his mentor/advisor Kekuhaupiʻo came out in this period, as did numerous similar works. Hula and other practices remained, some in public and some in private. As Davianna McGregor writes, the Hawaiian civic clubs emerged in these times, seeking both to save what elements of the culture that they could, while also preparing Hawaiians to thrive individually under the American empire. Success in both was limited by the circumstances of empire and the fact that the two goals were often at cross-purposes. Between these various efforts and the already sizeable repository of Hawaiian knowledge in the newspaper archives, enough of Ka Wā ʻŌiwi Wale culture remained to seed a renaissance in the 1960s, a renaissance that continues into today.[31]

Taken together, the body of work created by Silva, Osorio, Kameʻeleihiwa, and others has created a strong foundation for understanding Kanaka negotiations between the values, institutions, and ideas rooted in Ka Wā ʻŌiwi Wale and those introduced from foreign lands. While the specific subject of these negotiations differed from case to case, period to period, the core of these negotiations and conflicts remained the same: the value of Ka Wā ʻŌiwi Wale as a path for the future of Hawaiʻi. Without question, foreign interests that stood to gain power by devaluing all things connected to Ka Wā ʻŌiwi Wale – particularly the Kānaka – influenced such negotiations and fed, even led, many of the conflicts. Until the Overthrow and Annexation, however, the primary decision makers in these negotiations and conflicts were Kānaka, be they the various monarchs, the aliʻi, the makaʻainana, or the lāhui as a whole. As these histories have shown, the value they placed in Ka Wā ʻŌiwi Wale influenced the way they envisioned the relationships with one another and with the European and American powers.

While this Native-driven historiography has created a strong foundation for this book and other works, it should be noted that the often explicit and always powerful desire to counter the imperial apologists who had previously dominated Hawaiian history has resulted in its own problems. The historiography of Hawaiʻi remains quite tightly focused on Native engagements with various official and unofficial projects of

---

[31] Davianna Pomaikaʻi McGregor, "ʻĀina Hoʻopulapula: Hawaiian Homesteading," *Hawaiian Journal of History* 24 (1990): 4–5; Stephen Desha, *Kamehameha and His Warrior Kekūhaupiʻo* (Honolulu, HI: Kamehameha Press, 2000).

American imperialism and the resulting changes in Kanaka relationships with one another. Unfortunately, this heavy emphasis on relationships between the United States and Hawaiʻi has still left us with an incomplete and ahistorical understanding of the Hawaiian past by placing the imperial American present at the center of Hawaiian history. In accepting the idea that the only worthwhile outside relationship to study is between Kānaka and their past/present/future imperial rulers, historians have reinforced such thinking and in doing so, intentionally or unintentionally, naturalized empire. Furthermore, if Hawaiian historians *only* conceive Hawaiian history through interactions with empire, it makes it very difficult to truly understand that past or envision a Hawaiian future without empire. This problem is hardly unique to Hawaiian history; indeed it can be found throughout Oceanic history, where island group and national histories tend to focus largely on relationships with past or present imperial masters. Even when done to validate or historicize nationalist or anticolonial sentiments, they still reify both the normality of those relationships and the political borders created by such relationships.

While the recent wave of Native-centered yet imperially focused works of history may have contributed to this particular type of myopia, they have also helped create the necessary conditions to begin curing it. As the anti-imperial upstarts have become the new canon, the driving need to push back against imperial apologetics has eased. Though the simple realities of nineteenth-century Hawaiian history dictate that such imperial projects must be acknowledged and addressed, the work done by this new canon has created room for new subjects of inquiry, many of whom have received little to no study in the period of imperial apologetics or in the more recent push back against those apologetics.

Among those neglected subjects of inquiry are Kanaka ties and connections to parts and peoples of the world other than the "Great Powers," as well as the associated Kanaka understandings of those connections. There are a few major exceptions, however, including several studies of Kānaka on the West Coast of the United States.[32] Nancy Morris's dissertation on Native Hawaiian missionaries provides an overview of the motivations, training, and lives of Native Hawaiian

---

[32] Jean Barman and Bruce McIntyre Watson, *Leaving Paradise: Indigenous Hawaiians in the Pacific Northwest, 1787–1898* (Honolulu: University of Hawaiʻi Press, 2006); Tom Koppel, *Kanaka: The Untold Story of Hawaiian Pioneers in British Columbia and the Pacific Northwest* (Vancouver, BC: Whitecap Books, 1995).

missionaries in Oceania. In addition to being of tremendous aid in the development of Chapters 1 and 2 of this book, it is also probably the fullest exploration of the lives of Kānaka living overseas as individuals and families.[33] Perhaps the most significant work looking at Hawaiians beyond the US/Hawaiian binary has been David Chang's *The World and All the Things upon It*, which includes not just substantial examinations of Hawaiian connections to and travels within the broader world, but the way Kānaka have envisioned their ties and relationships with the peoples around the world. Anchored in examinations of Kanaka travelers and writers in the nineteenth century, Chang argues that Kānaka sought to intellectually and physically explore the world beyond Hawaiʻi's shores. Furthermore, they used travel, education, religion, and other means to develop a framework for understanding both the world and Hawaiʻi's relationships to it. Rather than seeing themselves as an isolated and inferior people, a view American missionaries and other foreigners often tried to promote, Kānaka understood themselves as connected into and engaged with that world, when at home or abroad.

In a similar vein, *Return to Kahiki* helps to improve our understanding of Hawaiian history by examining Kānaka through their relationships with other peoples of Oceania. Part of the impetus for doing so is simply to help develop a fuller and more nuanced understanding of Hawaiian and Oceanic history while also providing historical context for modern relationships between Hawaiʻi and other parts of Oceania. At the same time, this focus on Oceanic ties also destabilizes the America-centric vision of Hawaiʻi's connections to the world beyond its shores, envisioning Kānaka Maoli as a people eager to explore their existing connections to the wider world and eager to develop and shape further connections beyond their future imperial rulers. Furthermore, Kānaka retained a strong sense of their connections to the rest of Oceania, and at times explicitly sought to make use of those connections to maintain the religious, political, and cultural sovereignty of the lāhui in an age of empire. Where the empires and their representatives sought to repeatedly cast Hawaiʻi as either deviant or unqualified for independence in an imperial world, Kānaka repeatedly used their ties to Oceania to recast Hawaiʻi as part of a world independent of empire even if not entirely disconnected from it.

---

[33] Nancy Morris, "Hawaiian Missionaries Abroad, 1852–1909," PhD thesis, University of Hawaiʻi at Mānoa, 1987.

OCEANIA

While Hawaiian and other Oceanic histories have remained within the conceptual and geographical constraints of their imperial and anti-imperial pasts, the broader field of Oceanic studies, particularly the academics often lumped together as Native Pacific cultural studies, have moved toward an embrace of fluidity and movement as a way of understanding Oceanic pasts, presents, and futures. One of the defining moments for the field occurred in 1993, when Epeli Hau'ofa published the landmark essay "Our Sea of Islands." After visiting Hilo for an anthropology conference, Hau'ofa had taken a quick drive to the Kilauea volcano where he witnessed lava pouring into the sea, expanding the island. It seemed to him an appropriate metaphor for the continued growth and expansion of Oceanic peoples as well, one that ran counter to the imperial narratives of dying and increasingly invisible Natives. With the ease of communication and travel, Oceanic communities were growing: growing beyond our home islands, growing across Oceania, and growing Oceania beyond the physical boundaries of the Pacific.

Waiting for his flight back to Fiji at the end of his trip, Hau'ofa had a chance encounter with a Tongan friend, a frequent visitor to Suva who engaged in a small but profitable trade in kava between Fiji and the Oceanic community in Berkeley, California. The encounter helped birth Hau'ofa's vision of Oceanic travel creating and strengthening a network of islanders stretching across the ocean and the globe – spread wide, but not thin. This network, Hau'ofa argued, and particularly the relationships formed between different groups of islanders and island groups, could solve Oceania's problems where the outside world, namely empires and former empires, had failed – and in many cases not really tried. Hau'ofa also became a strong voice for thinking of the peoples of the Pacific Ocean not as Pacific Islanders, a term implying, to some at least, isolated specks of land scattered across the water, but instead as Oceanic peoples, peoples connected to each other through the ocean rather than separated by it.[34]

As Joni Madraiwiwi and others have noted, Hau'ofa's personal history of Oceanic travels provided the right sort of intellectual and cultural soil to nurture just such an idea. Born to Tongan missionaries in Papua New Guinea, Hau'ofa was educated in Tonga, Fiji, Canada, and Australia. Though he worked briefly for the Tongan government, he

[34] Epeli Hau'ofa, "Our Sea of Islands," *The Contemporary Pacific* 6, no. 1 (1994): 148–161.

spent most of his adult life as a professor at the University of the Pacific in Suva, eventually becoming a citizen of Fiji. He was best known for his fictional accounts of yet another island group, the fictional and yet all too real islands of Tiko.[35] By the 1990s, such trans-Oceanic life stories were increasingly common, as travels within and away from Oceania created pan-Oceanic communities and identities. While Hauʻofa would be one of the first within academia whose work examined and was informed by this trans-Oceanic world, he was certainly not the last.

At the same time that Hauʻofa was developing his "Sea of Islands" understanding of Oceania, a handful of Oceanic scholars were developing the intellectual foundation for what would eventually be referred to as Native Pacific cultural studies. Like Hauʻofa, many of these scholars came from personal and academic backgrounds that crisscrossed both Oceania and the Oceanic diaspora. One of the early contributors to the field, for instance, was Vince Diaz, of Filipino and Pohnpeian ancestry, born and raised on Guam, educated at the University of Hawaiʻi at Mānoa and the University of California, Santa Cruz. Teresia Teaiwa, another major contributor to the field, was an I-Kiribati who was born in Honolulu, raised in Fiji, received her doctorate from Santa Cruz, and taught in Fiji and Aotearoa. Furthermore, as she explains in her essay, "L(o)osing the Edge," her experiences meeting with and engaging with other Native Pacific Islander academics at academic conferences had proved essential in creating a broader sense of what Oceania was and what Oceanic scholarship could become. She also described the importance of the brief explosion of Oceanic students at UC Santa Cruz's History of Consciousness program in creating a cohort of academics that would go on to develop Native Pacific cultural studies, which included herself, Diaz, and Kēhaulani Kauanui. Like Diaz and Teaiwa, Kauanui's personal history lent itself to an understanding of Oceanic peoples as fluid, being a Kānaka ʻŌiwi born and raised in California, educated in part through the Māori studies program at the University of Auckland. Similarly, her research and thinking have been heavily influenced by her experiences studying, teaching, and working with Native American and First Nations scholars and activists within the continental United States as well as with other indigenous scholars from Oceania and elsewhere.[36]

[35] Joni Madraiwiwi, "Muse, Mediator, and Mentor," *The Contemporary Pacific* 22, no. 1 (2010): 104–105; Epeli Hauʻofa, *Tales of the Tikongs* (Honolulu: University of Hawaiʻi Press, 1994).

[36] Vicente Diaz, *Repositioning the Missionary: Rewriting the Histories of Colonialism, Native Catholicism, and Indigeneity in Guam* (Honolulu: University of Hawaiʻi Press,

Considering their backgrounds, it should come as no surprise that many Native Pacific cultural studies scholars have envisioned and written about the peoples of Oceania not as isolated groupings separated by the sea, but rather as Hau'ofa did, as a people connected to and connected by the Pacific. Diaz's work, for instance, routinely questioned the geographic and cultural "fixedness" of Oceanic peoples, and even of islands. Teaiwa's work similarly examines Oceanic peoples articulations and rearticulations of their identities in response to international and local tensions, desires, and opportunities. Building on these initial works, other Oceanic scholars, many sharing the trans-Oceanic backgrounds of their predecessors, have further developed this understanding of the fluidity of islander cultures, identities, and communities. A Chamorro scholar educated in Guam and Hawai'i, Keith Camacho's *Cultures of Commemoration* examines the role of historical memories among the Chamorro peoples of Guam and the Northern Marianas through the lens of World War II commemorations, critiquing the reification of imperial divisions within the island and the Chamorro, Japanese, and American roles in perpetuating them. Kamana Beamer's and Noenoe Silva's work in Hawaiian history also fit into this general vision of islanders as fluid and engaging the outside world without losing the connections to each other, 'Ōiwi culture, and to the lands that birthed them.[37]

Like Teaiwa and Hau'ofa, other recent Oceanic scholars have explicitly examined the connections and relationships between different Oceanic communities as an important part of understanding Oceania and its people as a whole. Hokulani Aikau's *A Chosen People* includes a significant discussion of the development of a pan-Polynesian community in Lā'ie, Hawai'i. Alice Te Punga Somerville, a Māori scholar who received her PhD at Cornell but who wrote her dissertation in Hawai'i, has explored such issues in her *Once Were Pacific*. *Once Were Pacific* examines how Māori writers such as Witi Ihimaera have understood and envisioned the Māori people as part of a broader Oceanic world. Though it is not the focal point of her work, Sommerville also includes enough historical context to argue that such understandings are not entirely new, indeed that

2010); Teresia Teaiwa, "L(o)osing the Edge," *The Contemporary Pacific* 13, no. 2 (2001): 349; J. Kēhaulani Kauanui, *Hawaiian Blood: Colonialism and the Politics of Sovereignty and Indigeneity* (Durham, NC: Duke University Press, 2008).

37 Teresia Teaiwa, "Militarism, Tourism and the Native: Articulations in Oceania," PhD thesis, University of California, Santa Cruz, 2001; Diaz, *Repositioning the Missionary*; Keith Camacho, *Cultures of Commemoration: The Politics of War, Memory, and History in the Mariana Islands* (Honolulu: University of Hawai'i Press, 2011).

this identification with other islanders extends to the life and work of Te Rangi Hiroa/Peter Buck in the early twentieth century, to Māori connections with the Raiatean navigator Tupaia in the 1760s, and even further back to the Oceanic origins of the Māori people. Finally, though not often seen as part of Native Pacific cultural studies, Nicholas Thomas's work in *Islanders* also contains significant discussions of trans-Oceanic travelers and settlers, and their importance in developing an overall understanding of the nineteenth-century Pacific.[38]

The recent group of scholars forming loosely under the banner of "Pacific Worlds" scholarship also deserves some mention as part of the intellectual environment in which this book is being released. Matt Matsuda's *Pacific Worlds,* probably being the most well known of these, lays out something of an agenda for reimagining the Pacific along the same lines as was done with Atlantic studies over the past few decades. Similar to Chang and many of the scholars mentioned in the preceding text, they imagine the Pacific in terms of movement and connection rather than a static collection of unrelated histories. While useful in terms of understanding connections between Asia, the Americas, and Oceania, for the most part Oceania's role in these histories seems largely incidental to the relationships between Asia and the Americas.[39]

WHY OCEANIA?

As noted previously, this book deals not only with Kānaka Maoli, but also with their relationships to other peoples within Oceania, a term I have chosen in part because of its mix of geographic flexibility and specificity. The following episode from King David Kalākaua's 1881 circumnavigation of the globe might help illustrate this point. During the voyage he received an invitation to visit with Sultan Abu Bakar, the Maharajah of Johor, today part of Malaysia. Kalākaua's missionary-descended travel companion, William Armstrong, seemed most interested in the

---

[38] Hokulani Aikau, *A Chosen People, a Promised Land: Mormonism and Race in Hawai'i* (Minneapolis: University of Minnesota Press, 2012); Alice Te Punga Somerville, *Once Were Pacific: Maori Connections with Oceania* (Minneapolis: University of Minnesota Press, 2012); Nicholas Thomas, *Islanders: The Pacific in the Age of Empire* (New Haven, CT: Yale University Press, 2012).

[39] Matt Matsuda, *Pacific Worlds: A History of Seas, Peoples, and Cultures* (Cambridge: Cambridge University Press, 2012).

Maharajah's displays of wealth, othering him as a decadent "Asiatic" ruler while reveling in his hospitality.[40]

Kalākaua's lasting impressions of the Maharajah, however, came not from his wealth or his otherness, but from the connections he and the Maharajah shared as descendants of the ancient Austronesian migration. Writing back to his brother-in-law, the king described the Maharajah as "a fine looking man [who] resembles the first Leleiohoku very much. If he could have spoken our language I would take him to be one of our people."[41] Leleiohoku, it should be noted, was an ali'i nui, a high chief, of the generation before Kalākaua. His widow, Princess Ruth Keli'iokalani, had adopted Kalākaua's brother and renamed him Leleiohoku in memory of her deceased husband. In 1877, the second Leleiohoku, then heir to the throne, had died as well. One can only imagine the potential emotional weight of such a moment, the near recognition of one's own kin in the face of a stranger a thousand miles from home.

The two monarchs quickly discovered a mutual interest in ethnography and began discussing the theory that the people of Polynesia had migrated from Malaysia. Though communicating largely in English, the two began exploring linguistic ties between their native languages, finding several similar terms between the two branches of what is now called the Malayo-Polynesian language family. The discussions satisfied the two monarchs of their shared connections not just as monarchs, but as "long-lost brothers." After a state dinner that evening, the two talked into the night, eagerly comparing legends and oral histories that further uncovered their shared Austronesian past. Though his visit with the Maharajah only lasted a single day, their conversations left a lasting impression on Kalākaua, who continued to cultivate personal and official ties to the Maharajah throughout his reign.[42]

Kalākaua's embrace of the Maharajah as kin, albeit distant kin, demonstrates a practical problem for any work seeking to examine this concept of distant kin tied together by the voyaging past, specifically what to call the geographical space in question and its inhabitants. *The Pacific* is simply too broad, while *Pacific Islands* and *Pacific Islanders* are too narrow, leaving no room for regions like Johor, tied to the Austronesian migration yet not considered as Pacific Islands. Both sets of terms are so commonly

[40] William Armstrong, *Around the World with a King* (New York: Frederick A. Stokes, 1904), 141–145.
[41] Richard A. Greer, "The Royal Tourist – Kalākaua's Letters Home from Tokio to London," *The Hawaiian Journal of History* 5 (1971): 82.
[42] Armstrong, *Around the World with a King*, 144–147.

used, however, that it can be difficult to avoid simply slipping back into them. *Kahiki*, though a useful concept for capturing ʻŌiwi Wale understandings of the world, is less useful for examining how Kānaka saw related peoples within the Pacific as *Kahiki* still referred to both Tahiti specifically and to foreign lands in general.

The vast majority of the events described in this book take place in the areas commonly referred to as Micronesia and Polynesia, but these terms are both too narrow and too divisive to frame this book. The historical usage of those terms as a way to divide the peoples of Oceania within colonial contexts and the potentially divisive use of those terms today presents a clear discursive problem. Though many of the Kānaka discussed in this book used the terms *Polynesia* and *Polynesian* to define the people and places they saw themselves as connected to, the geographic limits of that term ignore not just Micronesia and Melanesia, but chunks of Austronesian South East Asia as well. To a certain degree the use of the terms by Kānaka indicates the strength of these divisive European visions of the Pacific, although in some cases Kānaka used the terms in a much broader geographic sense. Kalākaua's proposed "Polynesian Confederacy," for instance, included parts of Micronesia, suggesting a certain fluidity in his usage. In the end, however, the common use of the term for a specific geographic area make it both problematic and inaccurate for the scope of this book. Despite this, in specific cases when sources used the terms *Polynesia* and *Polynesian*, that terminology will be maintained in this current work for the sake of accuracy.

In the past few decades the terms *Oceania* and *Oceanians* have increased in use among Pacific scholars, in large part through the influence of Epeli Hauʻofa. The focus on the ocean seems appropriate for descendants of the Austronesian voyagers, and the term has acquired a geographic flexibility under Hauʻofa's usage that can accommodate the Maharajah, the Mōʻī, and everyone in between. Though not a term used by many of the historical subjects of this work discussed within this book, its flexibility and connotations of ocean-based connectivity make it a useful term to refer to the broader area and people connected to the Lāhui Hawaiʻi through a shared connection to their voyaging ancestors.

SCOPE

This book examines three different trans-Oceanic projects initiated by Kānaka to better understand how they understood and shaped relationships to other peoples of Oceania: (1) Kanaka missionary efforts in

Micronesia and the Marquesas, (2) King Kalakaua's diplomatic legation to Sāmoa in 1887, and (3) politician and businessman John Tamatoa Baker's travels through Oceania in 1907. These projects were chosen in large part because of the written records they left behind. The missionaries and the diplomatic legation both left behind substantial archival records and Baker recorded his journey in a series of letters published by the Hawaiian-language newspaper *Ke Aloha Aina*. Thus this book is largely limited to examinations of the actions and thinking of various types of Kanaka elites. Less documented but arguably more common Kanaka interactions with other Oceanic peoples, namely through immigration to and from Hawai'i, are more difficult to trace and as such have largely been neglected in this study. In addition, to manage the scope of the project, non-Hawaiian Oceanians living in Hawai'i are not examined in any real depth except in cases in which they are relevant to other elements of this project, such as with Baker's grandfather, Steven Pupuhi of Tahiti.

CONTENTS

Chapters 1 and 2 focus on Kanaka missionaries working in Micronesia and the Marquesas between 1850 and 1900. Chapter 1 examines how the postmillennial worldview they inherited from the American missionaries in Hawai'i colored their understanding of the pre-Christian past as inherently na'aupō and provided the primary motivation for their own foreign mission work. This mission work allowed them to support the expansion of Christ's kingdom while also pushing back against the paternalism and racism of American missionaries in Hawai'i and in the field. Their understanding of a world separated between warring armies of Christ and Satan, combined with their insecurities over their closeness to the Hawaiian past, also led them to understand other islanders as archaic Kānaka Hawai'i, trapped in the na'aupō of their shared Oceanic/satanic past. Their portrayals and treatment of these other islanders display a clear attempt to display their own distance from Ka Wā 'Ōiwi Wale by making clear distinctions between themselves and their hosts, resulting in a general devaluing of the cultures, independence, and even lives of other islanders.

Chapter 2 continues this examination of Kanaka foreign mission work focusing on the efforts of these Kanaka missionaries to retain their own personal separation from the supposed na'aupō while in the mission field. Believing themselves beset by Satan at all sides, the missionaries

constantly feared that they would hoʻi hope (turn back) to the ways of
the naʻaupō. At times they did. This chapter examines those fears, the
handful of recorded incidents when the missionaries actually did hoʻi
hope, and the efforts of their fellow missionaries to deal with the spiritual and public fallout of such incidents. Taken as a whole, the incidents
and the response of other Kanaka missionaries mark out the boundaries of a Hawaiian Congregationalism that followed the central ideas of
Congregationalism while still quietly accommodating various aspects of
Ka Wā ʻŌiwi Wale.

Chapters 3 and 4 follow the diplomatic legation King David Kalākaua
sent to Sāmoa in 1886/1887 as a first step in building an explicitly anti-
imperial, Native-centered Oceanic confederacy. Chapter 3 examines the
dual set of appeals Kalākaua and his lead diplomat, John E. Bush, made
to Malietoa Laupepa and other Samoan leaders. To create a foundation
for such an unprecedentedly close alliance between two nations with
little previous diplomatic contact, the Hawaiian kingdom relied heavily on historic and cultural connections between the two peoples. At the
same time, the kingdom promoted itself as having both a firmer grasp of
Western naʻauao and greater access to global diplomatic networks. By
promising to use these to both shelter and tutor their Samoan kin, they
offered the Samoans possible salvation from the clear and present danger
of German imperial aggression.

Chapter 4 surveys the work of the legation after Malietoa Laupepa's
signing of the confederacy agreement in early February 1887. As the legation worked to secure support among other Samoan chiefs and to gather
information about Sāmoa, they also began to develop plans for what the
future relationship between Sāmoa and Hawaiʻi might look like. Overall
the legation planned to develop Sāmoa along the Hawaiian model, based
on a faulty understanding of the Samoans as underdeveloped Kānaka
Hawaiʻi. The legation's Envoy John E. Bush and its Secretary Henry Poor,
both of whom were hapa-Haole (part-Haole) Kalākaua loyalists, soon split
on the way such changes might be brought about. Bush's continued outreach to the Samoan people indicated a growing understanding of the role
of consent and local/regional independence within Samoan politics and a
desire to shape a relationship grounded largely in kinship and associated
responsibilities to one another. Poor, however, seemed far more willing to
envision and plan the relationship along imperial lines, with relatively little concern over Samoan consent and an eye toward the exploitation of
Samoan resources and lands. A coup by American settlers in Hawaiʻi and
a German invasion of Sāmoa killed the confederacy, leaving permanently

unanswered the question of whether the confederacy would wind up as a thinly veiled Hawaiian attempt at creating empire or fulfill its promise as a Native-driven bulwark against empire.

Chapters 5 and 6 follow former royal governor John Tamatoa Baker on a trans-Polynesian voyage in 1907 and his letters back to *Ke Aloha Aina*. Chapter 5 focuses on Baker's portrayal of the similarities and ties between the lāhui Hawai'i and other peoples of Oceania despite geographic distance and the imposition of imperial boundaries and rule across the Pacific. Baker presented the linguistic, cultural, and even geological similarities he found between Hawai'i and other areas of Oceania as evidence of Kanaka 'Ōiwi connections to a broad pan-Oceanic lāhui. This sense of Oceania-based belonging served as a direct counterpoint to American attempts to dismiss the Lāhui Hawai'i as isolated, archaic, and even aberrant according to American norms.

Chapter 6 follows Baker as he grappled with the future the Lāhui Hawai'i faced under American empire and by extension the futures various other Oceanic lāhui faced under their own respective empires. Based on his personal success, Baker heavily promoted the creation of small-scale agricultural entrepreneurship envisioning a future dominated by Oceanic yeomen touting Native identities and capitalist values. From the very start of his journey, however, Baker met with other Oceanic peoples who forced him to acknowledge the potentially destructive nature of capitalism, particularly the value systems underlying it. The most powerful of these critiques focused on the noticeable lack of a culturally defined upper limit on economic desire. By expanding this critique to the political and cultural sphere, Baker was able to develop it into an Oceanic critique of imperial aggression as not just destructive, but also abnormal and deviant.

SOURCES AND TRANSLATIONS

The three specific projects covered in this book all generated sizeable written records. The Native Hawaiian missionaries produced thousands of pages worth of reports, letters, and accounts that are now held in the Hawai'i Mission Children's Society Archives. Originally written in Hawaiian, most were translated some time ago by a descendant of the missionary Judd family, though a sizeable fraction are still only available in Hawaiian. Portions of both the translations and the Hawaiian originals are available on microfilm through the Pacific Manuscript Bureau. Awaiaulu.org's D. Nakila Steele, Puakea Nogelmeier, and Bryan Kamaoli

Kuwada have transcribed and translated the letters of one prominent missionary, Reverend John Kekela, as well as several articles he wrote. Awaiaulu's Dr. Puakea Nogelmeier was kind enough to lend me an electronic, and thus searchable, copy of the unpublished compilation. This proved very useful during the development of the first two chapters.

Due to the turmoil of the 1887 Bayonet Constitution, the overthrow, and the Republic Era, the various records of the Sāmoa legation are scattered in different locations in Hawai'i. A sizeable portion of the legation's records have been lost, destroyed, or were never placed in the archive, such as King Kalākaua's letters to Bush. The majority, however, can be found in the A. C. Carter letters and the Foreign and Executive Office files at the Hawai'i State Archive. Typescript versions of Walter Murray Gibson's correspondence with the legation are bound with other Miscellaneous Foreign Office and Executive correspondence, and Kalākaua's letters to Malietoa Laupepa and George Tupou of Tonga can be found in various forms in the Executive Correspondence-Outgoing folders. Smaller portions of the legation's documentation can be found at the Bishop Museum and some of Henry Poor's drafts and personal letters from the trip can be found at the Hawaiian Historical Society (Folder MS 327 H31).

Baker recorded his trip in a series of letters he wrote to *Ke Aloha Aina*, which were then published as a serial between 1907 and 1908. These are available digitally on the website Nupepa.org. After a badly damaged January 11, 1908 issue, there are no available copies of *Ke Aloha Aina* until October of that year. Except for a brief portion of Baker's account of Hong Kong, nothing else is available from his time in Asia. If any future reader knows of further copies of *Ke Aloha Aina*, or has other access to Baker's letters, please let me know. Baker's impressions of Asia, particularly his month-long stay in Japan, would be useful for examining Native Hawaiian understandings of Asia. The Māori scholar Paul Meredith has also provided a transcription and translation of an article about and an interview with Baker from the September 1907 issue of the Māori newspaper *Te Pipiwharauroa*.

All other translations directly from the Hawaiian-language sources are mine unless noted. When a translation was not available for Hawaiian Board of Commissioners for Foreign Missions (HBCFM) missionary records, the translations are mine as well, specifically in the cases of Samuel Kaaia's letters, Simeon Kahelemauna's letters, Samuel Kekuewa's letters, David Kanoa's letters after 1880, and Robert Maka's letters from 1887 and 1888. When using the available translations for the other letters, I backtracked at certain places to verify the original language when relevant and to seek some of the detail lost in translation. William Lono's journal was partially translated by his daughter and I used her translations as a general guide, but verified or did my own translations of relevant parts. Translations taken from the Samoan-language documents in the fourth chapter were all taken from official translations or staff translations available in the same collections.

In some cases, the specific Hawaiian-language words or phrases used in the original are significant to the arguments of the paper. In such cases I have left the word or phrase in Hawaiian but provided the rest of the quotation in English. At times this has meant editing the translations of others by searching out and restoring some of the original wording.

I

Ke Ao A Me Ka Pō

Postmillennial Thought and Kanaka Foreign Mission Work

In 1852, just thirty years after the first American missionaries arrived in Hawaii, Kānaka Hawai'i were embarking on foreign missions of their own. Among the first to leave for the mission field was the Reverend James Kekela. Though best known for his nearly half-century of mission work in the Marquesas, Kekela got his first taste of mission life as an observer on the inaugural mission to Micronesia, a joint effort between the ABCFM and the HBCFM. At the launch of that voyage he announced to a gathering at the Seamen's Bethel in Honolulu, "I am a native of these Islands, my parents were idolaters, and I was born in times of darkness." Saved by the coming of Christ in the form of American missionaries, he and the lāhui Hāwai'i had finally received the call to become missionaries. The people of Micronesia, he declared, were "what we were a short time ago," languishing as "degraded, wretched idolaters" in the darkness of Satan. Now the Lāhui Hawai'i would answer the call from those mired in darkness, bringing them both civilization and Ke Ao, the light of Christendom.[1]

Twenty-eight years later, Henry Nalimu, one of the Kanaka missionaries who followed in Kekela's footsteps, stood in front of a massive pyre of burning flesh on Tabiteauea atoll. Earlier that day an army of converts had put 600 "idolaters" to the sword and burned their bodies on the battlefield, some not yet dead when thrown into the flames. The Tabiteauean converts, students of Nalimu and his colleague Reverend W. B. Kapu, had literally conquered the atoll for Christianity. The HBCFM later investigated the roles of Nalimu and Kapu in the massacre. They removed

[1] "Remarks of Rev. Mr. Kekela," *The Friend*, August 1852, 30–31.

Nalimu from mission work, finding him partially responsible for the battle and having failed to properly remonstrate at the sight of the burning bodies. Kapu would be excused and sent back to continue teaching the Tabiteaueans the importance of expanding the realm of Christ.[2]

In the period between 1853 and 1908, several hundred Kānaka left Hawai'i as missionaries, assistant missionaries, missionary wives, domestics, unofficial helpers, and teachers. The hoahānau (cousins/brethren), as Kanaka members of the Hawaiian Congregational church referred to themselves, provided the missions with nearly $112,000 for salaries and supplies as well as an outpouring of moral support.[3] These Kanaka missionaries and their supporters turned to foreign mission work as an expression of their faith and as a collective action that would maintain their place in and devotion to the realm of Christ. Under the banner of the HBCFM, they dedicated and sometimes sacrificed their lives to expanding Ke Ao. Some went to Micronesia, where the joint Hawaiian and American mission field spread through the Carolines, the Marshalls, and Kiribati. Others, like Kekela, went to the Marquesas, where the HBCFM operated largely independently, answering the call of a Marquesan chief, Matuunui, who had come to Hawai'i asking for missionaries just as the HBCFM was getting underway.[4]

The Native Hawaiian zeal for foreign mission work came largely from the postmillennial perspective that Kanaka Congregationalists adopted and adapted from their American missionary teachers, who they often referred to as their mākua, or parents. In particular, they inherited their mākua's belief in a strict division of the world between the Ke Ao, the light of the kingdom of Christ, and Ka Pō, the darkness of the kingdom of Satan. They also inherited the belief that it was the responsibility of all within Ke Ao to expand it to prepare the Earth for the return of Christ. The American missionaries all too often used this theology as an excuse

---

[2] H. E. Maude and H. C. Maude, "Tioba and the Tabiteauean Religious Wars," *The Journal of the Polynesian Society* 90, no. 3 (1981): 324, 327; HBCFM, "Report of the Commission on Foreign Missions Respecting Messrs. Kapu and Nalimu," June 23, 1882, Micronesian Mission Archives, HMCS.

[3] Simeon Kahelemauna Nawaa, "The Hawaiian Mission to Micronesia and Marquesas," 1852, HEA Archives-HMCS.

[4] For a thorough examination of the training, lives, and legacy of the Kānaka missionaries see Nancy Morris, "Hawaiian Missionaries Abroad, 1852–1909," PhD thesis, University of Hawai'i at Mānoa, 1987. In addition to a thorough examination of the missionaries as a group, Morris has also included short biographies on each of the HBCFM's missionaries and assistant missionaries, both of which were an incredible aid when conducting the research this chapter and the next are based on.

to subvert the independence of the hoahānau, and at times the kingdom, deeming Kānaka too chronologically and culturally close to Ka Pō to handle their own religious, social, or political affairs. Kanaka missionaries like Kekela, however, used their efforts to proclaim the collective maturity of the Lāhui Hawai'i as a Christian people; their equality with other Christian peoples, including the Americans; and their commitment to remain pa'a, or firm, in the Christian fold.

The manner in which the Kanaka missionaries interacted with the peoples of the Marquesas and Micronesia, however, complicates this convenient and relatively comfortable argument about Kanaka agency and religious adaptation. The same belief in a world split between Christ and Satan gave the Kanaka missionaries an incentive to denounce and demonize the islanders among whom they worked. By portraying other Oceanic peoples as the *true* minions of Satan, they rhetorically distanced themselves from their hosts and strengthened their position as the soldiers of Christ. They also positioned themselves, like the ABCFM missionaries did in Hawai'i, as the authorities on and keepers of the boundary between Ke Ao and Ka Pō. Such thinking, predictably, led to waging spiritual war against the forces of Satan at all costs, including the independence, culture, and in some cases even the lives of other Oceanic peoples.

KE AO, KA PŌ, AND THE MOTIVATIONS FOR MISSION WORK

The Kanaka zeal for foreign mission work derived in large part from the postmillennial worldview their American mākua brought to the islands. Even before the Second Great Awakening, American religious sentiment had been shifting, strengthening beliefs in the importance of agency while also leaving much of the American public "drunk on the millennium." Many mainline American Protestants, including key figures who inspired or were active in the ABCFM, came to believe that a millennium of peace under the kingdom of God must be made manifest through the good works of Christians before Christ would return. Furthermore, many became convinced that the newly founded United States would be central in bringing about this Christian millennium.[5]

By no coincidence, these ideas flourished with the growth of American expansionism. Future Yale President Reverend Timothy Dwight, for

[5] Ernest R. Sandeen, *The Roots of Fundamentalism, British and American Millenarianism 1800–1930* (Chicago: University of Chicago Press, 1970), 42.

instance, proudly displayed the confluence of Christian postmillennialism and American expansionism in his epic poem, "The Conquest of Canaan," an allegory for a Christian American conquest of North America. While most of the focus of American expansionism and American religious fervor focused on North America, many sought to expand both the kingdom of Christ and American influence abroad through foreign mission work. Following the lead of the London Missionary Society (LMS) in England, students of Dwight founded the ABCFM in New England.[6] The ABCFM missionaries and their faith found great success in Hawai'i, and within thirty years of their arrival their students, the Kanaka Congregationalists, were prepared to carry their own postmillennial vision deeper into Oceania.

As Kānaka engaged this new Christian millenarianism, they and their mākua used existing Native concepts as a lens to understand the new belief systems. In doing so, they altered both sets of understandings, Native-izing Christianity while Christianizing Native understandings of time and space. To describe the growing kingdom of Christ, for instance, they used *mālamalama, ao,* and other terms that connoted light. Words connoting darkness, such as *pō* and *pōuli* came to symbolize the non-Christian world, the dreaded realm of Satan. Missionary Samuela Kaaia described the goal of the mission on Tabiteauea as encircling the island with "the malamalama of [Christ's] victory." Similarly, missionary James Kekela urged his fellow Kānaka to pray to God on behalf of the pagans of Hiva Oa, that they would be turned "from the pouli to the astounding malamalama of Christ."[7] One source of such light metaphors can be found in traditional Christian imagery. The biblical passage 1 John 1:5 (KJV) states, "God is light, and in him is no darkness at all." The Baibala Hemolele, the ABCFM's Hawaiian-language translation of the Bible, renders this as "he malamalama ke Akua, aohe pouli iki iloko ona."

6 Timothy Dwight, *The Conquest of Canaan: A Poem in Eleven Books* (Hartford, CT: Elisha Babcock, 1785); Richard Lee Rogers, "'A Bright and New Constellation': Millennial Narratives and the Origins of American Foreign Missions," in *North American Foreign Missions, 1810–1914: Theology, Theory, and Practice*, ed. Wilbert R. Shenk (Grand Rapids, MI: Eerdmans, 2004); David W. Kling, "The New Divinity and the Origins of the American Board of Commissioners for Foreign Missions," in *North American Foreign Missions, 1810–1914: Theology, Theory, and Practice*, ed. Wilbert R. Shenk (Grand Rapids, MI: Eerdmans, 2004).
7 Samuela Kaai to Forbes, October 17, 1887, Micronesia Mission Archives, HMCS; James Kekela to Gulick, August 7, 1867, RJKC, Awaiaulu.

Pre-Christian Hawaiian culture, however, contained culturally specific understandings of terms such as *ao* and *pō*. Even when used in a Christian context, such words retained pre-Christian connotations. *Ao* meant light or daytime, but also the time/space that mankind exists in, specifically the current era and the physical world. *Pō* meant the night and generic darkness, but also the time and being that was the primordial darkness. In the epic genealogical chants, the central repositories of the Kanaka Maoli cosmogony, Ka Pō covered the first half of existence, birthing much of the world and its contents. Ka Pō, in a way, is the ancestor of people, the akua (gods) and even Ke Ao, thus it is a space/time/being of great power, importance, and reverence. At the same time, Ka Pō is a space parallel to Ke Ao, the temporal world; Ka Pō is the time/space of the divine, mostly inaccessible to living man, but inhabited in part by ancestors and deities. Thus Kānaka imagined Ka Pō as a space and time of potential wholeness and reunion beyond Ke Ao while also being a potentially dangerous realm of powerful beings and uncontrollable forces.[8]

For the hoahānau the meanings of the terms *ao* and *pō* remained relatively stable while the values surrounding them changed dramatically. As Dorothy Barrere and Marshal Sahlins have argued, the strength of ao and po as pre-Christian concepts and their similarities to existing Christian rhetoric made them a powerful and frequently used pair of concepts for missionaries and converts alike – but not without some significant changes. Even in pre-Christian times, Kānaka saw ao and pō as an oppositional pair, but only through the new theology did they assign them opposite values. Ao became unequivocally positive, pō unequivocally negative. As both a time and a space, Ka Pō remained the realm of the akua and the ancestors, but the mission's teachings transformed the akua into the demonic agents of Satan and the ancestors into their minions and victims. Toketa, one of a number of Tahitian Christians serving the Hawaiian royal courts in the first half of the nineteenth century stated this quite clearly in his journal: "The greatest thing of value is the realm of light – Ao – of the god Jehovah ... There are two roads souls travel after death – the soul of the sinful man goes to his dwelling place in the Po, and that of the good man to the Ao." Spatially Ka Pō gained an added dimension. Where previously

[8] Mary Kawena Pukui, E. W. Haertig, and Catherine A. Lee, *Nana I Ke Kumu* (Honolulu, HI: Hui Hānai, 1972), 35, 40; Mary Kawena Pukui and Samuel Elbert, *Hawaiian Dictionary, Revised and Enlarged Edition* (Honolulu: University of Hawaii Press, 1986), 333; Valerio Valeri, *Kingship and Sacrifice: Ritual and Society in Ancient Hawaii*, trans. Paula Wissing (Chicago: University of Chicago Press, 1985), 3–7, 35–36.

it had been a separate sacred space, now it included parts of the earthly realm, specifically those dominated by the unsaved.[9]

In both the Christian and polytheistic views, Kānaka understood Ka Pō not just as an abstract or metaphor, but as a very "real" presence that overlapped Ke Ao around certain times, places, and people. In both views these overlaps held great spiritual significance. In the pre-Christian view, such overlaps represented great and dangerous powers that could be negotiated with and understood through knowledge, ritual, and kapu. Certain places, spaces, and people – particularly those of high geneal-ogy – contained elements of both Ka Pō and Ke Ao. These people and spaces allowed Hawaiians to interact with and even manipulate Ka Pō from within Ke Ao, while also representing a dangerous manifestation of unearthly powers on the earthly plane.

Most Native Congregationalists, however, viewed the overlap between Ke Ao and Ka Pō specifically as spaces of confrontation between the kingdoms of Christ and Satan. Such overlaps continued to be points of both opportunity and danger. The mission field, domestic or foreign, was a space dominated by Ka Pō, and thus an opportunity for those on the side of Christ to expand Ke Ao. Native missionaries celebrated every step toward the conversion of their hosts as a victory within the larger conflict of Ke Ao and Ka Pō. Christian marriage, for instance, showed a people taking a first step toward eradicating the darkness, a "Kukui hooma-lamalama," an illuminating lamp, penetrating an otherwise dark land. This sort of overlap, where Ke Ao encroached upon or penetrated Ka Pō, excited the hearts of Native Congregationalists.[10]

EQUALITY AND MISSION WORK

As stated in the preceding text, nineteenth-century American postmil-lennialism placed a heavy emphasis on the importance of human action in expanding the kingdom of Christ and bringing about his return. Both the ABCFM and HBCFM formed in part out of a desire to fulfill this prophecy and thus fulfill their duty as Christians as well. But another major motivation for Hawaiian mission work came from the anxiety

[9] Dorothy Barrere and Marshall Sahlins, "Tahitians in the Early History of Hawaii: The Journal of Taketa," *Hawaiian Journal of History* 13 (1979): 29. For a broader Oceanic view of similar changes in the meaning of these concepts see Christa Bausch, "*Po* and *Ao*, Analysis of an Ideological Conflict in Polynesia," *Journal de la Société des Océanistes* 34, no. 61 (1976): 169–185.

[10] Hezekiah Aea to Clark, January 16, 1864, Micronesian Mission Archive, HMCS.

among Kanaka Congregationalists over the lāhui's recently acquired status as a Christian people. Similar things could be said of the original ABCFM, which emerged partly out of fear that America was squandering its Christian expansionist birthright. Mission work provided a focus for collective action, strengthening the devotion of congregations at home while also displaying that devotion to the world, to Christ, and to themselves.[11] In the case of Kanaka Congregationalists, however, their anxiety came not from straying from an imagined destiny, but rather by their collective ties to a past their ABCFM mākua decried as inherently satanic.

In theory, the ABCFM's vision of postmillennialism was relatively inclusive. They believed all the peoples of the Earth, including the Lāhui Hawaiʻi, could and would acquire unity and equality under the kingdom of Christ. Yet the ABCFM's postmillennial theology competed with other, less inclusive, discourses promoting the inherent cultural and racial superiority of white Americans. Thus, the American missionaries were only too happy to encourage the Kānaka to believe that the stain of Ka Wā ʻŌiwi Wale was so strong that the Lāhui Hawaiʻi, a less capable race, would require white American guidance for the foreseeable future – perhaps even until Christ's eventual return.

To further this vision, ABCFM schools and preachers portrayed Ka Wā ʻŌiwi Wale as a time of naʻaupō (ignorance) and pushed Kānaka converts to actively condemn it. Students at the ABCFM's Lahainaluna seminary, for instance, seemed to have been encouraged to denounce their collective past and their ancestors. An 1834 article in the Lahainaluna newspaper, *Ka Lama Hawaiʻi*, follows such a pattern. The author, quite possibly a student, claimed that both pono (proper) and hewa (sinful or sin) practices existed in the old days, but only details the hewa. The article describes the hewa as ignorance, polytheism, polygamy, hula, and "indulgent games."[12] In an 1841 essay, a student named Kaluau lists the things that marked his ancestors as naʻaupō, ranging from illiteracy to hula. In the same essay Kaluau claimed that in respect to marriage, "In the old days, the way of living was not pono, therefore the man did not properly take the woman [as his wife], also, the children and the parents were not properly cared for." Another 1841 essay by future missionary

---

[11] John A. Andrew, *Rebuilding the Christian Commonwealth: New England Congregationalists and Foreign Missions, 1800–1830* (Lexington: University Press of Kentucky, 1976).

[12] "No Ka Pono Kahiko a Me Ka Pono Hou," *Ka Lama Hawaii*, February 21, 1834.

David Aumai stated that the people before the coming of the word were na'aupō and that the na'aupō were the same as animals.[13]

Even among the most devoted Kānaka the fear that they might ho'i hope (backslide) into Ka Pō remained constant. Individually and collectively the hoahānau had undergone a conversion experience, giving them some confidence in their immediate place within Christ's kingdom – but to convert was no guarantee of future salvation. Indeed, the belief in salvation that can be brought about through human agency came with a matching belief that damnation could come about through human agency as well. Combined with the belief that Satan and his agents were actively seeking to undermine the converted, the Kanaka Congregationalists lived with the constant anxiety that they, their fellows, or even their whole nation might ho'i hope at anytime. As a way of averting such disaster the hoahānau maintained a vigorous schedule of worship, prayer, bible study, and fellowship, work that assured they remain firm, rather than inaction that offered a window to ho'i hope.[14] Foreign mission work, with its intensive fundraising, high levels of personal and collective sacrifice, and direct attacks on Satan's realm, provided a productive outlet for their anxiety and a bulwark against backsliding. Their supposed proximity to Ka Pō may have been a source of considerable anxiety as Christians, but their efforts to expand Ke Ao would prove to their doubters and themselves that they stood firmly within the kingdom of Christ and would do whatever it took to remain there.

The chronological proximity of the na'aupō remained so pertinent to Native Hawaiian Protestants in part because many of the practices that marked the supposed na'aupō of their past had never really ended. The American missionaries had deemed the entirety of Ka Wā 'Ōiwi Wale as inherently na'aupō, so any connections to that period could be seen as remnants of the Satanic past. Hula, for instance, provided a favorite target for the anti-na'aupō crusaders, Kānaka and American alike. Much to the distress of Reverend Kekela and others among the hoahānau, public hula resurged in the 1850s despite repeated efforts to suppress it.[15] The American missionaries also frequently reported on the stubborn popularity of hula and sought repeatedly to ban

[13] Daniel P. Aumai, "Lahainaluna Essay," 1841, HEA, HMCS; Kaluau, "Lahainaluna Essay," 1841, HEA, HMCS; my translations.
[14] Richard Armstrong and Sheldon Dibble, *Ka Wehewehela, Oia Hoi Ka Hulikanaka* (Oahu, HI: Mea Pai Palapala a na Misionari, 1847), 78–88.
[15] James Kekela, "J. Kekela's Farewell Letter to All of the Church Members Here in Hawaii Pt 2," *Ka Hae Hawaii*, January26, 1859, RJKC, Awaiaulu.

it.[16] By focusing on such supposed acts of naʻaupō, the resident American missionaries provided a convenient and time-tested excuse to maintain their stranglehold on the administration of and ordination within the supposedly independent Hawaiian church. Similarly, it justified their efforts to gain and hold influence over the political, economic, and social life of the kingdom. Peculiarly, they never seem to have argued that elements of supposed naʻaupō in New England had condemned their own homeland to a place of eternal Christian immaturity and unreadiness for independence from the British.

While the ABCFM missionaries *in* Hawaiʻi sought to develop and maintain control over the islands, the home office of the ABCFM pushed for greater autonomy for Kanaka Congregationalists. Starting in the 1840s, Dr. Rufus Anderson, the Secretary of the ABCFM, traveled to Hawaiʻi and pushed the Sandwich Islands Mission toward the creation of a self-sufficient church. This meant not only a financially self-sufficient church, but also a church that no longer depended on Americans for its ministers and management. As Anderson argued in 1846, the Hawaiian church could not obtain its independence without the cultivation of a Kanaka ministry. This step would also lessen the Hawaiian churches' economic reliance on the ABCFM, as American ministers collected significantly higher wages than Kānaka.[17]

The ABCFM's resident missionaries, however, fought doggedly against increased independence for Kanaka Christians and the creation of a substantive Kanaka ministry. In the late 1840s they made a token gesture, ordaining a trickle of Kanaka ministers, many of whom, like Reverend Kekela, primarily served in the foreign mission field. In a further effort to avoid criticism from Anderson and the Kānaka church members, the Sandwich Islands Mission officially disbanded in 1854 and reorganized itself as the Hawaiian Evangelical Association (HEA), a supposedly independent church with ties to the ABCFM. They promptly resumed business as usual, with the American mission families maintaining control over thriving and overwhelmingly Kanaka congregations.[18]

It took a second visit and more arm-twisting from Anderson before the HEA agreed to the ordination of significant numbers of Kanaka ministers

[16] Lowell Smith, "Sandwich Islands: A Letter from Mr. L. Smith," *Missionary Herald* 50, no. 11 (1854), 341; Noenoe Silva, "He Kanawai E Hoopau i na Hula Kuolo Hawaiʻi: The Political Economy of Banning the Hula," *Hawaiian Journal of History* 34 (2000): 29–48.
[17] Ralph Kuykendall, *The Hawaiian Kingdom: 1778–1854, Foundation and Transformation* (Honolulu: University of Hawaii Press, 1968), 337.
[18] Ibid., 339–341.

in 1865. Even former doubters such as Reverend Lorenzo Lyons soon conceded that the new Kanaka ministers were more than capable colleagues. Until the 1900s, however, the American mission families retained control over the administration of the HEA, arguing that three generations into Ke Ao the Lāhui Hawaiʻi was still too close to Ka Pō to administer an independent church.[19] Such efforts also extended into attempts to control the general public and political life of the kingdom, culminating in the US-backed overthrow in 1893.

As far back as the 1850s, however, the desire to shake off the control and paternalism of the American missionaries led to a number of major changes in Hawaiian religious life, including the royal adoption of Anglicanism and the growth of Catholicism.[20] The most loyal among the hoahānau, however, remained in the Congregationalist flock and turned to foreign mission work as a time-tested way of proving their maturity as a Christian people and strengthening and fortifying their own spiritual progress. During Ka Wā ʻŌiwi Wale, Kahiki in the sense of foreign lands had been remembered as a source of religious power and authority, a source of mana. Now Kahiki, and specifically the Marshalls, Carolines, Kiribati, and the Marquesas, would once again be a source of mana, but now a source of Christian mana. As the people who carried Ke Ao into the dark realms of Satan's Pacific holdings, the Lāhui Hawaiʻi would prove once and for all their full equality as soldiers of Christ.

The hoahānau also used mission work to actively recast the paternalistic relationship between themselves and their American teachers. Hawaiian missionaries openly expressed their gratitude to the American missionaries through filial language, referring to the missionaries as their *mākua* and expressing their gratefulness directly. Yet the Kanaka missionaries also showed a clear desire to be perceived as the equals of the ABCFM missionaries, peers in practice, children in gratitude. In 1858 unordained mission printer Simeon Kanakaole asserted this Christian equality in the field, writing to the HBCFM, "You, the Makua [plural], brought the Gospel of Christ to the Kingdom of Hawaii ... and now

[19] ABCFM, *Missionary Herald* 59, no. 11 (1863), 332; Lorenzo Lyons, "Letter from Mr. Lyons, May 1865," *Missionary Herald* 61, no. 9 (1865): 261–262; Nancy Morris, "Hawaiian Missionaries Abroad, 1852–1909," PhD thesis, University of Hawaiʻi at Mānoa, 1987, 188–190.
[20] Ralph Kuykendall, *The Hawaiian Kingdom: 1854–1874, Twenty Critical Years* (Honolulu: University of Hawaii Press, 1966), 91–93; Ralph Kuykendall, *The Hawaiian Kingdom: 1778–1854*, 140–146, 163–166, 341–344; Rufus Anderson, *Missionary Herald* 60, no. 11 (1864): 339–340.

Hawaii stands and goes to dark lands to spread the Gospel of Christ and joins with America in mission work." Though acknowledging the communal sense of indebtedness to the American missionaries by referring to them as "makua," he also used Hawaiian mission work to place Hawai'i on an equal footing with America in doing Christ's work. Missionary Hezekiah Aea echoed this sentiment in an 1865 letter to Gulick, describing himself as "Your child," in his greetings, but as Gulick's "hoa kauwa," fellow servant, when discussing his work.[21]

The Kanaka missionaries also fiercely protected their status in the field. Berita Kaaikaula was one of the first Kanaka "assistant missionaries" sent to Pohnpei and a man of some wealth and status in Hawai'i. Reverend Albert Sturges, the ABCFM missionary in charge of the station on Pohnpei, saw the Kānaka as little more than domestic servants and treated them as such. He also tried to misappropriate a rocking chair that a Hawaiian church sent to Kaaikaula, arguing Kānaka were simply too big for such chairs anyway. Fed up with the treatment of the American missionaries, Kaaikaula moved to a plot of land given to him by a local chief and built a home there, living and working separately from the American missionaries.[22]

Kaaikaula's resistance to being converted from a servant of Christ to a servant of Sturges led Reverend Sturges to write a scathing letter to the HBCFM, declaring that he and his fellow ABCFM missionaries did not welcome any Kānaka who came expecting to be an equal. The Kanaka missionaries, he continued, should be answerable to himself or another white missionary who could control their wages and labor. They lacked the intelligence and linguistic skills to be real missionaries and were fit only for domestic work. Not coincidentally, he also noted that without someone to do their domestic work the American missionaries would be in dire straits. Forced to cook and clean for themselves they would likely starve, and certainly would not have any time to evangelize. The American mission families in charge of the HBCFM replied that they had a great deal of sympathy for Sturges's position, but that the Kanaka Congregations simply would not support such an arrangement. Indeed, Hawaiian congregations and prospective missionaries were already threatening to withhold further support based on reports of Kaaikaula's

---

[21] Hezekiah Aea to Gulick, September 15, 1865, Micronesian Mission Archive-HMCS; George Haina, "Parish Report of Tarawa," 1871, Micronesian Mission Archive-HMCS; Simeon Kanakaole to Clark, January 15, 1858, Micronesian Mission Archive-HMCS.

[22] Berita Kaaikaula to Clark, January 31, 1854, Micronesian Mission Archive-HMCS; Morris, "Hawaiian Missionaries Abroad," 289–290.

treatment. As a compromise, they disciplined Kaaikaula and sent the Sturges family a stipend to pay for domestic help from the HBCFM funds – at a rate that just happened to be equal to the pay of a Kanaka missionary. Finally, they vowed to assign American and Kanaka missionaries to separate stations in the future, with the Kānaka typically assigned to the atolls and the Americans to the more comfortable high islands.[23]

The Kanaka missionaries in the Marquesas proved particularly keen to project themselves as the equals of the Americans. The Kānaka proudly embraced the fact that a Marquesan chief had come to *them* for missionaries – although it was later revealed that he really came for guns but his Kanaka son-in-law advised him to ask for missionaries first.[24] The Marquesan mission remained an almost entirely Kanaka affair. With the exception of unordained American missionary James Bicknell and a few French-language teachers, Kānaka made up the entirety of the mission's personnel. The Marquesas mission also represented the possibility for Kanaka missionaries to succeed where ABCFM and LMS missionaries had both failed. In the 1830s ABCFM missionaries from the Sandwich Islands Mission had only lasted for eight months in the Marquesas before fleeing. LMS attempts had not lasted much longer. Rather than discourage the Kānaka, the failures of the Americans and the British inspired them. In 1860 Kauwealoha wrote to the HBCFM:

[ABCFM Missionary] Armstrong and his associates who left Nuuhiva … if they stayed there until now, then they would have had converts and some persons who wished to learn writing. We men do not know God's thoughts for this people. In human thought, God has abandoned this people for the land being full of filthiness and corruption, all evils of this world.

In my opinion God has not deserted this people at all … If God had the idea of abandoning this people, why has he frequently sent workers to this parish and to work?

Kauwealoha's insinuation was clear, the LMS and ABCFM may have abandoned the Marquesas but God and Lāhui Hawai'i would not.[25]

---

[23] Berita Kaaikaula to Clark, January 12, 1856, Micronesian Mission Archive, HMCS; L. Smith, "General Letter to the American Missionaries at Ascension, 10 July 1857," Micronesian Mission Archive, HMCS.

[24] Samuel Kauwealoha to Emerson, February 18, 1892, Micronesian Mission Archive, HMCS.

[25] Hiram Bingham, *A Residence of Twenty-One Years in the Sandwich Islands* (Hartford, CT: H. Huntington, 1848), 459–466; Samuel Kauwealoha to Smith, January 7, 1860, Marquesas Mission Archive, HMCS.

The Kanaka missionaries may have considered the Marquesas a chance for an explicitly Kanaka success, but the haole leadership of both the HBCFM and the ABCFM saw it as an inevitable disaster *because* it was an explicitly Kanaka venture. Moreover, they were willing to starve out and undercut the Kanaka missionaries to prove it. After Bicknell left they ignored cries for more missionaries, cut the Kānaka's salaries to starvation levels, and stopped sending the ABCFM's supply vessel to the Marquesas. At one point, they even tried to push the Marquesas mission over to the control of the LMS, which Isaiah Kaiwi equated with abandoning one's children. Despite decades of understaffing, minimal material support, and repeated attempts to close the mission, the Kanaka missionaries persisted, seeing their successes and failures as the success and failures of the lāhui as a whole. Kauwealoha summed up their position in a letter to the HBCFM, "[T]his is a parish given by God, for the Christian people of Hawai'i, so we should be very sinful if we abandon this parish and return to Hawai'i."[26]

While often relying on Kanaka chronological and cultural proximity to Ka Pō to justify their control over both the HEA and the HBCFM, American missionary actions and language also contained a fair amount of explicit and implicit racism. Sturges's treatment of Kaaikaula and insistence on Kanaka subservience provide a relatively clear-cut example. During the second half of the nineteenth century, tensions arose as Americans raised in an era of widely accepted racial power structures came to work in the same mission fields as Kānaka. In the 1880s, ABCFM missionaries in Micronesia even requested that the HBCFM grant white missionaries the freedom to punish and eject Kanaka Missionaries without due process. The board expressed sympathy to their position and replied that the white missionaries technically had that power all along, but encouraged them not to use it as the Hawaiian churches might cease their support.[27]

Racism on the part of Haole in the Pacific was such a normative part of late-nineteenth-century life that Kānaka were as likely to comment on its absence as its presence. Aboard a mission ship in 1858, Isaiah Kaiwi

---

[26] "He Ahaolelo Misionari Ma Ko Nuuhiva Pae Aina," 1861, Marquesas Mission Archive, HMCS; "He Ahaolelo Misionari Ma Ko Nuuhiva Pae Aina," 1862, Marquesas Mission Archive, HMCS; Isaiah Kaiwi to Smith, April 9, 1861, Marquesas Mission Archive, HMCS; Samuel Kauwealoha to Smith, May 4, 1862, Marquesas Mission Archive, HMCS; Morris, *Hawaiian Missionaries Abroad*, 105.

[27] HBCFM, "Special Report of the Committee on Foreign Missions," May 1882, HCMS – Micronesia, HMHHA.

experienced what he perceived to be an amazing lack of racism on the part of the ship's captain and crew:

The Lord is planting seeds of love in the poe keokeo [white people]. Normally the iliulaula [redskin/used here to refer to Kānaka] and the Haole do not mix. They greatly despise the iliulaula, but the work of the Lord is entirely different, here there is gathering together, socializing together, sitting together, eating together.

Kānaka of Kaiwi's time apparently had little experience with Haole who did not "despise" them, including Kānaka who had long experiences specifically with American missionaries. Like Kaiwi, Robert Maka saw his equal treatment during a trip in 1865 as worthy of mention, noting in a letter, "The captain took good care of us aboard the ship just like he cared for the white people."[28]

While Kaiwi and Maka may have marveled at the courtesy and treatment they received, such treatment was far from guaranteed. Poor treatment aboard the mission packet *Morning Star* prompted Samuel Nawaa to write the following in 1877:

The main point of this letter is that we were not well treated by the captain of the ship. Our food was like the sailors'. We had to associate with smokers – the ship's officers – and the tobacco smoke was awful when we were lying down. Is it right to put workers in distress? Is this a proper thing for you white people? Are the Hawaiian missionaries dogs? Shall they eat the crumbs of the white people?

Father, without hypocrisy and fear I declare that the captain of the Morning Star hates us Hawaiians evilly, but wants you white people.

Let us Christians consider this carefully as we are of one blood, have one spirit and one God who made us.[29]

Nawaa's statement not only described what he considered racial discrimination on the part of the captain, but also displayed his personal expectation of equal treatment as a fellow servant of Christ.

Almost a decade after Nawaa's voyage, the HBCFM and ABCFM still supported segregated accommodations aboard the mission ships. Though the Kānaka no longer complained about the conditions in their official reports, they still expressed their anger through quiet protests, including snubbing ABCFM missionaries who failed to support their fellow servants of Christ. Reverend Alfred Walkup mockingly reported on the Kanaka missionaries' protests on the way to Kiribati, "[T]hey feel aggrieved at not having the same accommodations and fare as the white

---

[28] Isaiah Kaiwi to Smith, February 19, 1858, Marquesas Mission Archive, HMCS; Robert Maka to Parker, August 14, 1865, Micronesian Mission Archive, HMCS.

[29] Samuel Nawaa to Bingham, October 26, 1877, Micronesian Mission Archive, HMCS.

people did. A certain degree of civilization puffeth up!" His statement, made in an official report, implies that he saw such racist thinking as normative and that he expected the Haole-run HBCFM to sympathize with his perspective. Based on their earlier and later actions, they most likely did.[30]

While the Kanaka missionaries clearly hoped that the board and the Haole missionaries might eventually treat them with a Christian sense of equality, their lack of official protest after 1877 indicates that they may have accepted the racial limits of Christian brotherhood. The fact that the board removed Nawaa from the field in 1881 may have helped stifle their criticism to a certain degree.[31] Kanaka missionaries continued to face racial segregation and unequal treatment aboard ABCFM mission ships into the 1890s, when Reverend W. N. Lono returned to Hawaii. In his memoir – but not his official reports – he recalled that the Haole missionaries received a level of courtesy and privileges openly denied the Kānaka, something he appears to have become accustomed to after twenty-two years as a missionary.[32]

THE MISSION FIELD

Viewed through the lens of the Kānaka/Haole relationship, the story of Kanaka foreign mission work reads as a celebratory account of Kanaka agency and adaptation. Realizing the potential of the theological division of the world that their American teachers used to *deny* their equality, the hoahānau in general and the Kanaka missionaries in particular adapted that division to *proclaim* that equality. Yet this narrative, like many narratives about Hawai'i, fails to examine the range of Kanaka existence outside of the Haole/Kanaka dynamic. In examining how the Kanaka missionaries understood and interacted with their Oceanic hosts a more complex picture of these missionaries emerges. In particular such an examination uncovers the somewhat disastrous effects of Kānaka defining themselves so ardently through their desire to expand the kingdom of Christ and defeat the forces of Satan. This same theological reasoning that allowed them to claim a measure of equality to

[30] Alfred Walkup, Annual Report, Gilbert Islands 1886–7, Micronesian Mission Archive, HMCS.
[31] HBCFM, "Foreign Missions Committee Report," 1881, Micronesian Mission Archive, HMCS.
[32] Lono, "Lono, W. N. Journal," undated.

and independence from the American missionaries also gave them a motive and a rationale for denying the same independence and equality to other islanders.

In their desire to show that they were securely on the side of Christ, the Kanaka missionaries attempted to create a sharp rhetorical divide between themselves and non-Christian islanders – the supposed forces of Satan. In some cases, they did this as bluntly and literally as possible. Perhaps feeding off the rhetoric of the US Civil War, Hezekiah Aea described resistance to the mission on Ebon as coming from "na puali koa kipi malalo iho o general Satano," the rebel soldiers under General Satan.[33] Dehumanizing language proved another common favorite tactic for establishing separation between the Kanaka missionaries and other islanders, such as when Reverend William N. Lono referred to the Kiribati people as "na ilio hihiu o ka moana Pakipika," the wild dogs of the Pacific.[34]

While blanket denunciations provided a convenient shorthand for separating themselves from unconverted islanders, the missionaries eagerly described in more detail the forms of wrongdoing practiced by the "wild dogs" upon whose lands they were living. Violence, ranging from simple assaults to murder and warfare, featured prominently in the picture the missionaries painted for their audiences in Hawai'i. In 1881 J. W. Kanoa described Butaritari as superior to all others in "drinking rum, hanging oneself and shooting in the belly." He also described some of the violence in detail in 1875, including drunken assaults and a husband biting his wife's toe off. Kanoa witnessed three Kanaka seamen murdered in his home by a chief in 1871, one bullet nearly striking Kanoa and one of the bodies apparently falling on or near Kanoa's young child. The chief had been angered over his inability to purchase guns off the ship on which the three were serving.[35] Kanoa was not the only missionary to witness or even experience such violence first hand. In the Marquesas, Reverend Paulo Kapohaku and his family barely escaped a fiery death at the hands of a female chief who had initially welcomed them to settle in her valley. After chasing him out three times, she burned down his home and stole his tools. Reverend Joel Mahoe was grievously wounded when the

[33] Hezekiah Aea to Smith, November 11, 1864, Micronesian Mission Archive, HMCS.

[34] Lono, "Lono, W. N. Journal," undated.

[35] J. W. Kanoa, "Butaritari Parish Report," 1872, Micronesian Mission Archive, HMCS; J. W. Kanoa, "News from Micronesia," 1875, Micronesian Mission Archive, HMCS; J. W. Kanoa, "He Wahi Moolelo No Ke Kihapai O Butaritari," June 26, 1881, Micronesian Mission Archive, HMCS.

mission station on Abaiang was sacked during a war, an incident that eventually resulted in a show of force by the USS *Jamestown*.[36]

At times, the missionaries' letters also reported years of prolonged warfare and violence. William Lono on Maiana reported several major wars in his reports, including a war on Tarawa in 1871, a vague reference to fighting and preparations for a war of retaliation against Abemama in 1876, and a civil war related to the Abemama war that lasted intermittently from 1876 until 1878. The missionaries reported some major form of warfare on Tarawa, Abaiang, Butaritari, Tabiteauea, Fatu Hiva, and Hiva Oa. The missionaries rarely discussed the underlying causes of these wars, however, typically blaming them on Satan, single incidents like Abemama's king slaying people of Maiana, or just on the consumption of alcohol.[37]

In 1854 Kauwealoha and Kekela both wrote letters naming the love or preoccupation with war as one of the major characteristics of the Fatu Hiva people. Kauwealoha simply called them, "He poe kanaka puni kaua," a war-loving people. Kekela elaborated, "[T]he people's existence in this land is not good, nor is it protected – an ignorant race – he poe puni kaua. They war back and forth against each other." The idea of an individual or people who were puni kaua appears frequently in nineteenth-century Hawaiian historical writing, often associated with ali'i nui like Kalaniopu'u, but by the 1850s such a desire for war, let alone the opportunity for it, would be beyond the experiences of any but the oldest Kānaka. With no battles in Hawai'i since the early 1820s and no significant warfare since the turn of the century, these accounts of violence must have both shocked and titillated Kanaka audiences, while presenting clear evidence of their separation from the na'aupō of these non-Christian islanders.[38]

[36] Alexander Kaukau to Smith, January 3, 1861, Marquesas Mission Archive, HMCS; J. W. Kanoa to Gulick, October 12, 1868, Micronesian Mission Archive, HMCS; Morris, *Hawaiian Missionaries Abroad*, 388.

[37] George Haina, "Parish Report of Tarawa, 1878–79," 1879, Micronesian Mission Archive, HMCS; Paulo Kapohaku to Smith, September 18, 1859, Marquesas Mission Archive, HMCS; James Kekela to Clark, December 29, 1854, RJKC, Awaiaulu; William Lono to Pogue, October 17, 1871, Micronesian Mission Archive, HMCS; William Lono to Pogue, July 19, 1876, Micronesian Mission Archive, HMCS; William Lono to Pogue, February 9, 1877, Micronesian Mission Archive, HMCS; William Nehemiah Lono to Pogue, July 17, 1878, Micronesian Mission Archive, HMCS; Nalimu, "Tapiteauea Church Repot, 1878–1879," undated, Micronesian Mission Archive, HMCS.

[38] Samuel Kauwealoha to Baldwin, February 4, 1854, Marquesas Mission Archive, HMCS; James Kekela to Hunnewell, April 2, 1854, RJKC, Awaiaulu.

The missionaries were also eager to portray their hosts as thieves, frequently listing theft as one of the many evils of their hosts. They seemed particularly concerned about the theft of their own belongings, as on Jaluit where the only specific theft Reverend Kapali ever mentioned was the theft of missionary crops. Kekela described the situation in the Marquesas as far more dire, writing:

Only with constant vigilance night and day do we save the clothes, the adzes, digging sticks, kettles, knives and everything else. Things of ours that are lost to thievery are completely lost, never to be gotten again if we go to find them. They are not embarrassed when wearing in our presence things that they've stolen.[39]

Since Magellan, outsiders have characterized the people of Oceania as thieves, often amazed that those who had seemed genuinely friendly would also take things from them openly and boldly.[40] While outsiders saw simple theft as a sin as well as a violation of their person through their property, Oceanic peoples often perceived their actions as correcting imbalances of one sort or another. Thus the Marquesans and the people of Jaluit may have targeted the HBCFM missionaries so often because the HBCFM missionaries failed to act according to the expectations of their hosts. Kekela seems to have understood this, even though his Protestant training recoiled at the implications. He noted of the people of Fatu Hiva, "[T]hey are pleasant when paid, and that is what is right when we spend what we have, that it be in trade or for work. If their goods come to us through sale without them being pleased, there is then grumbling, and they'll just come and steal." On occasion, however, their hosts simply used theft to let the missionaries know their welcome had worn thin, as when the people of Hanaipa bluntly told Alexander Kaukau, "O ko makou aihue iho la ia a hele oe, alaila pau": With regards to our theft, when you leave, then it will end.[41]

The missionaries also incorporated many ethnographic details to tantalize their audience and accentuate the otherness of their hosts. In Kiribati, funerary practices provided the Kanaka missionaries with a textbook example of the macabre "other." Henry Nalimu described these

[39] David Kapali to Pogue, June 28, 1877, Micronesian Mission Archive, HMCS; James Kekela, "J. Kekela's Farewell Letter to All of the Church Members Here in Hawaii Pt 7," *Ka Hae Hawaii*, March 9, 1859, RJKC, Awaiaulu.

[40] Kuykendall, *The Hawaiian Kingdom 1778–1854*, 14, 18–19.

[41] Alexander Kaukau to Clark, February 25, 1864, Marquesas Mission Archive, HMCS; James Kekela, "J. Kekela's Farewell Letter to All of the Church Members Here in Hawaii Pt 6," *Ka Hae Hawaii*, March 2, 1859, RJKC, Awaiaulu.

practices in 1872, "If a corpse is well beloved by his people, he is not buried in the earth. He is placed above to become putrid then taken outside to be rubbed with coconut oil to become shiny. The persons whose deeds were regarded as evil were buried below." In the Marquesas, the missionaries frequently reported on another practice, ʻai kanaka, or cannibalism. Paulo Kapohaku, for instance, reported on one female chief in 1859 eating part of a female prisoner. Such practices may have been particularly meaningful for Kānaka Hawaiʻi, in part because they echoed similar practices from Ka Wā ʻŌiwi Wale, demonstrating how drastically the lāhui had distanced themselves from the naʻaupō of both their ancestors and other islanders.[42]

HANA LEʻALEʻA

In addition to reports on the murder, warfare, and cannibalism of their hosts, the missionaries were particularly fond of describing and denouncing the hana leʻaleʻa (pastimes), of their hosts. The term *hana leʻaleʻa* covered a number of different activities that the HBCFM missionaries and their ABCFM forefathers saw as sinfully pleasurable. Sports and games, for instance, were clear signs of Satan undermining the naʻauao. The 1870–71 report for Abaiang reported a general season of hana leʻaleʻa:

> In the third week of April 1871 sports were awakened in every place throughout the land. Here are the recreations: the hula, flying kites, swinging, baseball, canoe racing, attracting the old men and old women, young men and young women, and small children. They gave up working in their taro patches and were devoted to laziness. So some seekers gave up their support of Jesus' Kingdom, returning to darkness, forsaking good works, attending the hula and many sporting events, indulging in adultery, giving up education.[43]

While the missionaries distrusted all forms of hana leʻaleʻa, they expressed the most concern over hula.[44] Hula drew missionary contempt

[42] Henry Nalimu to Pogue, July 26, 1872, Marquesas Mission Archive, HMCS; Paulo Kapohaku to Smith, September 18, 1859, Marquesas Mission Archive, HMCS.

[43] Joel Mahoe, "Apaiang Parish Report, 1870–71," Micronesian Mission Archive, HMCS.

[44] In reality, the many different forms of Native dance described here as hula cover a broad array of forms, functions, and meanings that fall beyond the definition of hula, a term for a specific range of Hawaiian dances. The missionaries used the term *hula* to denote, and decry, all forms of Native dance. Seeing all Native dance as evil and a sign of the naʻaupō, they saw little difference to distinguish different forms. Because this chapter is primarily concerned with how these missionaries saw and shaped their relationship with other islanders, I have followed their thinking and also used *hula* to denote all Native dance the missionaries encountered.

not just for being one of the most popular and persistent forms of hana le'ale'a in both Hawai'i and the mission field, but also for its religious and sexual connotations. In their descriptions of hula in the mission field, the HBCFM missionaries worked hard to maintain that cultural stigma. In 1882, complaining about the continued success of hula instructors while his own school struggled to find students, Lono wrote, "[I]n the school house is my student, in the hula house, the student of Satan." In 1862 Hapuku equated hula and polytheism with murder and cannibalism, describing the people of Hiva Oa as "A people who greatly desire the spirits of their ancestors, hula, unjustified plundering, cannibalism, and all the evil customs."[45]

A major part of missionary discontent with hula and hana le'ale'a in general was that these activities promoted the body as a source of pleasure, connecting them to sex and sensuality. The term *le'ale'a* can even be used to infer sex when more direct terms are not desired. Like the ABCFM before them, the Kanaka missionaries felt a clear desire to investigate and report on this particular type of le'ale'a among their hosts. In 1862 Kauwealoha reported to *Ka Hoku Loa*, "They sleep around, even the old and mature, living together etc, raising children and grandchildren, they go to one another like animals. One woman, four or five men, one man, several women. When ships come, the women go out and the men help them." The allusions to multiple partners, "even among the old and mature," maritime prostitution, and nonnuclear families assured the readers that this was clearly a practice of a very different type of people than the modern Kanaka Congregationalist, perhaps even the behaviors of "animals."[46]

Reports equating changes in sexual behavior with conversion also provided the missionaries and their readers with proof of the moral superiority inherent in Christendom, while also reassuring them that their commitment to Christ might ease their own sexual desires. Surely the hoahānau would be safe if sexual adventures occurred only among the unsaved, such as one of the chiefs J. D. Ahia described on Apaiang: "[H]e is the younger brother of the deceased king ... he has pulled a part of the town to the hula and the assembling at night of men and women for fornication." Reinforcing the equation between salvation and an end to sexual impropriety, Ahia added that, "[T]he sister of R. Kaiea has turned to

[45] Zakaria Hapuku to Clark, March 13, 1862, Marquesas Mission Archive, HMCS; William Lono to Forbes, March 25, 1882, Micronesian Mission Archive, HMCS.
[46] Samuel Kauwealoha, "No Hivaoa," *Ka Hoku Loa*, March 1862.

righteousness. She was utterly devoted to pleasure formerly with young men to indulge in sensuality at night. This woman dragged in young girls to engage in fornication with young boys. And God turned her into a religious woman to do his will."[47]

Like most places in the Pacific, Hawai'i still had its fair share of hana le'ale'a, indeed Hawaiian devotion to hana le'ale'a was a favorite attack among ABCFM missionaries and their descendants whenever they felt the need or desire to deride the maturity of Hawaiian Christendom. For the devout like Kekela, hula, sex outside of Christian marriage, and other resilient forms of hana le'ale'a provided a constant source of anxiety, particularly when associated with the possibility of ho'i hope. During a visit home in 1858–59, Kekela was deeply troubled to see that hula, a form of hana le'ale'a he railed against in Nukuhiva, was still alive and well in his homeland. In Hawai'i things were worse, he argued, for the people of Hawai'i had been educated, they had heard and read the word of the Lord and still they chose to ignore him. Worst of all, Kekela had noted that some of those indulging themselves in this manner were hoahānau who had fallen back into the na'aupō. Despite numerous signs of success, the fear of the nation slipping back into darkness remained foremost on his mind, and he was quick to point out any signs of slippage. Alongside his condemnations of hana le'ale'a abroad, Kekela's fears on his voyage home illustrate the anxiety of the hoahānau that their individual and collective place within Ke Ao could easily be lost without constant vigilance and action.[48]

In defining their hosts almost solely through their hana le'ale'a and other na'aupō, however, the missionaries left room for Kānaka to still claim moral superiority. In Hawai'i these behaviors were exceptions and outrages rather than the norm. In the minds of the sober Hawaiian Congregationalists, reports of widespread hana le'ale'a solidified the na'aupō of the Marquesans and their inferiority to the hoahānau, who avoided such behaviors – at least in public. While the American missionaries may have complained about hula in Hawai'i, the hoahānau who read Kekela's reports could find some security in the fact that things were far, far worse in the truly heathen lands of the south. At the same time, these accounts gave an extra deterrent to members who might be inclined

[47] J. D. Ahia to Forbes, April 20, 1871, Micronesian Mission Archive, HMCS.
[48] James Kekela, "J. Kekela's Farewell Letter to All of the Church Members Here in Hawaii Pt 1," January 12, 1859, RJKC, Awaiaulu; James Kekela, "J. Kekela's Farewell Letter to All of the Church Members Here in Hawaii Pt 2," *Ka Hae Hawaii*, January 26, 1859, RJKC, Awaiaulu.

to enjoy or participate in hula now and then or those who excused or condoned the hula of others. To do so would lower oneself to the level of the wild dogs of the south, firm in Ka Pō rather than Ke Ao.

NATIVES, MISSIONARIES, AND EMPIRES

The Kanaka missionaries, zealous as they were of promoting their own equality and independence as a Christian people, frequently supported acts of imperial aggression against other islanders. As long as the empires' colonial projects aided the mission or weakened the will and independence of their hosts, the missionaries tended to cheer the empires on and collaborate with them whenever possible. Furthermore, portraying themselves as aligned with these explicitly Christian empires allowed them to display both their own Christian standing as well as their separation from the non-Christian islanders targeted by those empires.

Surprisingly, this included the French in the Marquesas. The Kanaka missionaries viewed the French as both potential allies and potential foes, following the New England Protestant understanding of Catholicism as being – at best – marginally within the kingdom of Christ. In the 1830s, the rabid anti-Catholicism of the ABCFM had led to the persecution of Catholic converts and the expulsion of Catholic missionaries from Hawai'i, specifically French Catholic missionaries, in 1831. Though French diplomatic and military pressure had resulted in Kamehameha III declaring an edict of toleration in 1839, both Kanaka and Haole Congregationalists in Hawai'i retained distinctly anti-Catholic attitudes. The Kanaka missionaries' distaste for Catholicism shines through in their reports, which typically referred to Catholics by the pejorative term *Ho'omana Pope,* the Hawaiian equivalent of Papist, rather than the more neutral term *Katolika.*[49]

Despite their anti-Catholic sentiments, the HBCFM missionaries felt encouraged when a French administrator in Tahiti welcomed them and granted them permission to establish a mission in the Marquesas. He also sent a French warship to accompany them to Fatu Hiva, much to their happiness and surprise. A few days later, a second French warship arrived with a Catholic mission and the Kanaka missionaries' begrudging appreciation evaporated. Over the next twenty-two years the HBCFM

---

[49] James Kekela to Clark, September 3, 1853, RJKC, Awaiaulu. In the collected works provided by Awaiaulu, Kekela used the term *katolika* only five times, compared to nearly 200 uses of *pope.*

missionaries' views of the French followed this pattern, alternating between eagerness for cooperation and outright distrust and contempt of French Catholicism.[50]

In 1875 when French warships arrived in Hiva Oa to avenge the killing of a colonial official, the Hawaiian mission seemed to have no qualms about supporting a Roman Catholic empire. Zachariah Hapuku celebrated the French soldiers coming to "teach" the Marquesans, and reported approvingly of the French willingness to shoot those who do not obey their "teachings." He then argued for more Kānaka to come to the Marquesas, as the French would protect them from the Marquesans. In 1880 he further celebrated the French occupation. New laws forced children into schools, punished and returned any student that ran from the schools, and forced the adults to fund them. This was a definite boon for the Hawaiian missionaries, whose schools had minimal success in attracting or retaining students until the French occupation. The Lord had finally seen fit to fill their schools, albeit at the point of a Catholic bayonet.[51]

Kekela felt particularly encouraged during the second French invasion in 1880, when the French sought and destroyed numerous Marquesan religious artifacts and structures. The French, he noted approvingly, also forced the Marquesans to build roads around the island, "as they do in enlightened nations." During that same period Hapuku noted, in passing, that the people of Hiva Oa were literally whipped into performing this work. The presence of roads and churches was the mark of an enlightened land, and the HBCFM missionaries welcomed any progress toward ending the naʻaupō, even if it cost the Marquesans their personal freedom and the very skin off their backs.[52]

Since 1868 Samuel Kauwealoha had cooperated with the more established French presence on Uapou, where he doggedly attempted to build a school. He held an exhibition for the French governor's visit in 1869, although a student "accidentally" burned the school down the next day. The peculiar timing of this incident hints at the possibility his students were not as eager to collaborate with the French empire as Kauwealoha was. He also wrote approvingly of the 1880 occupation of Hiva Oa, noting that in addition to overturning the old kapu and destroying the

[50] Ibid.

[51] Zakaria Hapuku to Clark, June 27, 1875, Marquesas Mission Archive, HMCS; Zakaria Hapuku to Bingham, October 9, 1880, Marquesas Mission Archive, HMCS.

[52] James Kekela to the Hawaiian Board, March 1881, RJKC, Awaiaulu; Zakaria Hapuku to Bingham, October 9, 1880, Marquesas Mission Archive, HMCS.

sacred places, the French captured Hiva Oa's two most prominent kāula (prophets). Imprisoning them in a pit and "encouraging" women to walk over their heads, the French effectively stripped them of their mana and their utility as foci for resistance. The result of these actions, Kauwealoha reported jubilantly, was that after decades of extremely limited success, many chiefs came to beg the HBCFM missionaries for teachers and a mission station.[53]

As the French empire maintained its occupation following the 1880 invasion, the mission continued to collaborate with the French in "teaching" the Marquesans and the schools remained the key point of interaction. Things were complicated, however, by an 1881 decree that all schools had to teach in French. The French were slow to enforce this, allowing the Kānaka a few years to obtain a French Protestant teacher from Tahiti. Kauwealoha, who had a long relationship with the French on Uapou, continued to praise them into the nineties when French authorities sent police to enforce school attendance and payments.[54]

Reverend Kekela, however, had begun souring on the French by 1882, accusing them of being deceitful and attempting to suppress the Protestant church. In 1895, while staying at the home of a French administrator, "a kind man, [who] hosts me and my daughter well," Kekela universally condemned the French administration as "arrogant and law-breaking." In 1898 Kekela denounced the French as second-rate colonizers, wishing that the British or Americans should have taken over, as they had in "Australia, New Zealand, Fiji, Samoa and Hawai'i, the 'Paradise' of the Pacific," where colonization had brought true progress. Furthermore, the French were racists, as "they look to their own kind, not to the ili ulaula."[55]

The relationship between Kanaka missionaries and the British in Kiribati was noticeably less strained. To start with, the British were not just Protestant, but also associated with the LMS, a close ally of and

[53] Samuel Kauwealoha to Gulick, July 4, 1868, Marquesas Mission Archive, HMCS; Samuel Kauwealoha to Miss Chamberlain, July 20, 1869, Marquesas Mission Archive, HMCS; Kauwealoha to Forbes, July 28, 1881, Marquesas Mission Archive, HMCS.

[54] Samuel Kauwealoha to Forbes, March 23, 1881, Marquesas Mission Archive, HMCS; Kauwealoha to Hall, February 22, 1882, Marquesas Mission Archive, HMCS; Samuel Kauwealoha to Emerson, January 26, 1892, Marquesas Mission Archive, HMCS.

[55] James Kekela to Hyde, July 21, 1882, RJKC, Awaiaulu; Kekela to Emerson, September 22, 1895, RJKC, Awaiaulu; James Kekela to Emerson, September 12, 1898, RJKC, Awaiaulu; James Kekela to Emerson, June 31, 1898, RJKC, Awaiaulu. It should be noted that Kekela was among the few Native Hawaiians that backed both the overthrow and annexation: James Kekela to Hyde, May 15, 1895, RJKC, Awaiaulu.

inspiration for the ABCFM. In addition, formal occupation and administration only occurred in 1892, when the HBCFM as a whole was in its last gasps. The islands did, however, fall under informal British authority for the entire span of the Kiribati mission. This led to frequent interactions with the Royal Navy, which claimed the right to enforce sanctions in those islands as they saw fit. In nearly every case, the missionaries and the British imperial representatives saw and treated one another as allies.

Holding the island of Abaiang captive to flush out the killer of a British citizen, the captain of one British warship sought out ABCFM missionary Reverend Taylor and HBCFM missionaries Leleo and Haina. In the likely event that the British bombarded the island, the missionaries and their families would first be offered refuge aboard the ship. Later, upon hearing of the eventual capture and execution of the murderer, Reverend Lono equated mission teachings and the "teachings" of British naval justice, writing, "[H]e obtained the last of the disobedience of the instructions of the missionaries. To disobey is death, to listen is life." Robert Maka happily reported an 1887 British law forbidding the sale of alcohol to the Kiribati people. Though the establishment of formal British authority in 1892 resulted in the forcible removal of former missionary W. N. Kapu from the islands, many of Kapu's former colleagues supported his removal, particularly Peter Kaaia, who accused him of questionable trading and being a disruptive presence. Worse, he suspected Kapu of supporting the recently established Catholic mission.[56]

The attempted murder of HBCFM missionary Joel Mahoe and the destruction of the ABCFM/HBCFM mission station on Abaiang also brought American naval "justice" into the picture in 1870. In response to an outcry by ABCFM supporters in New England, the navy ordered the USS *Jamestown* to visit the region and protect American interests. This apparently included the HBCFM missionaries. Through displays of overwhelming firepower and a thinly veiled desire to use it on Native homes and bodies, Captain William Truxton of the *Jamestown* managed to get compensation for the damages to the mission as well as guarantees for the future safety of Haole and Kanaka missionaries. Though he intended to hunt down Mahoe's assailants, the Abaiang people told the

[56] Samuela Kaai, "Na Mea Hoike No Ke Kipakuia O Kapu Mai Tabiteuea," 1892, Micronesian Mission Archive, HMCS; Leleo to Pogue, April 24, 1876, Micronesian Mission Archive, HMCS; Lono to Pogue, July 19, 1876, HMCS-Micronesia, HMHHA; Robert Maka to Forbes, August 31, 1887, Micronesian Mission Archive, HMCS.

disappointed Captain Truxton that the two had been killed earlier that year. The *Jamestown* then visited various islands and atolls throughout Micronesia, meeting with missionaries and local leaders to assure the safety of the missionaries and resident Americans.[57]

Some of the missionaries seemed to be keen to ride the American's imperial coattails in the Marshalls, such as Mary Kaaialii, wife of Simeon Kahelemauna. When the *Jamestown* "visited" Mili, Mr. Kahelemauna reported that he and the chief they lived under, Drime, met with Captain Truxton of the *Jamestown*. Truxton had forced Drime to sign a promise of good conduct, guaranteeing the missionaries' safety. Soon after the visit of the *Jamestown*, Kaaialii decided to purposefully violate the kapu around graveyards to prove the falseness of her hosts' religion. She wrote, "I went right in, entered the graveyard and stood at the head of the grave of the son of that chief. At this time the chief himself called to me: 'Oh woman do not go there lest you die.'" When she did not die, Kaaialii declared the incident a success for the side of God, disproving the superstitions of the heathens. Another reading of the incident, however, was that she purposefully desecrated a gravesite and avoided the very real and worldly punishments for such violations because the people of Mili knew the consequences of attacking missionaries.[58]

Seeing the concrete ways that the power and influence of empire benefited mission work, the HBCFM missionaries' greatest complaint about empires seemed to be that they lacked one themselves. Most importantly, they lacked the firepower of an empire. In 1861 Alexander Kaukau reported that the chiefs and warriors of a neighboring valley had overtaken the valley Kauwealoha lived in. The chiefs harassed the missionaries, threatening to kill them and mocking them for having no warship to protect them. George Leleo witnessed the execution of the murder suspect from Abaiang, who was tied to the cannon of a British warship and fired through in the manner made famous after the Indian Rebellion of 1857. Leleo's only regret was not the brutality of the spectacle but that the king of Butaritari who had murdered three Kānaka still walked free. If the Hawaiian kingdom had a warship, it seems Leleo would be eager

---

[57] HMCS, *Annual Report of the Hawaiian Mission Children's' Society* (San Francisco: C. W. Gordon Steam Printer, 1880), 42; Simeon Kahelemauna to Pogue, June 1, 1872, HMCS-Micronesia, HMHHA; Morris, *Hawaiian Missionaries Abroad*, 141.

[58] Mary Kaaialii Kahelemauna, "Reminiscence of Her Life on Milli (Mulgrave) Written in 1877 after Her Husband Simeon Died," February 18–May 24, 1877, translation from *Ka Lahui Hawaii*, Micronesia Collection Archive, HMCS; Kahelemauna to Pogue, June 1, 1872, Micronesian Mission Archive, HMCS.

to see it used to ensure that Kānaka Maoli would receive the same respect as the British.[59]

While they lacked warships, the Kanaka missionaries did not lack for imperial ambition. During the Kalākaua era, when both Hawaiian nationalism and the king's foreign policy ambitions peaked, several of the missionaries tried to promote the creation, or at least the illusion, of a Hawaiian empire to strengthen their work. On Butaritari, Kanoa and Robert Maka encouraged their chiefly patron, Nanteitei, to request a Hawaiian protectorate over the island in 1882. Remarkably similar petitions from Tabiteauea in 1878 and Abaiang in 1882 also hint at missionary inspiration, as these were among the most successful of the Kiribati stations.[60]

Though the kingdom never actually created any such protectorates, George Haina acted as if one existed while trying to end hostilities on Abaiang. He reported telling the warring parties, "You are friends of Kalakaua because your names are written in his book. His thoughts are ao and he commands us to talk to you folks, to live peacefully together, among one another." One of the chiefs then responded, "'We don't want war,' because he respected the enlightening words of Kalakaua." At another time Haina told them, "You are friends of Kalakaua, for you are living under the Hawaiian flag." Like Haina on Abaiang, Henry Nalimu on Tabiteauea favored a Hawaiian protectorate and sought to convince both the local chiefs and the Hawaiian government of the benefits of one. In a letter on the subject, he wrote, "[T]his will be a good thing in our opinion if the government of Hawaii should regulate the evil deeds of these islands. This would speed up the advancement of the work of God in the Gilberts."[61]

TABITEAUEA: CHRIST AND TIOBA

While Nalimu failed at getting a Hawaiian protectorate established, he and his colleague, Reverend W. B. Kapu, did find massive success in converting the people of northern Tabiteauea. Kapu had trained under

---

[59] Alexander Kaukau to Smith, January 3, 1861, Marquesas Mission Archive, HMCS; Leleo to Pogue, April 24, 1876, Micronesian Mission Archive, HMCS.

[60] Kuykendall, *The Hawaiian Kingdom, 1778–1854*, 313–314.

[61] George Haina to Bingham, November 27, 1878, Micronesia Collection Archive, HMCS; George Haina, "Parish Report of Tarawa, 1878–79," HMCS-Micronesia; Henry Nalimu to Bingham, February 4, 1879, Micronesian Mission Archive, HMCS.

Reverend Titus Coan, a fire-and-brimstone revivalist in the style of Reverend Charles Finney. In the 1830s and 1840s Coan had duplicated Finney's style and success in Hilo, and now Kapu duplicated Coan's style and success in Tabiteauea. By Nalimu's arrival as an unordained catechist in 1870, Kapu already had a substantial following in the north of the atoll. Energized by Kapu's preaching, his converts destroyed all religious artifacts that tied them to the supposed na'aupō and sought to spread the kingdom of Christ as quickly as possible to the south of the atoll – whether the people there wanted to convert or not.[62]

Most in the south did not express any real desire to convert; they were quite vocal about keeping the Congregationalists out. This was especially true of the followers of the Tioba faith, a recent indigenous form of evangelical Christianity based on prophetic visions. In 1879 open conflict broke out between the two faiths, sparked in large part by Kapu and Nalimu's attempts to proselytize in Tioban territory and the desecrations committed by their followers as they accompanied the two Hawaiians. On June 15, a battle broke out between the Tioba people and the Congregationalists, resulting in fourteen dead on the Tioban side. In a second battle in September of 1880, Kapu and Nalimu's converts massacred the Tioban warriors, seized their lands, and burned the dead and wounded in a massive pyre.[63]

While Kapu and Nalimu did not lead the battle themselves, they certainly held a great deal of responsibility for both the battle and its gruesome outcome. Several historians, including H. E. and H. C. Maude, have documented the missionaries' efforts to instigate the conflict through fiery rhetoric and goading the Tiobans into battle. Some accounts even have them preparing battle plans for their followers though they stopped short of participating in the fighting. HBCFM investigators found many Tabiteaueans who claimed that Nalimu personally invigorated them with a sermon before the battle and encouraged the massacre. More importantly, however, Kapu and Nalimu provided the theological rationale that allowed their followers to overturn established Tabiteauean military tradition and commit acts of communal violence unlike anything in the living memory of the atoll.[64]

---

[62] Maude and Maude, "Tioba and the Tabiteauean Religious Wars," 311.
[63] Ibid., 312, 316, 318–323.
[64] Ibid., 328; HBCFM, "Report of Committee on Gilbert Islands on the Tabiteauea Massacre," August 27, 1881, Micronesian Mission Archive, HMCS.

The Tioban forces largely stuck to traditional battle protocols favoring duels intended to wound. A death on the battlefield marked an official end to hostilities and required compensation to the family of the slain. On an atoll as small as Tabiteauea, such protocols allowed for warfare while minimizing the social disruption of revenge killing, large-scale warfare, and wars of conquest. The Congregationalist forces, however, fought a war of annihilation, seeking to kill as many of their opponents as possible. The families of the dead received no compensation, instead the majority of their lands were taken and split among the victors, including Kapu and Nalimu. Those who fled the battle were pursued and slaughtered, as were any who surrendered or were wounded on the field.[65]

While traditional rivalries and a desire for control over the lands and resources of the south certainly provided some of the inspiration for the battle, these had existed long before the coming of Kapu and Nalimu. They had not, however, been strong enough to break the battle protocols alone. These were only broken once the northerners accepted the postmillennial division of the world between two distinct and irreconcilable forces, Ke Ao and Ka Pō. Furthermore they seem to have accepted, quite enthusiastically, the dehumanization and denouncement of all those who opposed Ke Ao. Finally, the theology the missionaries introduced established that those who did not actively participate in spiritual battle, those who did not seek to strengthen and expand Ke Ao, were not yet true followers of Christ. Thus in fighting the Tioba people, slaughtering them like wild animals, and taking control of their lands, Kapu and Nalimu's flock secured the island for the kingdom of Christ in as direct a means as possible. Like the Hawaiians before them they had taken the theology of their teachers to heart, made it their own, and applied it to their own agenda.

The ABCFM missionaries who brought postmillennial theology to Hawai'i frequently relied on it as a means of characterizing their Native flock as weak, immature, and needing a firm, American hand to guide all their spiritual and worldly doings. Though such rhetoric clearly affected the confidence of Kanaka Congregationalists, within thirty years they had made the theology their own. Following its logic, they fought for their full independence and equality in Christ's kingdom, highlighting their efforts to expand that kingdom through foreign mission work. They

[65] Maude and Maude, "Tioba and the Tabiteauean Religious Wars," 320–321.

also used this work to critique the racism of American missionaries of the era, even attacking their unchristian behavior and attitudes in official reports.

Yet in adapting this theology, the Native missionaries also gave themselves an incentive and a means to distance themselves from non-Christian Oceanians, to prove their place in Ke Ao by separating themselves from those lost within Ka Pō. They did so using rhetoric that placed other Oceanians directly within the realm of Satan or that deemed them less than fully human. They did so by cheering on and supporting imperial projects that denied other islanders the independence the Hawaiians guarded so jealously for themselves. And they did so by encouraging other islanders to adapt their worldview, creating, manipulating, and deepening social divisions – sometimes with horrific consequences.

2

Among the Wild Dogs

Negotiating the Boundaries of Hawaiian Christianity

Aneane kanakolu na makahiki o W. N. Lono i keia wa a ke hoouna nei ka
Haku ia ia i waena o na ilio hihiu o ka moana Pakipika.

> *W. N. Lono was nearly thirty when the Lord sent him*
> *among the wild dogs of the Pacific Ocean.*
> *– Memoir of William Nehemiah Lono,*
> *Missionary to Kiribati*

Like many of his HBCFM colleagues, William Nehemiah Lono did not
convert to Congregationalism, he was born into it. By the time of his birth
in 1840, the Congregational church dominated Hawai'i's religious sphere.
Lono's parents, dedicated both to their son and to their religion, saved
what little money they had for his education under ABCFM tutelage, first
at a day school in Kona and then as a boarder at the Lymans' School in
Hilo. He would later attend the seminary in Wailuku, where he would
eventually be chosen and trained to go to Kiribati as a missionary. In
addition to the twenty years he spent in Kiribati, Lono dedicated his entire
adult life to the church, as a student, deacon, and pastor upon returning
home from the mission field. His life, as laid out in his handwritten memoirs, was one lived entirely within the fold of Congregationalism.[1]

His memoir also reveals a side of Lono that reveled in a deep embrace
of the land of his birth and the Hawaiian culture that emerged out of
that land. His descriptions of his journeys around Hawai'i Island, both
as a youth and as an adult, follow the poetic traditions of Hawai'i.

---

[1] William N. Lono, "Lono, W. N. Journal," undated, Micronesian Mission Archive, HMCS;
Nancy Morris, "Hawaiian Missionaries Abroad, 1852–1909," 374.

He narrates his journeys as a path between wahi pana, famous places, referencing significant and well-known attributes of those places. His travels on the north of the island took him from the chilly winds of Waimea, to the falls of Hiʻilawe, to the sands of Hamakua. He drank from the bubbling waters of Kāwā, was soaked by the Hāʻao rain of Kaʻu, and wept when gazing upon his birth sands, reciting the lines of a famous oli "Kona kai opua i ka lai, Pua hinano i ka malie" (Kona, calm sea of billowing clouds, a Hinano blossom in the tranquility).[2]

While exemplary in many ways, Lono still reflects the experiences of many Kanaka Congregationalists of his era. Raised and educated within the church, they devoted themselves to the teachings of Christ and to the continued progress of Ke Ao in their own lives, in Hawaiʻi, and in the world in general. Yet they remained just as strongly rooted in the culture of Hawaiʻi, its oral traditions, its cultural and social norms, and many of the logics and values rooted in Ka Wā ʻŌiwi Wale. As a result, this generation was essential in defining and institutionalizing a specifically Hawaiian Congregationalism. While they embraced and promoted key tenets of nineteenth-century Congregationalism, such as the advancement of Ke Ao, they also accommodated elements of Hawaiian culture that many American Congregationalists would have been simply incapable of understanding as the thoughts and actions of a Christian people.

Life "among the wild dogs," provided the Kanaka missionaries with a novel location to develop such a Hawaiian Congregationalism. While Kanaka missionaries fully embraced Christianity and sought to rid themselves of all traces of supposed naʻaupō, their experiences in the mission field offer a glimpse into a complex landscape of power, belief, and tradition. Their proximity to non-Christian islanders, their isolation from their homelands, and the realities of everyday life in the mission field offered considerable temptations to stray from their rigid moral path. While for the most part the missionaries did not hoʻi hope (backslide, *lit.* turn back) at times the pressures of the mission field and the temptation to commit individual acts of hewa (sin) were simply too strong.

As opponents of the Native Hawaiian missionaries were quick to point out, incidents of Kanaka missionary hewa called into question the solidity of the division between the naʻauao of the Kanaka missionaries and the naʻaupō of their host cultures. Nancy Morris has argued, convincingly, that the specific nature of several of these incidents reflects a much closer cultural proximity to both Ka Wā ʻŌiwi Wale and non-Christian

---

[2] Lono, "Lono, W. N. Journal," undated.

Islanders than the Kanaka missionaries would be willing to admit.[3] These incidents do not, however, illustrate an inability of the Kanaka missionaries to fully embrace Christianity. Instead Kanaka missionaries were developing and reflecting a specifically Hawaiian Congregationalism that actively negotiated the spiritually and politically fraught terrain between two different versions of the division between Ke Ao and Ka Pō.

The first version echoed the theology and politics of American Congregationalism, which made it necessary to develop and create a stark line between Kanaka Christianity and the Hawaiian/Oceanic past according to the benchmarks set by orthodox American Congregationalism. This division allowed the Kanaka missionaries to not just separate themselves from Ka Pō, but also to promote themselves as the spiritual equals of the ABCFM and other Haole Protestants. The second division, which was practiced more than proclaimed, defined Ke Ao in ways that quietly accommodated values and practices from Ka Wā ʻŌiwi Wale that were neither shared nor accepted by their ABCFM brethren and mākua. By its very nature this unofficial and largely implicit Kanaka-defined vision of Ke Ao was being constantly renegotiated and defined, often through disciplinary actions within the Kanaka mission community. When individual Kanaka missionaries transgressed either of the two versions of the Ao/Pō divide, the reactions of the Kanaka and Haole mission communities demonstrated how the two groups defined the divide and in doing so defined themselves.

SILENCE AND PURGE

The letters and reports that the Kanaka missionaries sent back to the Haole-dominated HBCFM provide considerable insight into how they perceived and handled the failings or alleged failings of other missionaries. Some missionaries, such as the unusually quarrelsome Reverend W. B. Kapu, peppered their correspondence with gossip and accusations about other missionaries, but this was the exception rather than the norm. Individual and group correspondence rarely discussed any possible wrongdoings by fellow missionaries, and when they did the reports often sought to stifle or silence accusations against individual missionaries that may have reached the HBCFM in Honolulu.

On occasion, however, individual missionaries committed acts of hewa so egregious and/or so public that they required intervention by

[3] Morris, "Hawaiian Missionaries Abroad, 1852–1909," 235.

other missionaries. In such cases, the Kanaka mission community often sought to spiritually and physically expel the missionary or mission family in question from the mission field, maintaining the public separation between the remaining missionaries and the naʻaupō. Two cases investigated by the 1873 Gilbert Islands General Meeting, convened and run by the Kanaka missionaries, demonstrate how they sought to silence perceptions of missionary hewa in some cases while purging offending colleagues in others.

One of the first orders of business for the 1873 general meeting was an effort to untangle a series of accusations and counteraccusations between HBCFM missionaries W. B Kapu and Henry Nalimu on Tabiteauea – the two missionaries implicated in the Tabiteauea massacre some eight years later.[4] By 1873, Kapu had already earned a reputation for conflict with other missionaries. In 1866 he wrote a letter hinting at ongoing disputes with three other missionaries, Daniel Aumai, George Haina, and J. W. Kanoa. Kanoa, he wrote, had told Kapu and Daniel Aumai that they must obey him, but "Kanoa is not our Lord." Haina meanwhile had reported that conflicts between Aumai and Kapu were having a negative effect on the work. This was nonsense, Kapu wrote, the work was slow by nature and the conflict between himself and Aumai was of minor consequence. In a masterstroke of passive aggressive deflection, he added that he was sorry to hear that Haina's wife and child had fallen into hewa and went over to the hula, the only mention by a Kanaka missionary that such a thing had occurred.[5]

Compared to the eventual strife between Kapu and Nalimu, Kapu's 1866 letter and the clashes it hinted at were relatively minor. The exact origins of the conflict between Kapu and Nalimu are hard to pin down, but after Nalimu joined Kapu on Tabiteauea, the two quickly began to accuse each other of numerous hewa. According to Kapu's 1872 report, Nalimu was spreading rumors that Kapu promoted idolatry, hula, and false teachings regarding the proper starting time for the Sabbath. Kapu retaliated by claiming it was Nalimu who spread false teachings about the Sabbath and, furthermore, Nalimu taught that drinking was acceptable. Later that year he again accused Nalimu of telling the people that drinking was acceptable and clarified that Nalimu taught that fishing, farming, and the lighting of cooking fires were all permissible on the

---

[4] Gilbert Islands Mission, "General Meeting Annual Report, 1873," Micronesian Mission Archive, HMCS.
[5] W. B. Kapu to Gulick, June 19, 1866, Micronesian Mission Archive, HMCS.

Sabbath despite restrictions on such acts in Hawai'i. In a letter from July of the same year, Nalimu accused Kapu of a range of minor and major hewa, including letting his female domestics gossip, selling tobacco, threatening Nalimu with a stick, threatening the people of Tabiteauea with a warship, and accusing Nalimu of killing his dog.[6]

In 1873 the Gilbert Islands General Meeting, which brought together the entire Gilbert Islands Mission, examined both sets of accusations. At the meeting the two repeated and expanded their claims in person. Kapu claimed that Nalimu told the people that hula and drinking were acceptable and that Nalimu was seen drunk on a visiting ship. Nalimu repeated the charges that Kapu had purchased tobacco and used it to pay the builders of the schoolhouse, as well as using the children who lived with him to sell tobacco while hiding his own dealings. Almost any of the accusations laid out against Kapu and Nalimu, if found to be true, would have been grounds for expulsion from the mission, clear evidence of the na'aupō of the accused.[7]

The assembled missionaries, however, spent almost no effort in examining the accusations. They instead pushed Nalimu and Kapu to end their dispute, pressuring each to admit that their charges were based entirely on hearsay, which was not admissible as evidence in a formal investigation. Unlike in other cases, the general meeting did not seek out any witnesses who might have given direct testimony against either Kapu or Nalimu. In response to accusations of distributing tobacco and alcohol against J. D. Ahia during that same 1873 meeting, the missionaries called forth multiple witnesses from across Kiribati and recorded testimonies over multiple days. They did the same for later accusations against Joel Mahoe, Kaluhine Haina, and George Haina in 1885. In the case of the Nalimu/Kapu dispute, however, the general meeting concluded it was a simple personality conflict between the two ministers and that the charges had no real merit. The two were then pressed to shake hands as a mark of the end of their disagreement.[8]

Kapu, however, was intent on getting the last word. In 1874 he wrote that Nalimu had struck Mrs. Nalimu and only the presence of the local

---

[6] W. B. Kapu to Pogue, July 15, 1872, Micronesian Mission Archive, HMCS; W. B. Kapu, "Parish Report, Tapiteauea," 1872, Micronesian Mission Archive, HMCS; Nalimu to Pogue, July 26, 1872, Micronesian Mission Archive, HMCS.

[7] Robert Maka, "Minutes of the Gilbert Islands General Meeting, 1873," Micronesian Mission Archive, HMCS.

[8] Ibid.; William N. Lono, "Minutes of the Gilbert Islands General Meeting, 1885," Micronesian Mission Archive, HMCS.

people, who pulled Nalimu off and threw him in a spring, prevented a severe beating. As with the rest of Kapu's allegations the HBCFM and his fellow missionaries chose to ignore these claims. Kapu and Nalimu's dispute soon came to an end, however, as they focused their ire and energy on a shared foe, the followers of the Tioba religion on the southern side of the atoll.[9]

As Nancy Morris has argued, in cases of interpersonal conflict the Kanaka mission community preferred to employ either a formal or informal process of hoʻoponopono, a Hawaiian practice that aimed for restoring peace rather than punishing wrongdoing. The handling of the Kapu/Nalimu conflict shares many characteristics of hoʻoponopono, including multiple group prayers, an airing of grievances, and an effort to reach a point of mutual forgiveness and fellowship before moving on.[10] In this particular case such methods might have been far more useful to the collected missionaries than an investigation, as the threat to the mission seemed to come not from conduct that fractured the carefully constructed rhetorical wall between themselves and Ka Pō, but rather from a lack of collegiality and a willingness to gossip. If left to simmer the bad blood between Nalimu and Kapu would inevitably cause greater problems, particularly because many of the rumors surrounding their behavior came from those considered to be within Ka Pō, such as foreign traders opposed to the mission and the unconverted of Tabiteauea. To maintain their Christian superiority, the Hawaiian missionaries needed to maintain at least some semblance of Christian unity. The practice of hoʻoponopono was constructed specifically for such a purpose, allowing the missionaries to restore unity and stability. Furthermore, by focusing on the dispute as the source of the various accusations, the missionaries in Kiribati could silence, at least formally, the accusations of hewa that would have tarnished their collective reputation if proven true.

On occasion, accusations of hewa were so considerable or so public that they required action. The 1873 General Meeting also investigated and began the process of expelling missionary Timoteo Kaehuaea, a man as conflict prone as Kapu but with a far more violent temperament. The most well-known incident, and the one that forced the rest of the missionaries in Kiribati to investigate Kaehuaea, involved a bloody attack on

9   W. B. Kapu to Pogue, July 31, 1874, Micronesian Mission Archive, HMCS.
10 Morris, "Hawaiian Missionaries Abroad, 1852–1909," 195; Mary Pukui, E. W. Haertig, and Catherine Lee, *Nana I Ke Kumu (Look to the Source)*, (Honolulu, HI: Queen Liliuokalani Children's Center, 1972), 60–64.

an I-Kiribati man. According to George Leleo, who lived near Kaehuaea, the man had been helping Kaehuaea build a house and argued with him over payment. Kaehuaea then attacked and cut the man with a hatchet. Materialism-driven and hatchet-based violence appears to have been a theme for Kaehuaea. In another case, he chased down and terrorized an I-Kiribati woman with his hatchet after her dog bit, but did not kill, one of Kaehuaea's pigs. In yet another incident Kaehuaea, apparently unable to find his favorite hatchet, used either a Kiribati spear or a war club to terrorize some local children who he believed had stolen some of his chicks.[11]

Kaehuaea also seemed unusually trigger-happy for a missionary, once shooting at and beating a young servant in the employ of fellow missionary George Leleo. Kaehuaea suspected, incorrectly, that the boy had stolen goods from his home. In another case, a local man had gone to Kaehuaea's place to discuss something with him, but Kaehuaea was busy and told the other man to leave. When the other man refused Kaehuaea ran into his house and returned with a gun and a large knife, prompting the man to hide beneath a pandanus tree until he had a chance to flee. In a final incident, a man had been carrying a barrel for Kaehuaea when the top fell off. Kaehuaea grabbed his gun, put it against the man's forehead and asked whether he would enjoy having his own barrel cracked open.[12]

While some of Kaehuaea's fellow missionaries may have shared his frustrations over suspected thefts and property damage, these violent episodes were a direct threat to the work of the mission. Despite Kaehuaea's repentance, the meeting recommended that he be sent home, which the HBCFM board agreed to do.[13] Allowing Kaehuaea to remain as a missionary was a clear practical threat to their work, as such incidents hardly endeared them to the I-Kiribati. Furthermore, Kaehuaea's violence clearly and quite irrevocably transgressed the boundary between Ke Ao and Ka Pō in a way that the other missionaries, and the board, simply could not ignore. This is not to say that missionaries disapproved of violence entirely, as they certainly accepted a certain degree of disciplinary violence. They enthusiastically approved of disciplinary violence carried out by empires, for instance, applauding the French invasions of the

---

[11] Maka, "Minutes of the Gilbert Islands General Meeting, 1873"; George Leleo to Bingham, September 8, 1873 (located in Kaehuaea folder), Micronesian Mission Archive, HMCS.

[12] Leleo to Bingham, September 8, 1873, HMCS – Micronesia, Kaehuaea folder, HMHHA.

[13] Maka, "Minutes of the Gilbert Islands General Meeting, 1873." Kaehuaea, however, initially refused to return home and instead briefly took up copra trading for a few years before retuning. Morris, *Hawaiian Missionaries Abroad*, 292–293.

Marquesas, French whipping of forced labor on Hiva Oa, and the British blowing a suspected murderer from a cannon in the Marshalls.[14] Even in Hawai'i, ABCFM-associated teachers used physical violence to cow Kanaka and Haole students into submission at Lahainaluna, Punahou, and the Royal School.[15] Having been trained in the mission schools, it seems quite likely that at least some of the Kanaka missionaries had been the target of disciplinary violence in their training and perpetrators of it in the mission field.

Yet the irrational interpersonal violence that Kaehuaea was prone to was exactly the sort of behavior that the missionaries portrayed as belonging within Ka Pō. The Marshallese, I-Kiribati, and Marquesan violence the missionaries reported on served as an excellent rhetorical device to contrast Ke Ao and Ka Pō. Kaehuaea's violence threatened the very basis of this worldview, therefore Kaehuaea would have to be purged from the mission. Interestingly, ABCFM Reverend Benjamin Snow on Ebon, often eager to decry the Kānaka as weak-willed sinners, felt that the board and the general meeting had overreacted. He recommended that Kaehuaea simply be transferred to another station, perhaps because the only one harmed in the incident had been an I-Kiribati. Kaehuaea seemed to agree, refusing to return home and remaining in Kiribati at his own expense for several more years.[16]

As seen in the 1873 Gilbert Islands General Meeting, the behavior of individual missionaries occasionally required interventions by the broader mission community. When the missionaries in question were not believed to have committed major hewa, such as in the dispute between Kapu and Nalimu, every effort was made to resolve and move past the issue for the sake of the mission. When this was not possible or desirable, as in the case of Kaehuaea, the mission community moved quickly to purge themselves of the taint of na'aupō carried by their fallen colleagues.

---

[14] George Leleo to Pogue, April 24, 1876, Micronesian Mission Archive, HMCS; Zakaria Hapuku to Clark, June 27, 1875, Marquesas Mission Archive, HMCS; James Kekela to the Hawaiian Board, March 1881, RJKC, Awaiaulu.

[15] For information on corporal punishment at Lahainaluna see Paul William Harris, *Nothing but Christ: Rufus Anderson and the Ideology of Protestant Foreign Missions* (New York: Oxford University Press, 2000), 50. For information on corporal punishment at Punahou see Joy Schulz, "Empire of the Young: Missionary Children in Hawai'i and the Birth of U.S. Colonialism in the Pacific, 1820–1898," PhD thesis, University of Nebraska, 2011, 125–126. For information on corporal punishment at the Royal School see Linda K. Menton, "A Christian and 'Civilized' Education: The Hawaiian Chiefs' Children's School, 1839–50," *History of Education Quarterly* 32, no. 2 (1992), 228.

[16] Morris, "Hawaiian Missionaries Abroad, 1852–1909," 292–293.

ALOHA, MADNESS, AND WITCHCRAFT
IN THE MISSION FIELD

While personality conflicts and violence could easily cause cracks in the carefully built separation between Kanaka missionaries and Ka Pō, some of the most spectacular and deepest challenges to that separation came not from anger but from aloha (love). In several cases, a missionary's aloha for a sick or deceased family member led to behavior that marked them as na'aupō rather than na'auao, at least under normal circumstances. These events sometimes lead to the use of practices associated with pre-Christian Hawaiian spirituality or with local spiritual practices condemned by ABCFM missionaries as vestiges of the lingering na'aupō. The use of such practices in times of distress highlighted the permeability of the border between the na'auao of the Hawaiian Christians and the na'aupō of their "pagan" hosts. The reactions of fellow Hawaiian missionaries similarly acknowledged the fragility of the wall separating these groups, either quietly overlooking slippages or anxiously purging transgressors to reestablish the appearance of a separation.

In two cases, those of the Reverend Kapu and John Nua, the deaths of missionary wives lead to practices that echoed traditional Hawaiian practices of mourning, memory, and spiritualism in ways that Haole missionaries in Micronesia saw as disqualifying them from mission work. Though only in the mission field between 1892 and 1895, Nua initially achieved some success thanks, according to later accounts by Catholic missionary Father Sabatier, to a "pretty wife" with an even prettier singing voice.[17] When she died, ABCFM missionary Reverend Alfred Walkup reported that Nua had gone mad, prophesizing and committing other acts Walkup considered unacceptable for a missionary. Nua's fellow Kanaka missionaries took him in and attempted to shelter him from the judgment of the board, but Walkup successfully sought his removal. The HEA report for 1895, however, merely noted that Nua's wife had died and that he wished to return due to grief.[18] Nua eventually recovered enough of his sanity to return to service as a pastor once home in Hawai'i.[19]

Reverend Kapu of Tabiteauea also suffered substantial mental anguish over the 1876 death of his wife, Mary. While she was lying ill, the couple's

---

[17] Ernest Sabatier, *Astride the Equator: An Account of the Gilbert Islands,* trans. Ursula Nixon (Melbourne: Oxford University Press, 1977), 226.

[18] Morris, "Hawaiian Missionaries Abroad, 1852–1909," 437.

[19] HEA, *Thirty Second Annual Report of the Hawaiian Evangelical Association* (Honolulu: The Hawaiian Board, 1895), 61.

home burned down and Kapu was barely able to save her from the flames. The fire and the events around it, including the looting of their property and her exposure to the elements after the fire, did little for Mary's health. She soon died a proper martyr's death, calling out for the I-Kiribati to repent with her last breaths.[20] After Mary's death, various Haole observers reported that Kapu regularly communed with Mary's spirit, talking to her in an apparently open manner.[21]

In both these cases, the reactions of Kapu and Nua to their wives' deaths crossed the boundaries of what most non-Kanaka Congregationalists would consider acceptable Christian behavior, leading to Nua's removal and strengthening the growing misgivings surrounding Kapu. Neither case, however, seemed to raise much of a stir among the Native Hawaiian mission community, whose records are silent on Nua's supposed mental health issues or Kapu's communing with his wife.[22] They do, however, appear in accounts by ABCFM Reverend Walkup and other Haole. Part of the issue seems to be that Walkup and some other Haole were keen to disparage the Kanaka missionaries, grabbing onto and reporting whatever rumors came their way. At the same time, the Native Hawaiian missionaries were equally keen to silence scandals that might hurt the mission and their collective reputation.

Another possible cause, however, was that the Kanaka missionaries saw these events not through the lens of acceptable Christian behavior but rather through the lens of acceptable Kanaka mourning practices. While the American missionaries in Hawaiʻi succeeded in ending, or at least heavily curtailing many pre-Christian spiritual and cultural practices, they had less success regarding Kanaka expressions of grief. Somewhat stereotypical of New England expressions of emotion in general, the ABCFM missionaries preferred that mourning remain a largely private practice, tight-lipped and full of gravitas if undertaken at all. Kanaka practices, however, included a considerable amount of what Mary Pukui has referred to as "grief work," meant to both help heal the loss of a loved one and to express one's aloha for that person.[23]

---

[20] George Haina to Pogue, June 15, 1876, Micronesian Mission Archive, HMCS; J. W. Kapu to Chamberlain, April 26, 1876, Micronesian Mission Archive, HMCS.

[21] Morris, "Hawaiian Missionaries Abroad, 1852–1909," 237.

[22] I was unable to find any mention of either of these two issues in my own research and even Morris, whose examination of the mission archives was more in depth than my own, only cites non-Hawaiian sources.

[23] Mary Pukui, E. W. Haertig, and Catherine Lee, *Nana I Ke Kumu*, 132–148.

The greater the aloha one shared with the deceased, the more expressive was the required grief. Wailing, or uwe, was a common practice, loud mournful cries that often shocked and unnerved non-Kanaka observers.[24] Kanikau, chants commemorating the deceased, were also common, before and after the adoption of Christianity. Such practices continued throughout the nineteenth and twentieth centuries. To express their aloha and their associated grief in as prominent a manner as possible, many mourning Hawaiians included kanikau in letters to the Hawaiian language newspapers. *Ke Alula*, for instance, published a kanikau written by missionary Joel Mahoe in 1868, which he had written for his deceased infant daughter Mareka.[25] Overwhelmed by both the numbers of kanikau and by the expense of running a newspaper, the editor of *Nupepa Kuokoa* began to charge for publishing reader-submitted kanikau in 1867.[26]

Other common displays of grief for deceased family members or a beloved aliʻi included elements that shocked Haole Protestant sensibilities. American missionaries and other non-Kānaka seemed particularly fond of noting temporary or permanent disfigurement, including but not limited to cutting oneself or knocking out one's own teeth. Pukui noted similarly shocking behavior, especially in the case of the death of an aliʻi, such as people wearing clothes in a manner that displayed their genitals. Such actions would be considered as signs that an individual was "pupule," mentally ill, and under normal circumstances this would be a cause of concern for the family or community. In a mourning period, however, such actions could be and would be excused as temporary madness, an appropriate expression of grief and a clear demonstration of the depth of aloha felt for the deceased. As Morris has argued, Nua's actions reflect such practices, which may explain why his fellow Kanaka missionaries had little interest in sending him home. Both Kānaka and Haole may have seen his actions as pupule, but Kānaka may have seen such grief-derived pupule as appropriate under the circumstances. Just as Nua was removed from the mission field and later given a pastoral flock, other Hawaiian ministers were also briefly withdrawn from religious duties following the death of loved ones. In 1894 the Reverend Martina Lutera, a former Native Hawaiian missionary, was temporarily removed from the

---

[24] Ibid., 145.
[25] Joel Mahoe, "Ka Make Ana o Mareka K. Mahoe," *Ke Alaula*, April 1868. For a translation see Morris, "Hawaiian Missionaries Abroad, 1852–1909," 233.
[26] Puakea Nogelmeier, "Mai Paʻa I Ka Leo: Historical Voices in Hawaiian Primary Materials, Looking Forward and Listening Back," PhD thesis, University of Hawaiʻi, 2003, 135.

ministry after the death of his wife, Harriet. The grief weighed heavily on Lutera, whose actions led the HEA to deem him to be "unsound of mind."[27]

Often one's aloha for and grief over the deceased took on what could be considered spiritualist aspects that clashed with Congregationalist teachings. Morris has equated Kapu's communing with his wife's spirit with the practice of ʻunihipili, a practice of communing with the dead meant to both ease the pain of separation and to demonstrate one's aloha for the dead. Nua's "madness" and prophesizing follow similar mourning practices, which go beyond acting "pupule," and include prophesizing based on hōʻailona (signs) from the dead. Walkup and the HBCFM board interpreted Nua's grief-driven prophesizing as a lack of Christian fortitude, but his Kanaka colleagues may have seen it as an expression of his aloha for the deceased and part of the healing process.[28]

Yet such practices still betrayed the vision of cultural separation between the Kanaka missionaries and the supposed naʻaupō of the pre-Christian Hawaiian past. Furthermore, it put them more in line with the mourning practices of other "naʻaupō" islanders than with their ABCFM mission mākua. Early European visitors to the Marquesas noted cutting and wailing practices similar to those practiced by the Hawaiians. The HBCFM missionaries often disparaged Kiribati burial practices, which included the caring for the rotting bodies of the dead above ground and the retention of bones as family relics. In all cases, aloha was expressed through actions considered otherwise extreme, socially unacceptable, or dangerous; the more extreme the measure the greater the aloha for the dead.[29]

It should be noted that missionaries like Kapu and Nua were among the most dedicated and often most devoted of the Native Protestants in Hawaiʻi. Kapu, for instance, promoted an extremely rigid code of Christian conduct and established a strict system of fines and punishments for his flock on Tabiteauea.[30] Despite their Christian devotion and

[27] HEA, *Thirty Second Annual* Report (1895), p. 13; HEA, *Thirty Third Annual Report of the Hawaiian Evangelical Association* (Honolulu: The Hawaiian Board, 1896), 10; Morris, "Hawaiian Missionaries Abroad," 378; Pukui et al., *Nana I Ke Kumu*, 133.

[28] Morris, "Hawaiian Missionaries Abroad, 1852–1909," 235; Pukui et al., *Nana I Ke Kumu*, 133, 56.

[29] Edwin N. Ferdon, *Early Observations of Marquesan Culture, 1595–1813* (Tucson: University of Arizona Press, 1993), 81; Henry Nalimu to Pogue, July 26, 1872, Micronesian Mission Archives, HMCS.

[30] G. W. Kapu to Pogue, July 15, 1872, Micronesian Mission Archive, HMCS; Morris, "Hawaiian Missionaries Abroad, 1852–1909," 333–334.

their efforts to create a wall between themselves and Ka Pō, the Kanaka missionaries still retained and seemed willing to overlook mourning practices with ties not just to pre-Christian Hawaiian culture in general but to Oceanic spiritualism in particular. Such practices remained somewhat common in the twentieth century as well. The mental health workers who helped develop *Nana I Ke Kumu* with Mary Pukui noted such spiritual practices or echoes of such practices in the 1960s and 1970s.[31]

The strength and retention of such practices seems to indicate that their importance for Kānaka Maoli, even for the devout like Kapu and Nua, outweighed fears and insecurities about their proximity to Ka Pō. This strength and persistence likely stems from their association with aloha, and specifically the type of aloha one held for close family members. Such a value is not specific to Hawai'i or to Oceania, but the emphasis Kanaka placed on relationships between people and on expressions of aloha raises both the importance and acceptance of such seemingly extreme mourning practices. For these reasons, Kapu and Nua's Kanaka colleagues seemed perfectly content to overlook their actions, neither finding the need to condemn them as having falling into Ka Pō nor being particularly interested in discussing acts that they knew that the HBCFM and ABCFM would perceive as reeking of Ka Pō.

There were, of course, limits to what the Kanaka missionaries were willing to remain silent about, even during periods of mourning. Another investigation from the Gilbert Islands General Meeting in 1873 could help illustrate some of those limits as it resulted in the expulsion of missionary J. D. Ahia from the mission. The previous year, Ahia's wife, Nei Kalua, abandoned Ahia and their children and then died estranged from Ahia on Abaiang. Overcome with grief Ahia began, like Nua and Kapu, acting in ways uncharacteristic of a devout missionary, much to the chagrin of fellow missionary George Haina. Haina wrote home of his great aloha for Ahia, but also reported his great sorrow over Ahia's hewa and his "teaching the people to do wrong." According to Haina's account, Ahia had purchased tobacco and alcohol, used the tobacco to pay for the preparations for his wife's funeral, and served the alcohol to two I-Kiribati women in his house.[32]

Though Ahia denied any wrongdoing, the 1873 meeting called several witnesses over multiple days who testified that Ahia had indeed purchased tobacco to pay the man who had dug his wife's grave. Others testified that

[31] Pukui et al., *Nana I Ke Kumu*, 140–143.
[32] George Haina to Pogue, August 14, 1872, Micronesian Mission Archive, HMCS.

Ahia had purchased at least two bottles of alcohol, and the two I-Kiribati women testified that not only had he served them alcohol, but that he had drank some himself. While some wine was allowed in certain circumstances, the women testified that at least some of the alcohol had been clear, stored in a square bottle, and burned going down. It also made them very drunk; one of them testified that "human thought left us." The meeting found Ahia guilty of all the charges, and added in a final charge of lying to his fellow missionaries about his actions. Eager to purge Ahia and his sins from the mission fold, they recommended that he be recalled by the HBCFM at the soonest possible moment, which he quickly was.[33]

In some ways, the spiritualist aspects of Nua and Kapu's mourning might seem more threatening to the barrier between the Kanaka missionaries and Ka Pō, yet Ahia's actions generated a far sterner reaction from his fellow missionaries. Like in the case of Nua and Kapu, Ahia's actions might be seen as "pupule," an indication of the depth of his grief through drastically out-of-character acts. Ironically, considering their desire to promote themselves as separate from so much of the pre-Christian past, the missionaries may have condemned Ahia's specific expressions of grief in part because they were *not* rooted in that same past. Nua and Kapu mourned in ways that were culturally or spiritually familiar enough that their colleagues may have waived their normally strict interpretations of Christianity – though still recognizing the situation as potentially embarrassing enough to either cover up or ignore. Ahia's use and exchanges in tobacco and alcohol have less of a root in Hawaiian cultural expressions of grief than in introduced debauchery, perhaps one of the reasons the missionaries were less willing to forgive and forget his actions.

One could also argue that Kānaka often felt a stronger association with those elements of Christianity that most closely resembled elements of the pre-Christian kapu system. As the name indicates, the kapu system was heavily dependent on the creation and maintenance of various kapu, restrictions and prohibitions on specific actions during specific times. Thus Sabbath restrictions could easily be understood and promoted as a kapu day, in which certain actions were prohibited. Kanaka Congregationalists, it should be noted, often took Sabbath day restrictions particularly seriously as seen with the appropriately named Reverend W. B. Kapu's campaign against Sabbath-day cooking fires. It would be difficult for Kanaka Congregationalists to accept turning their backs on a deceased loved one and their spirit, but a straightforward kapu on alcohol or tobacco would

[33] Maka, "Minutes of the General Meeting, 1873."

be much simpler to accept and to maintain. Ahia had clearly violated the mission's kapu on both substances.

Furthermore, by distributing tobacco and alcohol Ahia not only committed what the other missionaries saw as hewa, he enabled and encouraged hewa among the I-Kiribati, "teaching the people to do wrong," as Haina had put it. In doing so he undermined the mission's presumptions of moral authority and presented ammunition for I-Kiribati and others opposed to the mission. This was in no way an abstract threat; islanders in the mission field often pushed back against Hawaiian spiritual authority.

In 1859 Reverend Kanoa had faced exactly that sort of opposition when the people of Abaiang noted that other Kānaka Maoli in the area smoked and danced. Why, they asked, was Kanoa claiming that the Kānaka Maoli were na'auao yet the I-Kiribati were na'aupō for doing the same things. Kanoa's response was that those other Kānaka were not missionaries, the true representatives of the Hawaiian na'auao. The damage was still done, however, leading Kanoa to write home about the importance of increasing church morality at home and among Kanaka sailors visiting the area.[34] In the case of Ahia, however, it *was* a missionary who committed such acts and worse, encouraged the I-Kiribati to commit them as well. For his erosion of the authority of the mission and his own moral failings, Ahia needed to be purged from the mission. There were acceptable ways to express his aloha for his dead wife; sharing tobacco and alcohol with I-Kiribati were not on the list.

The Marquesas mission faced its own aloha-driven controversy in 1892, when James Kekela and Samuel Kauwealoha accused fellow missionary Zachariah Hapuku of participating in witchcraft. The three were long-term colleagues in the Marquesas, Kekela and Kauwealoha having arrived in 1853 and Hapuku in 1861. Their families had even intermarried; Kekela's son Ioane married Hapuku's daughter Emele. In this particular case, it was Hapuku's aloha for the ailing Emele that lead to what Kekela, Kauwealoha, and the board all agreed to be an act of considerable hewa.

In 1892, the Hapuku family had traveled to Puamau to visit the Kekela's and to leave one of Ioane and Emele's children for James and Naomi Kekela to hānai (adopt/raise). Emele was pregnant with another child, likely their daughter Maria[35] and on the way back to Hapuku's

[34] J. W. Kanoa to Clark and Kawaiahao Members, November 25, 1859, Micronesian Mission Archive, HMCS.
[35] Based on the ages of children listed in: James Kekela to Parker and Emerson, November 5, 1896, RJKC, Awaiulu.

mission station at Atuona, Kekela caught up with them and gave Emele a horse to ride. According to Hapuku, a small local child told Emele that the horse had belonged to Vae Topetu, an ali'i wahine (female chief), who had recently died. Emele began to ache along the journey and by the time they arrived at Atuona she was quite ill, slowly worsening throughout the pregnancy and for several months after delivering her child.[36]

With Emele's strength leaving her, Hapuku and the rest of the family began to fear for her life. Another ali'i wahine, who was Emele's hānai mother, heard about her illness and came to visit and care for Emele. Hapuku described her as a "luahine lapaau" – an experienced female medical practitioner whose skills typically included not only the diagnosis and treatment of physical ailments, but spiritual ones as well. The luahine lapa'au told Hapuku that Emele had been cursed or possessed by a "daimonio" (demon), more specifically the spirit of Vae Topetu, whose horse had been kapu to pregnant women such as Emele. Hapuku and the luahine lapa'au spoke to the spirit, pleading for Emele's life. Speaking through Emele, the spirit at first denied that anything could prevent her from taking Emele's life, but eventually she decided that the horse must be given to her living daughter in Puamau. Then and only then would Emele be cured.[37]

At this point Hapuku wrote to Kekela, to whom they had returned the horse, asking that Kekela give the horse to the "daughter of the demon." Kekela refused, scandalized not only by Hapuku's actions but also that Hapuku had now involved him. Hapuku later claimed that Kekela had tried to switch horses to somehow trick the spirit, arriving in Atuana with the daughter of Vae Topetu and another horse. Kekela denied this and claimed he had simply opposed the entire business completely, but he did eventually did turn over the original horse. Emele soon recovered her health.[38]

Kekela and Kauwealoha quickly dashed off a letter to the HBCFM board explaining what had happened and requested that the board authorize a committee composed of themselves and a representative from the next mission ship to investigate the matter. They never disputed Emele's possession, but Hapuku, they argued, should have relied on the power of Christ to defeat the "demon" rather than making a deal

[36] Zachariah Hapuku to Emerson, September 5, 1893, Marquesas Mission Archive, HMCS.
[37] Ibid.
[38] Ibid.; James Kekela and Samuel Kauwealoha to the Hawaiian Board, December 22, 1892, Marquesas Mission Archive, HMCS.

with it. Hapuku's efforts to explain what happened to the board relied largely on the fact that he had not prayed to or sacrificed anything to any Marquesan or Hawaiian god's or spirits, he had merely given away a horse. Kekela and Kauwealoha, however, argued that in doing so he had committed an act of major hewa, and had clearly tumbled back into Ka Pō.[39]

This launched a series of angry denunciations between Kekela and Kauwealoha, on one side, and Hapuku, on the other. In 1893 Hapuku replied that Kekela and Kauwealoha were simply conspiring against him for personal reasons. The two had never fully trusted him as he had not attended the elite Lahainaluna seminary like the two of them. Furthermore, they were jealous of the success and popularity he and Emele had among both the Marquesans and the French authorities. Finally, he argued, his denouncers were known sinners as well. Kauwealoha was widely rumored to have slept with his Marquesan stepdaughters and Hapuku had met two Marquesan women who claimed to have slept with Kekela. In 1894 Hapuku reported that Kauwealoha was in debt to opium sellers and Kekela was sick in the head. The board sided with Kekela and Kauwealoha, however, and ejected Hapuku from the mission. Hapuku remained in the Marquesas and continued to preach and teach independently until 1897, when he repented and his fellow missionaries welcomed him back into the mission.[40]

Kekela and Kauwealoha, removed from the situation as it was not their child who was ill, enthusiastically and routinely condemned Hapuku until his repentance in 1897. His former colleagues argued that in giving the horse to the "demon," Hapuku had not only endangered his soul but the sanctity of the mission as a whole. In engaging with Marquesan spiritualism highly reflective of the supposed na'aupō of Hawaiian spiritualism, Hapuku's actions tarnished them all with the na'aupō of both their unconverted hosts and of Ka Wā 'Ōiwi Wale. When asked to give the horse to Vae's daughter, Kekela had replied that what the Hapuku family was engaged in was, "No ka po mai ia no Satana mai," of the pō of Satan, as well as "naaupo lapuwale," worthless ignorance, terms

[39] Kekela and Kauwealoha to the Hawaiian Board, December 22, 1892, Marquesas Mission Archive, HMCS; James Kekela to Emerson, October 19, 1893, RJKC, Awaiaulu.
[40] Zachariah Hapuku to Emerson, September 5, 1893, Marquesas Mission Archive, HMCS; Zachariah Hapuku to Emerson, February 26, 1894, Marquesas Mission Archive, HMCS; Zachariah Hapuku to Emerson, May 6, 1897, Marquesas Mission Archive, HMCS; James Kekela to Emerson, September 22, 1895, RJKC, Awaiaulu; James Kekela to Emerson, April 2, 1897, RJKC, Awaiaulu.

the missionaries normally reserved for the actions of the Marquesans, Marshallese, and I-Kiribati.[41]

Worse, however, such actions were witnessed by the Marquesans, including Catholics and other opponents of the mission, weakening the authority of the missionaries. In December 1892, the two noted that the 'Ohana Hapuku were "planting the seeds of the kingdom of Satan," as news of the incident was spreading around the island. In 1893 Kekela complained that:

The natives of Nuuhiva laugh and tease, saying, "One would have thought Jesus was the god of those Kekela folks, but it turns out that you are people who believe in demonic spirits," meaning the corpses of the dead. "Ha, we don't believe in such things. Hah! You people are liars." "How is it that Hapuku folks gave the horse on behalf of the demon?" It is not possible to reply. The Catholics laugh teasingly along with some foreign traders, and the same is true of some French officials.

For Kekela and Kauwealoha, the actions of the Hapuku family dealt a lasting and potentially fatal blow to the mission's claims of Christian superiority. The Hapuku family needed to be expelled from the mission for the mission to ever recover.[42]

While Kekela and Kauwealoha feared for the maintenance of their spiritual authority, the 'Ohana Hapuku feared only for Emele. Like Kapu and Nua, the 'Ohana Hapuku's aloha trumped a missionary project built in part upon policing the boundary between Kānaka Hawai'i and other islanders. Moments of crisis such as this broke down the artificial line between Marquesans and Hawaiians, revealing their cultural and spiritual kinship. The similarity between Marquesan and Hawaiian spiritualism prompted Hapuku to seek out Marquesan spiritual authority and defer to a Marquesan woman's metaphysical knowledge. When questioned by the missionary authorities Hapuku attempted to renegotiate the boundaries between Ke Ao and Ka Pō, arguing that he had not transgressed the boundaries as he neither prayed to nor gave offerings to the spirit. His wife, Hana, was far more direct in her defense, "What about it, did my daughter die? A horse is a minor thing to me, the life of my daughter is what is important."[43]

---

[41] Kekela and Kauwealoha to the Hawaiian Board, December 22, 1892, Marquesas Mission Archive, HMCS.

[42] Ibid.; James Kekela to Emerson, October 19, 1893, RJKC, Awaiaulu; Samuel Kauwealoha to Emerson, December 8, 1892, Marquesas Mission Archive, HMCS.

[43] Hapuku to Emerson, September 5, 1893, Marquesas Mission Archive, HMCS; Kekela, Kekela to Emerson, October 19, 1893, RJKC, Awaiaulu.

While all the Kanaka missionaries in the Marquesas seem to have agreed on the basic narrative of the events surrounding Emele's possession, the split between the 'Ohana Hapuku and those of Kekela and Kauwealoha show that even within the small, close-knit Marquesas mission events could force significant difference of opinion over the proper dividing lines between Ke Ao and Ka Pō. The cases of Nua and Kapu, however, show even greater differences between how Kanaka missionaries defined those lines and how their Haole counterparts did. Mission work and devotion to their religion required the Kanaka missionaries to sacrifice and even condemn vast swaths of the practices and beliefs they inherited from Ka Wā 'Ōiwi Wale, but it could not force them to sacrifice their aloha.

MOEKOLOHE: SEX AND THE MARRIED MISSIONARY

Of all the ways American missionaries sought to reshape Hawai'i, perhaps none was as ambitious as their efforts around sex and sexual relationships. Between their neo-Calvinist theology and their middle-class Victorian lionization of physical self-control, they arrived at an understanding of appropriate sex strictly defined by the confines of a church-sanctioned, monogamous, lifelong, patriarchal, heterosexual marriage. The sheer number of descendants the missionaries left behind indicates they certainly had no trouble with sex within such a marriage, but any sex outside of this very specific form of sexual relationship was a clear sign both of one's lack of self-control and lack of civilization. When they arrived in Hawai'i in 1820, they were shocked to find that this was almost the only form of sexual relationship *not* widely practiced among the population.

Like many of the peoples of Oceania, Kānaka Maoli had relatively little use for such a restrictive vision of sex as the specific economic, cultural, and social structures that benefitted from and promoted that vision simply did not exist in Hawai'i. Unencumbered by such limits, Kānaka enjoyed sex both within and outside of long-term relationships and with a lack of secrecy and shame that astounded, intrigued, and titillated Haole. Sex acts also occurred between people of the same sex and gender, with the same lack of secrecy and shame as other forms of sex. This is not to say that there were no sexual norms or restrictions, but the allowable range of sex acts was by all accounts broad and diverse. Kānaka Maoli participated in a diverse array of sexual and romantic relationships. As in many parts of the world, serial monogamy was a common arrangement, combining a shared domestic situation with an exclusive or near exclusive sexual relationship. The length of such relationships was largely determined by the interest of the two parties in maintaining it. Other relationships included what could be understood as polygamy or polygyny, with a single individual having established relationships with two or possibly more partners. There was even a term to define the relationship between two individuals who were both in sexual/romantic relationships with a third individual, they were each other's *punalua*.[44]

This was the sexual world that the ABCFM missionaries landed in and this was the sexual world they sought to remake in their own image. Unable to find an equivalent for adultery or fornication in the Hawaiian language, they created a new term, *moekolohe* (mischievous sleeping), to denote all sex outside of their rigidly proscribed norms. Once they defined moekolohe, they moved to stamp it out. They decried moekolohe from the pulpit, ejected perpetrators of moekolohe from their congregations, and convinced Ka'ahumanu and her circle of powerful chiefs to institute marriage laws and criminalize moekolohe. Despite legal, religious, and social condemnation, many Kānaka retained understandings of sexuality based on the less-constrictive norms of Ka Wā 'Ōiwi Wale. This can most commonly be seen through the persistence of serial monogamy despite the unwillingness of both church and state to grant divorces, making all subsequent relationships technically adultery. By the mid-nineteenth century, a combination of Kanaka sexual freedom and Neo-Calvinist condemnation led to an impasse where moekolohe was widely condemned and prosecuted yet frequently practiced.[45]

Beyond simply demonizing sex outside of marriage, the ABCFM missionaries also sought to normalize and promote their specific vision of marriage. In addition to monogamy, these introduced forms of marriage placed a heavy privilege on male authority and power within the relationship, including male control of female labor, sexuality, and mobility. New laws even allowed husbands to request that the courts track down and return wives who had left them, a dramatic change from the freedom of earlier times.[46] By no coincidence the ABCFM and

---

[44] For a more detailed survey of sex and relationships in Ka Wā 'Ōiwi Wale see Milton Diamond, "Sexual Behavior in Pre Contact Hawai'i: A Sexological Ethnography," *Revista Española del Pacífico* 16 (2004): 37–58.

[45] Sally Engle Merry, *Colonizing Hawai'i: The Cultural Power of Law* (Princeton, NJ: Princeton University Press, 2000), 247, 255–257.

[46] Ibid., 252–254.

the HBCFM required their missionaries to be married before going into the field, both to set an example of proper Christian marriage and to provide their missionaries with domestic, intellectual, and emotional support that they could, theoretically, command and control. Just as importantly it provided them with a sexual outlet, preventing them from being tempted to succumb to Ka Pō in the form of "heathen" women.

The mission field provided Kanaka missionaries with a moekolohe-rich contrast to their vision of properly restrained Congregationalist sexuality. Far from the eyes of other Kānaka and their American mākua, that same mission field provided numerous temptations to engage in relatively familiar sexual experiences and relationships that they publically condemned. While it is impossible to know how often members of the mission community may have committed moekolohe, accusations of moekolohe do appear with some frequency in connection to Kanaka missionaries. A review of the Kanaka missionaries' accounts shows that in cases in which moekolohe was the primary issue of concern, the Kanaka missionaries tended to either ignore the matter or to address it in as cursory a manner as possible – often to the exasperation of their Haole colleagues. In cases in which missionaries, or more commonly their wives, committed moekolohe within part of a broader set of acts that challenged the authority and privileged status of missionary husbands, the missionaries tended to react with far more fervor. Such moments also show that for at least some of the women within the mission, the surrender of their sexual and personal sovereignty was too high a price to pay for retaining the illusion of Kanaka conformity to Congregational sexual norms.

Of all the cases in which members of the mission family were accused of simple moekolohe – moekolohe absent of a larger pattern of actions calling into question male authority within marriage – only two resulted in disciplinary action. In both cases this disciplinary action was taken not by the Kanaka mission community, but by the HBCFM board in Honolulu. In 1891 the HBCFM board recalled Zadaio Paaluhi back to Hawai'i for an inquiry into rumors of his misconduct, specifically rumors about moekolohe with a thirteen-year-old neighbor. An article in the ABCFM's Hawai'i newspaper *The Friend* noted that the inquiry came about as the result of "[m]onths and even years" of scandalous rumors. Paaluhi's failure to address the rumors and the apparent failure of his colleagues in Kiribati to act on their own led to the board ordering Paaluhi home for the investigation. Paaluhi denied the charges and there was little evidence against him, but the board found him guilty and prevented his return to the mission field.[47]

In the other case, the 1885 Gilbert Islands General Meeting heard and granted longtime missionary J. W. Kanoa's request that he be allowed to remain in Kiribati and withdraw from the mission. The HBCFM had earlier ordered that Kanoa return home with his second wife Mary, a much younger I-Kiribati woman who had achieved a reputation for moekolohe that had spread to Honolulu and beyond. At the general meeting, Kanoa admitted to his wife's misdeeds, but stated that he wished to remain in Kiribati to continue aiding the mission in an unofficial and thus less damaging manner. In this particular case, the Kanaka missionaries' collective loyalty to one of their own seems to be the overriding concern, not Mary's reputation for moekolohe. If accounts of Mary's moekolohe had reached Honolulu, they had surely reached Kanoa's fellow missionaries first, but they took no official action to either end Mary's moekolohe or to purge her and her na'aupō from the mission community. This moekolohe was apparently seen as a private issue, one that did not require or even allow Kanoa's fellow missionaries to become involved in the management of his own household. Forced by the HBCFM to accept his removal from the mission, they softened the blow as much as possible by creating a space for him to operate independently.[48]

These two cases were exceptional in that they resulted in removal from the mission, but they were not unusual in their failure to generate any real desire among other Kanaka missionaries to purge the offenders and their na'aupō. In the Kanoa case they went out of their way to allow Kanoa to continue working with the mission *despite* the HBCFM board's decision to withdraw him from the field. In every case in which moekolohe and moekolohe alone threatened to pull a missionary back into Ka Pō, other Kanaka missionaries ignored the moekolohe unless other factors forced their hand. In the Marquesas, for instance, when Hapuku

---

[47] Morris, "Hawaiian Missionaries Abroad," 420; "Hawaiian Board," *The Friend*, November 1891, 89.

[48] Lono, "Minutes of the Gilbert Islands General Meeting, 1885." According to Hiram Bingham II, a close friend and former colleague of Kanoa, Kanoa continued to aid the mission without the benefit of pay or supplies in the hopes that Mary might change her ways. The HBCFM made an agreement with Kanoa that if she could avoid adultery or other unbecoming behavior for three years, they could rejoin the mission, but by Kanoa's death in 1897 they remained off the official mission rolls; see Hiram Bingham II, "Mr. Kanoa's Wife," *The Pacific Commercial Advertiser*, March 26, 1897, 5.

denounced both Kekela and Kauwealoha for moekolohe, his accusations
were clearly motivated not by the desire to purge the mission of moekolohe, but rather in retaliation. He claimed, after all, that such rumors
were widespread and that he had even met with two of the women, but
he had little interest in reporting or confronting Kekela and Kauwealoha
until after *they* had denounced *him* for suspected witchcraft.[49]

In the case of Levi Kaiwi, even an aggressive investigation and inter-
rogation by ABCFM missionary/HBCFM representative Dwight Baldwin
failed to prompt the 1862 Marquesas General Meeting to investigate
Kaiwi's supposed moekolohe. Kaiwi and his wife, Kapauana (sometimes
Pauana) were already scheduled to leave the mission due to her own
moekolohe, which will be examined in more detail later in this chapter.
Baldwin, however, felt the need to investigate rumors swirling around
Levi, namely his dealings in tobacco and alcohol. Visiting Vaitahu, the
valley on Tahuata where Kaiwi was stationed, Baldwin interviewed residents, gathering information on Levi and Pauana and discovering widespread accusations that Levi had also participated in moekolohe.[50]

At the ensuing general meeting, Baldwin pushed the Kanaka missionaries to formally investigate Levi. Much to Baldwin's surprise it took days
before the assembled Kanaka missionaries addressed the charges, with
Kaiwi continuing to participate in the meetings and worship. Following
the established pattern of avoiding controversy whenever possible, the
missionaries only reluctantly addressed Baldwin's accusations, perhaps
because Kaiwi was already scheduled to leave the islands. Kaiwi denied
the alcohol and tobacco charges and the Kanaka missionaries apparently
accepted him at his word and took no further action. They also refused to
address what Baldwin called, "the vastly graver charges of <u>moekolohe</u>."
Despite what the increasingly exasperated Baldwin considered Kaiwi's
guilty demeanor, neither denying nor admitting to the charges and acting
"like a wolf in a trap," the other missionaries refused to press the issue.[51]

Stunned by how the Kānaka, "shrank from the responsibility," Baldwin
spent even more time speaking to the people of Vaitahu about Levi and
Pauana, leaving convinced that the two had indeed sunk deep into Ka
Pō. According to these interviews, Levi had not only had numerous lovers, but he seemed to put little effort into keeping these affairs quiet as,

---

[49] Zachariah Hapuku to Emerson, September 5, 1893, Marquesas Mission Archive, HMCS.
[50] Dwight Baldwin, "Report of the 6th Voyage of the *Morning Star* to the Marquesas
     Islands," May 1862, Marquesas Mission Archive, HMCS.
[51] Ibid. Double underline in original.

"there was nobody at Vaitahu, native or foreigner, that did not know of his adulterous life." One woman told Baldwin, "Pauana was more better than Kaiwi, for she took only one man, but he had taken many women." The king of Tahuata also reportedly claimed that he did not wish for any more missionaries, as they were, "All a set of adulterers." Still the other Kanaka missionaries did and said nothing to address Kaiwi and his moekolohe. Reporting home about the departure of Kaiwi, Kekela described the reason for his return solely as "the moekolohe of his wife," an explanation that likely rankled Kaiwi's fellow passenger, Reverend Baldwin.[52]

In at least one other case Haole missionaries forced investigations of supposed moekolohe that Kānaka were willing to overlook. In June 1874, while her husband Simeon Kahelemauna was away, a bedridden and ill Mary Kaaialii received a massage from one of her female servants, a common medical practice throughout much of Oceania. When the female servant tired of massaging her, a young male servant took over the task. During the massage he attempted to kiss and grope her. Kaaialii grabbed him by the genitals and managed to push him off, but did not have the energy to remove him from the house, where he stayed overnight. After Simeon's return, she informed him of what happened. In his August letter to the HBCFM in August, Simeon included an account of the assault, writing that his wife had fallen into "moekolohe," though his description makes it clear that this was a case of attempted rape. For the Kahelemauna family the matter seemed settled, and based on the lack of mention in their writings the same seems to hold true for the other Kanaka missionaries.[53]

ABCFM missionary Benjamin Snow, however, soon found out and felt the need to intervene. Though Snow was sympathetic to her plight, in his eyes Kaaialii had fallen because she allowed the young man to massage her. Furthermore, she had touched his genitals, albeit in an effort to fight him off, and had failed to physically eject him from the house after the incident, despite being bedridden. After interviewing Kaaialii, Snow temporarily ejected her from the congregation, demanded she not participate in the next communion, and proceeded to "help" her write a confession, which he read to the congregation while Kaaialii stood on mute display. He then welcomed a properly humiliated Kaaialii back into the congregation.[54]

[52] Ibid.; James Kekela to Emerson, May 8, 1862, RJKC, Awaiaulu.
[53] Simeon Kahelemauna to Pogue, August 24, 1874, Micronesian Mission Archive, HMCS.
[54] Ibid.; Benjamin Snow to Pogue, December 28, 1874, Micronesian Mission Archive, HMCS.

In 1885 Kanaka missionaries *did* choose to investigate rumors about George Haina on Tarawa, but only after the rumors had become so pervasive that they threatened the good name of the Kiribati mission as a whole. The Gilberts' General Meeting addressed claims that Haina committed moekolohe with a married woman named Ntoka. Ntoka, her husband, and Haina all denied the accusations. Operating off some earlier groundwork, the meeting also interviewed Haina's daughter Sela. Sela testified that she had started the rumors in response to her father not allowing her to marry a Haole merchant. Hearing Sela's testimony the rest of the general meeting quickly declared the case closed.[55]

In all these cases the Kanaka mission community seemed highly reluctant to pursue accusations of moekolohe despite the widespread association between moekolohe and Ka Pō. As Morris has pointed out, the missionaries may have been uninterested in pursuing charges regarding moekolohe in part because they did not feel it was that significant an issue. Even in Hawaiʻi the full pressure of law and church failed to stomp out moekolohe. ABCFM missionaries continued to express amazement that even young men and women with good social standing and Christian upbringings had sexual histories the missionaries simply could not reconcile with as proper Christian behavior. For many Kānaka of the era, either at home or in the mission field, moekolohe was too common and too natural an act to place undue stress upon. If discovered, repentance was of course required, but the act lacked the particularly heavy sense of sinfulness that it did among the American mission community.[56]

While the Kanaka missionaries only reluctantly pursued investigations into moekolohe alone, they would prove keen to pursue investigations into and punish individuals whose moekolohe or other actions threatened mission husbands' power and authority over their wives. Indeed, defending the recently introduced institution of marriage would prove a far more important task than punishing the recently defined sin of moekolohe. Most of the cases discussed in the preceding text, for instance, involved moekolohe committed by Kanaka men. Such actions, though violating the sexual norms of Christian marriage, did little to threaten the authority of husbands over their wives. In fact, ignoring male moekolohe could easily be seen as propping up male power and authority, especially because the Kanaka missionaries did actively investigate and report on moekolohe of mission wives. Even in the cases of Kaaialii

---

[55] Lono, "Minutes of the Gilbert Islands General Meeting, 1885."
[56] Morris, "Hawaiian Missionaries Abroad, 1852–1909," 229–232.

Kahelemauna and Mary Kanoa, however, other Kanaka missionaries had little desire to intervene and purge the moekolohe from the mission in the way Snow and HBCFM board did. The sexual conduct of Mary and Mrs. Kahelemauna were the business of their husbands, not other missionaries. In other cases, the moekolohe of missionary wives *did* prove of significant concern for other Kanaka missionaries, particularly when the suspected moekolohe occurred during a husband's absence.

On two different occasions male missionaries accused Kaluahine Haina, the wife of George Haina, of moekolohe and similar acts that called into question her husband's sexual and domestic authority over her. The first set of accusations can be found in a letter fragment from missionary Daniel Aumai, likely from 1866, which details her sexual improprieties. While her husband was visiting Hawai'i for his health,[57] Kaluahine and the Haina children stayed on Abaiang with the Mahoe family, who had their hands full preventing Kaluahine from straying with I-Kiribati men. "Because of the talking and friendliness of this woman with the men," Aumai wrote, the men would come at night and call out to her. Kaluahine went to them and "sat upon the thighs of the pagan as though he was her husband." Aumai also claimed that a man named Ten Kimaoa, the younger brother of the king of Tarawa, called out to her at night when she was at the Mahoe home, asking her to bring him water. Mrs. Mahoe tried to stop her but she went out anyway, the insinuation being that she planned to bring him more than just water. According to Aumai, she also declared to the local people she had no husband and was sexually available or, as Aumai put it, "like a prostitute."[58] In addition to the implied moekolohe, the public manner in which she acted and the way Kaluahine not just *signaled* that she was free from the sexual control of her absent husband but actively *declared* herself to be free of him, were threatening enough for Aumai to report on her actions. After Haina returned, however, Aumai made no more reports. In Haina's absence it was the business of the mission to police his wife's behavior but when he returned to the mission field it became his business once again.

Some nineteen years later, the same general meeting that investigated and dismissed accusations about George's moekolohe once again brought Kaluahine under scrutiny. This time the issue was her relationship with

---

[57] This seems to be the same trip during which Haina reported tensions between Aumai and Kapu in response to which Kapu accused Kaluahine and one of the Haina children of having participated in hula.

[58] Daniel Aumai, Letter Fragment, Micronesian Mission Archive, HMCS.

her former host Joel Mahoe. Though the Mahoe family had returned home a decade earlier, Joel had returned aboard the *Morning Star* as a visiting representative of the HBCFM board. According to Likiak Sa, an I-Kiribati minister on Kosrae, Mahoe had come to Likiak's home when Mrs. Haina was staying there. As was the case some twenty-three years earlier, George was not present. Mahoe's interactions with Mrs. Haina had a domestic and intimate nature that did not sit right with Likiak or with his other houseguest, Kanaka missionary George Leleo. Mahoe apparently sat and ate with her privately, prayed with her, called her "Mama," and whispered with her in her room for some time. Leleo finally kicked Mahoe out and told him to stay away. The people of Kosrae, Likiak reported, were convinced that Mahoe and Kaluahine were having an affair.[59]

The general meeting publically admonished Mahoe for his actions, though neither he nor Kaluahine seemed to face any long-term sanctions. Mahoe returned as the HBCFM representative in 1889. Kaluahine returned to Honolulu for good in the 1890s, not because of the scandal but because her husband George died at sea while visiting another island. She would live on until 1903, when the Hawai'i Evangelical Association's annual report would remember her fondly as a long-time missionary wife and mother of eleven.[60]

As in the case of Aumai's reporting on Kaluahine in 1866, the general meeting's uncharacteristic zeal in investigating the incident between Joel Mahoe and Kaluahine can also be traced to their efforts to protect the marital authority of the absent Mr. Haina. As described earlier, no claims of moekolohe were explicitly made, though they were certainly implied. Rather the ire of Leleo and the other missionaries stemmed from the oddly intimate and domestic behavior publically exhibited between Mahoe and Kaluahine. The accusations and investigation focused largely on the incidents in Likiak Sa's home, such as the two eating together, whispering together, and Mahoe calling Haina, "Mama." What Mahoe was doing was more than trying to seduce Kaluahine; he almost seemed to be supplanting George Haina's domestic role within the Haina marriage.[61]

In other cases, the Kanaka missionary community intervened not because the actions of mission wives threatened the authority of their

---

[59] Lono, "Minutes of the Gilbert Islands General Meeting, 1885."
[60] Lono, "Minutes of the Gilbert Islands General Meeting, 1885"; HEA, *Fortieth Annual Report of the Hawaiian Evangelical Society* (Honolulu: The Hawaiian Board, 1903), 50.
[61] Lono, "Minutes of the Gilbert Islands General Meeting, 1885."

husbands, but rather because mission wives had negated that authority completely by "abandoning" their husbands, their children, and the mission. The term Kānaka used for this was *ha'alele*, which can mean to abandon, but it can also be used for simply leaving, rejecting, or giving up upon. The term carries less inherent judgment than abandonment, but many of the male missionaries certainly implied that judgment when mission wives chose to ha'alele. In the Marquesas, Ruta Kaiheekai, the wife of Alexander Kaukau, and Luisa Pauana, the wife of Levi Kaiwi, both left their husbands for other lovers. In both these cases, other Kanaka missionaries stepped in, both to purge the offending women and their husbands from the mission and to encourage the women to return to their husbands and to Hawai'i. In neither case were they successful. In a third case, this time in Kiribati, Nei Kalua left her husband, J. D. Ahia. Nei Kalua's death soon after negated the need to purge her from the mission, but it also helped pitch Ahia into the grief that led to his own fall into Ka Pō.[62]

In the case of Pauana, rumors of her affair with Kale, a Kānaka Maoli living in the Marquesas, reached the rest of the Marquesas mission sometime in 1860 or 1861. When confronted by Kekela and some of the other missionaries in 1861, Pauana admitted to the affair and repented in front of the other missionaries and visiting HBCFM representative Dr. Sidney Gulick. Though Kekela wrote that it was probably best if the Kaiwi 'Ōhana returned to Hawai'i, he assured the HBCFM that they had accepted her repentance and that "the missionary leaders in Hawaii should not be concerned." It is hard to tell to what degree Gulick prompted the investigation or the Kanaka missionaries did, but Kekela's reports of Pauana's contrast with his lack of reporting on Levi's supposed moekolohe a year later.[63]

Things between Pauana and her lover were not quite as over as Kekela and his colleagues had believed. In February 1862, Kekela reported back to the HBCFM that Pauana had abandoned Kaiwi and was living with Kale. Later that year, the *Morning Star* and HBCFM Representative/ABCFM missionary Reverend Dwight Baldwin arrived in the Marquesas with instructions to retrieve the Kaiwi family. When the mission ship arrived at Vaitahu only Levi and his children were at the station; Pauana had not only abandoned her husband, she had fled to the opposite site

---

[62] Based on her name, Nei Kalua may have been I-Kiribati rather than Native Hawaiian. Morris, "Hawaiian Missionaries Abroad, 1852–1909," 268.

[63] James Kekela to Smith, April 10, 1861, RJKC, Awaiaulu.

of the island with her lover. The "king" of the valley agreed to send word to her, but to Baldwin's chagrin he would not force her to return against her will.[64] It appears Pauana never did return to either Kaiwi or Hawai'i. Alexander Kaukau was still discussing efforts to send her back to Hawai'i in 1865. Reverend Coan reported that Pauana died in the Marquesas sometime soon after his visit there in 1867, however there does not seem to be any mention of her death in the writings of any of the Kanaka missionaries living in the Marquesas.[65]

In 1864 another adultery scandal rocked the Marquesas mission, this time involving the wife of Alexander Kaukau, Ruta Kaiheekai. Soon after arriving at their new station at Hanavave, Fatuiva, Kaiheekai began an affair with the two young chiefs who held the land the mission was built upon. This continued for four months until Bill Kekuku, another Kānaka Maoli who lived at the station, discovered the affair and told Kaukau. At first Kaukau refused to believe that Kaiheekai was having an affair, then he saw a distinctive set of scratches across her back. Soon after Kaiheekai fled to live with the two chiefs while Kaukau attempted to care for both the mission and the couple's children.[66]

Despite repeated efforts to convince her to return, Kaiheekai remained with the chiefs for several years. Although Kekela sought to have Kaukau removed from the field as soon as possible, Kaukau remained for several years as well, hoping to convince his wife to return to him. He reported praying with and teaching her, at one point even believing he had made progress in "taming her," but nothing could persuade her to return. In 1867 he wrote that she "pays no attention to me because of her love for the young chiefs." Kaukau returned home that year, crushed by Kaiheekai's abandonment and the accidental death of his son soon after.[67]

---

[64] James Kekela to Smith, February 24, 1862, RJKC, Awaiaulu; Dwight Baldwin, "Report of the 6th Voyage of the *Morning Star* to the Marquesas Islands," May 1862, Marquesas Mission Archive, HMCS.

[65] Morris, "Hawaiian Missionaries Abroad, 1852–1909," 305; Alexander Kaukau to Gulick, October 13, 1865, Marquesas Mission Archive, HMCS; Titus Coan, *Life in Hawaii: An Autobiographic Sketch of Mission Life and Labors, 1835–1881* (New York: Anson D. F. Randolph and Company, 1882), 207.

[66] Alexander Kaukau to Gulick, October 13, 1865, Marquesas Mission Archive, HMCS; Alexander Kaukau to the editor of the *Nupepa Kuokoa*, April 3, 1866, Marquesas Mission Archive, HMCS.

[67] James Kekela to Gulick, November 22, 1865, RJKC, Awaiaulu; Alexander Kaukau to Gulick, November 6, 1866, Marquesas Mission Archive, HMCS; Alexander Kaukau to Gulick, February 20, 1867, Marquesas Mission Archive, HMCS.

As long as Kaiheekai remained in the Marquesas, particularly as long as she continued openly living with the two young chiefs, she also remained an open sore upon the good name of the mission, a crack in their façade of separation from both Ka Pō and the sexually licentious young Marquesan chiefs who lived within it. The Kanaka missionaries continued to encourage her to return to her husband in Honolulu, but Kaukau's colleagues, as well as HBCFM representative Reverend Coan in 1867 and HBCFM representative Reverend Smith in 1868, all failed to convince her. By 1869 she refused outright to meet with HBCFM representative Reverend Pogue. According to Coan she, like Pauana, died some time after.[68]

In both these cases, the Kanaka missionaries were deeply concerned not just with moekolohe, but with the broader challenge of mission wives rejecting the authority of their husbands. Thus while the Kanaka missionaries rarely reported on moekolohe, Kekela not only reported on Pauana and Kaiheekai leaving their husbands, he absolutely bemoaned their actions. In a 1862 letter Kekela dismissed the importance of deadly battles in his valley, drought, and famine, writing, "he mea ole wale no ia. Hookahi no pilikia nui loa i loaa mai iwaena o makou. Oia ka haule ana o ka wahine a L. Kaiwi iloko o ka moe kolohe." (They are as naught. There is only one great problem found among us. This is the fall of L. Kaiwi's wife into moekolohe.) Similarly, in his 1865 letter to Gulick he briefly states that some of the mission community had died of small-pox, and possibly some of their bodies had been eaten, before a long and emotional recounting of Kaiheekai's fall and its effect on the emotional state of the mission.[69]

Considering how strongly the Congregationalist vision of marriage asserted male authority and control, it seems little wonder that Kekela and his colleagues reacted so strongly when mission wives fled – or that those mission wives chose to flee in the first place. The imposition of American sexual and domestic norms through the institution of marriage left much to be desired for women still familiar with the greater personal autonomy of Ka Wā ʻŌiwi Wale. Hawaiian customs allowed women not just room for the occasional affair, but more importantly

---

[68] J. F. Pogue, "Morning Star Report, 1869," Marquesas Mission Archive, HMCS; Lowell Smith, "Morning Star Report, 1868," Marquesas Mission Archive, HMCS; Coan, *Life in Hawaiʻi*, 207.

[69] James Kekela to Smith, February 24, 1862, RJKC, Awaiaulu; James Kekela to Gulick, November 22, 1865, RJKC, Awaiaulu.

they also allowed women to haʻalele at will and to start a new relationship without anyone's approval or consent other than that of herself and her new partner. Even in the late nineteenth century many women continued to follow patterns of serial monogamy despite a legal system that forced women to return to husbands they had "abandoned" or to be fined and imprisoned as "adulterers."[70] For centuries, serial monogamy had been the norm in Hawaiʻi, other parts of Oceania, and indeed over large swaths of the world. In taking new partners, Pauana, Kaiheekai, Nei Kalua, and perhaps even Kaluahine Haina and Mary Kanoa would have been following far more established customs than Christian marriage.

Within the new system men were entitled to their wives' domestic labor as well, which was vital in the mission field. This domestic labor, including the raising of children without the support of the extended family, may have provided further incentive for missionary wives to seek a temporary, or even permanent, break from their husbands. Women in the new system of marriage were also geographically constrained, being expected to remain either in or near the home or with their husbands. Kanaka Maoli women, like Kanaka Maoli men, frequently traveled to visit family and friends, often independent of whatever man they may have been partnered with. Native women were unlikely to enjoy the geographic constraints expected of married Christian women, particularly because their husbands were still free to travel while their wives raised the children and maintained the home. For the mission wives, whose husbands were frequently traveling to teach and to preach, this would have added to an already heavy burden while removing the social and emotional benefits found in travel.[71]

The frequency with which members of the Kanaka mission community were accused of moekolohe, and the reluctance of that community to address moekolohe, indicate a major deviation from the official understanding of the sexual lines between Ke Ao and Ka Pō. Though not openly questioning the belief that moekolohe was evidence of the naʻaupō, Kanaka missionaries simply lacked the zeal of their American mākua in stamping it out. In many ways their thinking on sex retained strong influences from Ka Wā ʻŌiwi Wale, a time when moekolohe was not even a concept, let alone a concern. The mission's husbands were, however, deeply concerned with maintaining the institution of Christian marriage,

---

[70] Merry, *Colonizing Hawaiʻi*, 250–252.
[71] Ibid., 252–254.

which gave them considerable power over their wives. When missionary wives, or even other missionaries, acted in ways that questioned a husband's authority over his wife the mission community reacted far more decisively. At least some mission wives were less interested in maintaining this new form of marriage, choosing instead to embrace another remnant of Ka Wā 'Ōiwi Wale and ha'alele. If that meant leaving the mission community and Ke Ao as well as leaving their husbands, then so be it.

Kanaka missionaries and other devout Kānaka Maoli considered it imperative that in the battle between Christ and Satan, between Ke Ao and Ka Pō, they remain solidly within Ke Ao. Their devotion to their religion ran deep, and for some it ran so deep that they were willing to spend – and risk – their lives and that of their families in the mission field. While they publicly espoused an understanding of the boundaries between Ke Ao and Ka Pō that closely mirrored that of their American mākua, in practice Kanaka missionaries were often willing to redefine those boundaries as they saw fit.

The lives, writings, and scandals of the Kanaka missionaries hint at the evolution of a flexible Christianity, which maintained its central beliefs and teachings despite being radically reshaped to better fit Kanaka cultural needs and expectations. The various hewa the Kanaka missionaries chose to ignore, particularly those associated with moekolohe and grief, do not show the failures of the missionaries to act as Christians, but rather their participation in defining and normalizing a new type of Christianity. These first-, second-, and sometimes third-generation Christians were in the midst of a broader effort to develop a Christianity that allowed them both to claim a space in the Christian world while still allowing for elements of Ka Wā 'Ōiwi Wale they did not feel willing to reject, at least in private. Ironically, this new strain of Christianity allowed them to retain considerable similarities and common ground with the very people they spent so much effort to separate themselves from: their ancestors and the "wild dogs" among whom they worked.

The flexibility of this Christianity can be seen in the memoirs of W. N. Lono, written sometime after being installed as the pastor of Kaumakapili church in 1901. Lono remained committed to the church, but he also remained very much immersed in the culture of his birth and of his ancestors. His memoir, as mentioned earlier, transitioned seamlessly between descriptions of his Christian education and his culturally informed treks around the island. In discussing his travels he did more than just express aloha 'āina and a Hawaiian sense of place; however, he also explicitly called upon the gods and supernatural forces from Ka Wā ʻŌiwi Wale to illustrate his story.

In the forests of Panaʻewa he described himself as being guided through the forest by the beauty of "Paliuli or Laieikewai," two women described in moʻolelo of the area, women known both for their beauty and for the supernatural forces surrounding them. Describing the 1859 lava flow approaching the ocean at Kiholo, he described witnessing the glowing fires from higher ground, stating, "E auau kai ana ua wahine noho mauna la ia makahiki" (the lady who lives on the mountain will bathe in the ocean this year). The lady referred most likely[72] to Pele, the fire deity, a powerful force in the minds of any who lived on the lava-laced south side of Hawaiʻi Island. Even for a dedicated Hawaiian Congregationalist like Lono, Christ may have lit the path to Ke Ao, but Pele still lit the path to the sea.[73]

---

[72] Poliahu, the female deity of snow has also been referred to as "ka wahine noho mauna," but in the context of his discussing the lava flowing from Mauna Loa to Kiholo, it seems far more likely that he was referring to Pele.

[73] Lono, "Lono, W. N. Journal," undated.

3

A Kindred People

Hawaiian Diplomacy in Sāmoa, 1887

In 1962, University of Hawai'i anthropology student William Pila Kikuchi traveled to the island of Aunu'u, just off the coast of Tutuila. Upon learning that Kikuchi was from Hawai'i, Salauve'a, a local chief, informed him that in 1887 two Hawaiian sailors, Aniani and Mahelona, had deserted a Hawaiian naval ship and taken refuge on Aunu'u. Later, when asylum seekers from Tutuila, being pursued by their enemies, asked for shelter on Aunu'u, the local people offered their aid. The two sailors and a Kanaka storekeeper named Manoa planned the defense, set up kill zones, and manned the cannons. Setting up an ambush in a pass through the coral reef the Aunu'u people defeated the pursuers in such a devastating manner that Aunu'u was never threatened from Tutuila again. The people of Aunu'u still remembered the Kānaka Hawai'i for their contributions and their descendants continued to live on Aunu'u.[1]

In many ways, this alliance of Kanaka deserters and Samoan villagers was the most concrete result of the diplomatic project the sailors had once been a part of: King David Kalākaua's grand dream of creating a trans-Oceanic "Polynesian Confederacy" of independent Native states as a bulwark against the aggression of foreign empires. Though its political impetus came from the increasing rapaciousness of the "Great Powers," the confederacy's internal logics emerged from Kalākaua's vision of Hawaiian success that embraced both Native and foreign sources of knowledge and culture. Best known for developing such ideas through his domestic policies, the king also incorporated them into his foreign

---

[1] William Pila, "A Legend of Kaimiloa Hawaiians in American Samoa," *Hawaiian Historical Society Review* (1964): 268–269.

policy efforts. Throughout his reign, he consistently promoted Hawai'i as part of the European/American diplomatic and cultural world while still deeply enmeshed in Ka Wā 'Ōiwi Wale. He also began to develop a vision of Hawai'i as closely connected to other Oceanic and even Asian peoples through culture, history, and their shared fears of imperial aggression.

Recognizing the risk posed by this aggression, Kalākaua sought to use Hawai'i's diplomatic status and connections to pull other Oceanic peoples out from under the threat of empire. In doing so, he hoped to preserve the independence of the Hawaiian kingdom, at that point the lone recognized nation-state in a region the empires had marked for acquisition. In January 1887 he put into place the most concrete effort to advance such ideas, sending a diplomatic legation[2] to Sāmoa, Tonga, and other island groups throughout Oceania to lay the groundwork for a confederacy of independent Oceanic states. By February, Malietoa Laupepa, the King of Sāmoa under the most recent constitution, had signed a treaty of alliance with Hawai'i, the first such treaty between Oceanic peoples. With the arrival of the Hawaiian naval training ship HHMS *Kaimiloa* in June, the legation began to prepare for the short journey to Tonga where they hoped to duplicate their success.

They never made it to Tonga. A combination of a July coup by the "mission faction" in Hawai'i and the German invasion of Sāmoa in August brought the confederacy and the legation to a grinding halt. On the diplomatic and political front the confederacy was a clear failure, having done little more than provide fuel for existing agitation among white supremacists in Honolulu and German expansionists in Berlin and Apia. From the perspective of the Great Powers and many other white observers, the brief life of the confederacy seemed to be a naïve, perplexing, and altogether annoying incident. In addition to the simple affront of a Native kingdom assuming the right to participate in world affairs, Hawaiian actions threatened to upset tenuous negotiations over the imperial partitioning of Oceania, providing further proof of the need for white control of the Pacific.

The few historians of Hawai'i and the Pacific who have examined the confederacy have largely portrayed it as its contemporary detractors did; a gin-fueled, incompetent attempt at empire building by a naïve Native

---

[2] Within nineteenth-century diplomatic practice, a legation was a diplomatic mission or office one step lower than an embassy. The key distinction was that a legation was headed by an envoy extraordinary and minister plenipotentiay rather than an ambassador.

monarch and a set of buffoonish amateurs.[3] Ralph Kuykendall largely let a grad student write his account of the confederacy. In *Dismembering Lāhui*, Jon Osorio mentions the confederacy briefly and acknowledges Kalākaua's anti-imperial motives for the project, but accepts the dominant narrative of the legation as a complete debacle. Gavan Daws meanwhile, reveled in the seeming ludicrousness of the confederacy, presenting it as an example of Kalākaua's ego and Minister Walter Murray Gibson's desire for glory. Many other historians of Hawai'i and the Pacific simply ignore it. Like the mission faction and the Germans before them, they have left the confederacy and Kalākaua's dreams to rot on the trash heap of history. As Klaus Neumann has argued, however, you can learn a great deal about history by digging through its trash.[4]

Failure or not, the confederacy and the Hawaiian legation to Sāmoa offer a unique view into how Kalākaua administration viewed the Hawaiian past, other islanders, and the role of each in the Hawaiian future. This chapter examines the Hawaiian legation's time in Sāmoa, particularly its appeals to the Malietoa government and other Samoan decision makers. It starts with an examination of the legation's lead personnel, two accomplished part-Haole Kānaka with strong ties to the Kalākaua administration. The chapter continues with a brief narrative of the events leading to the signing of a treaty between Hawai'i and Sāmoa, followed by an examination of the dual set of appeals used by the legation to obtain Samoan support for the treaty.

The administration and the legation relied heavily on a discourse of kinship based on genealogical and historical ties between Sāmoa and Hawai'i, hoping to build a relationship that would form the foundation for future alliances. Where the Kanaka missionaries in Micronesia and the Marquesas had sought to use other islanders to distance themselves from Ka Wā 'Ōiwi Wale, the legation sought to use Ka Wā 'Ōiwi Wale to pull themselves closer to the Samoans. Having established this kinship, the legation employed an already established belief in Hawai'i's superior na'auao and access to global networks of power, culture, and

---

[3] See Ralph Kuykendall, *The Hawaiian Kingdom, 1874–1893: The Kalakaua Dynasty* (Honolulu: University of Hawaii Press, 1967), 322–340. Kuykendall seemed to have little interest in examining the topic, relying largely on the work of one of his graduate students, Jeremy Horn.

[4] Klaus Neumann, "Starting from Trash," in *Remembrance of Pacific Pasts: An Invitation to Remake History*, ed. Robert Borofsky (Honolulu: University of Hawai'i Press, 2000), 62–77.

trade denied to the Samoans. Though this discourse of Hawaiian exceptionalism separated the Kānaka Maoli and the Samoans, the confederacy
offered the possibility that the Samoans would be able to acquire similar
status and access under the tutelage of their northern kin.

KALĀKAUA AND THE POLYNESIAN CONFEDERACY

When Kalākaua became Mōʻī, or ruling monarch, in 1874, one has
to wonder whether he regretted ever having campaigned for the job.
Elected by the legislature, Kalākaua continued to face widespread dissent
from the supporters of his opponent, Queen Emma Rooke, the widow
of Kamehameha IV Alexander Liholiho. Upon hearing of Kalākaua's
electoral victory, Emma's supporters rioted, tearing apart the royal car-
riage and using pieces of it to beat pro-Kalākaua legislators. Beyond the
simmering resentment of Emma's supporters, the country faced larger
economic and political problems. The end of the US Civil War meant
a massive drop in sugar prices, dragging down the islands' economy.
Kalākaua's lukewarm support for a reciprocity treaty had secured him
the equally lukewarm support of the sugar industry. That same group,
however, along with others within the foreign community were growing
increasingly vocal about the belief that they, not the Kānaka Maoli or
their Kanaka monarch, deserved to rule the islands. Furthermore, foreign
diseases continued to devastate the lāhui: between 1853 and 1872, the
Kānaka population had dropped from 71,109 to 51,531, a 27 percent
drop in less than twenty years.[5]

By 1880, the challenges facing Kalākaua were only marginally
smaller. Kalākaua's success at obtaining a reciprocity treaty had allowed
the sugar industry to rebound at the cost of further alienating many
of Emma's strongest supporters. Despite their alliance over reciprocity, the king still needed to deal with the contentious mission faction,
a combination of American missionary families and sugar-based Haole
businessmen. Despite a certain amount of lip service to the idea of an
independent Hawaiʻi, the mission faction continued to express their
desire to rule over both Kalākaua and the islands. Taking advantage of
political missteps around the appointment of international con artist
Celso Moreno to a cabinet position, the mission faction used threats

⁵ Robert C. Schmitt, *Demographic Statistics of Hawaii: 1778–1965* (Honolulu:University
    of Hawaiʻi Press, 1968), 74.

of violence and unrest to force the appointment of an all-Haole cabinet composed of their allies.[6]

If the king's domestic problems were not enough, Europe and the United States were at the start of a period of rapid imperial expansion. The Berlin conference, which would split up Africa, was only a few years away. The French were seizing more and more of Southeast Asia as well as expanding their control over the Marquesas and New Caledonia. The ever-expanding British Empire was seizing colonies great and small, including Fiji in the South Pacific, and was a few years from formally splitting New Guinea with the Dutch and Germans. The Germans were also actively fomenting instability in Sāmoa in the hopes of acquiring the islands. The settler states of the United States, Canada, Australia, and New Zealand, meanwhile, continued to kill and dispossess indigenous peoples for the benefit of white settlers and agricultural concerns.

As many national executives of the twentieth century would later do, Kalākaua decided to sidestep his domestic problems and further his foreign policy in a single stroke, a well-publicized trip abroad. In 1881 he left Hawai'i to become the first reigning executive to circumnavigate the globe, hoping to increase Hawai'i's diplomatic visibility and seek out new sources of immigration. As part of a deal to prevent Haole rebellion against his regent, Lili'uokalani, the mission faction saddled the king with two of their own as escorts. One of those escorts, mission scion William Armstrong, later wrote a memoir of the journey, noting that he and the rest of the mission faction hoped the journey might cow the king into accepting the superiority of "Anglo-Saxon traditions" in governance. In short, they hoped the journey might somehow convince him to turn the kingdom over to Haole rule. They were sorely disappointed.[7]

The journey instead strengthened Kalākaua's commitment to Hawai'i's independence and reinforced three major components of the king's understanding of the world. The first was the clear threat of empire. Everywhere the king went the empires were either in control or seeking control. A noted Anglophile, the king even began critiquing the British Empire, describing British troubles in India as getting their fingers burned for sticking them in someone else's business. Second, the voyage made the

[6] Jon K. K. Osorio, *Dismembering Lāhui: A History of the Hawaiian Nation to 1887* (Honolulu: University of Hawai'i Press, 2002), 147–159, 166–173; Kukendall, *The Hawaiian Kingdom, 1874–1893*, 218–220.

[7] William Armstrong, *Around the World with a King* (New York: Frederick A. Stokes Company, 1904), 23–26.

king aware of the diversity, depth, and achievements of other supposedly na'aupō peoples around the world. The Japanese in particular struck the king as a model of how the targets of empire were capable of both maintaining the dignity of their own civilizations and embracing useful outside influences. Third, the king came to believe that the best path forward for the independent peoples of the globe would come from collective action, formal alliances, and mutual aid to counteract the rapid growth of European and American empires across the world.[8]

The king used the voyage to act upon these ideas, even engaging in preliminary discussions with Japan's Emperor Mutsuhito about a massive alliance of the independent peoples of Asia and Oceania. The emperor agreed about the importance of such an alliance, later writing, "to do this is a pressing necessity for the Eastern Kingdoms, and in so doing depend their lives." Those countries most successful at modernizing and gaining international recognition, specifically Japan and Hawai'i, would help the others "prove" their capability for self-governance, hopefully removing them from the threat of imperial aggression. This in turn would strengthen the security of Hawai'i and Japan, who would become the model for Asian and Oceanic nations rather than the exceptions among them.[9]

It was a grand and glorious scheme, a Third World movement more than a half-century before its time. Like such ideas tend to do, it died quickly and quietly. A year after the king's visit the emperor sent him a letter regretfully informing him that the time simply was not right for such a plan. A proposed marriage alliance, uniting the two nations by uniting their royal lines, was also declined, with the emperor citing Japanese tradition. Kalākaua would continue to seek such international solutions, however, including the Polynesian Confederacy that is covered in these pages. He would also maintain his hopes of geographically broader alliances, including 1887 plans for an economic "Policy of Combination" between Hawai'i, Japan, China, Thailand, Johor, and the West Coast of South America.[10]

But first, however, he needed to wrest domestic control back from the mission faction. After his return, Kalākaua embarked on a series of domestic and foreign initiatives intended to protect the kingdom both

[8] Ibid., 170; David Kalākaua, "Transcript of a Voyage around the World, Especially Japan," 1881, Monarchy Collection, BMA.
[9] Kuykendall, *The Hawaiian Kingdom, 1874–1893*, 229.
[10] David Kalākaua to Robert Irwin, 14 January 1887, Irwin Papers, I'olani Palace Archive.

from the aggression of foreign powers and of the foreign community in Hawai'i. Politically, Kalākaua and his supporters portrayed the mission faction as a greedy, power-hungry group hostile to continued Hawaiian independence. After decades of missionary teachings about the inherent evil of Kanaka ways and the inherent superiority of the United States, this was not a difficult sell. Despite an alliance between the mission faction and the Kanaka supporters of Queen Emma the king held onto a majority of the legislature in 1882 and build on that majority in the next two elections.[11]

Kalākaua also met with considerable success on the cultural front, attacking the missionary discourse equating Ka Wā 'Ōiwi Wale with the na'aupō by celebrating a national culture as enmeshed in the Hawaiian past as it was in the global present. Building off the legacy of Kamehameha IV and V, Kalākaua confronted missionary discourses directly with his 1883 coronation, a multiday celebration of Kalākaua as the king of a people rooted in both Ka Wā 'Ōiwi Wale and an embrace of world cultures and knowledge. Emissaries from across the world were greeted with European-style state dinners and balls as well as massive lū'au (feasts) and publicly funded demonstrations of hula and oli that went deep into the night. Enormous crowds of Kānaka came from across the kingdom, celebrating the king, but more importantly celebrating his public embrace of their shared Native past.[12]

The mission party was furious, claiming that the hula and other celebrations were obscene remnants of the na'aupō, proof of continued Native incapacity for self-rule. They even demanded that the printers of the event program be arrested for obscenity, not realizing that the offending parties were the publishers of their own "party organ." The overwhelming success of the event, however, both among the Native population and foreign representatives, made it clear that the mission faction's ability to define the Hawaiian past was now relegated to the past. By the time of the king's jubilee in 1886, the mission party effectively admitted their own defeat, barely raising an eyebrow at the displays of hula and other traditions.[13]

At the same time that he was securing domestic support, Kalākaua expanded his foreign policy agenda. Despite Japanese reluctance to move

---

[11] Osorio, *Dismembering Lāhui*, 193–229.
[12] Noenoe Silva, *Aloha Betrayed: Native Hawaiian Resistance to American Colonialism* (Durham, NC: Duke University Press, 2004), 108–120.
[13] Ibid., 109–110, 116–117.

forward on a broader Asia-Pacific coalition, Kalākaua decided to develop a smaller coalition against the increasingly aggressive empires circling Oceania. Since the 1840s, Hawai'i had depended on its formal diplomatic recognition to protect it from colonization. Should the rest of Oceania fall, however, diplomatic protections would likely do little to protect a small independent Native state such as Hawai'i. In 1884 Kalākaua's Minister of Foreign Affairs Walter Murray Gibson sent out a diplomatic protest arguing that the kingdom could not remain "silent about or indifferent to acts of intervention in contiguous and kindred groups which menace [the kingdom's] own situation."[14] The Great Powers, as one might imagine, ignored the protest almost entirely.

Assuming – correctly – that such diplomatic appeals would do little to protect Oceania, Kalākaua and Gibson set out to create a scaled-down version of the proposed plan with Mutsuhito, a "Polynesian Confederacy"[15] between Hawai'i, Tonga, Sāmoa, and whatever other independent islands or island groups could be persuaded to join. In the short term, they hoped to use Hawaiian diplomatic ties to shield the confederacy as a whole, giving them time to develop both the internal political stability and the collective diplomatic clout to shield them all in the long term. Furthermore, the composition of the three core confederated states would likely solidify the existing Pacific stalemate between the major imperial aggressors: the United States, Germany, and the United Kingdom. By 1886 American interests in Sāmoa and Hawai'i, British interests in Tonga and to a lesser degree Sāmoa, and German interests in Sāmoa had created a situation in which all major imperial expansion into Polynesia had halted until the Samoan situation could be untangled.[16] A formal confederacy such as the one Kalākaua proposed would further complicate the issue, possibly even complicating it to the point that further imperial expansion in Polynesia would be postponed indefinitely. Finally, the confederacy and Kalākaua's leadership of it would be a display of mana, increasing the status of the king and the kingdom in a manner understood by Kānaka and foreign powers alike.

---

[14] Walter Murray Gibson, *Report of the Minister of Foreign Affairs*, 1884, Appendix C, FOEX, HSA.

[15] Though the king and others often referred to the project as "the Polynesian Confederacy," the planned confederacy would also include then independent parts of Kiribati and the Marshalls and thus would extend past the area typically referred to as Polynesia.

[16] For more on this see: Paul Kennedy, *The Samoan Tangle: A Study in Anglo-German-American Relations, 1878–1900* (St. Lucia: University of Queensland Press, 1974).

If Kalākaua and Gibson wanted to develop such a confederacy they would need to move fast. By 1886 word had spread that the Great Powers, hoping to find an end to the stalemate, were planning a conference along the lines of the 1884 Berlin conference that had partitioned Africa. Though technically the meeting would revolve around the future of Sāmoa, discussion of the future of Hawai'i and Tonga would likely occur as well.[17] With the clock ticking, the Kalākaua administration launched two diplomatic efforts. The first used Hawai'i's diplomatic connections in Washington, Berlin, and London to press for Hawaiian involvement in such a conference. The second was the diplomatic legation that is the focus of this chapter, which Kalākaua sent to develop treaties of confederation with Sāmoa and Tonga and otherwise develop the diplomatic groundwork for the confederacy. In December 1886, a diplomatic legation to Sāmoa and Tonga left Honolulu with the future of the confederacy, Hawai'i, and Oceania resting on their shoulders.[18]

KA NA'AUAO HAWAI'I: STAFFING THE LEGATION

On January 3, 1887, the Hawaiian diplomatic legation arrived in Apia, Sāmoa. The party included Envoy Extraordinaire and Minister Plenipotentiary John E. Bush; Secretary Henry F. Poor; Bush's wife Mary; his daughter Mollie; photographer, Joseph Strong[19]; staff members David Moehonua and Hiram Kaumuali'i; and a final individual named Kane. One account also listed two unnamed Samoans among the party. At some point, the legation also included an interpreter named Kanoa Kauwe, though it is unclear if he arrived later, who was a Kānaka Hawai'i already living in Sāmoa, or perhaps was one of the Samoans mentioned in the preceding text with a Hawaiianized name. Bush's orders instructed him to examine the situation on the ground, establish ties with Malietoa Laupepa, and work toward a resolution of hostilities between Laupepa and the "rebel"

---

[17] Indeed, the British and the Germans promoted a plan at the eventual conference essentially granting Sāmoa to the Germans, Hawai'i to the Americans, and Tonga to the British. The Americans rejected the plan and a similar plan in 1889, in large part, it seems, due to their desire to develop a naval base in Tutuila. Kuykendall, *The Hawaiian Kingdom, 1874–1893*, 338.

[18] Ibid., 325, 330.

[19] Strong was the husband of Isobel Osbourne, the step-daughter of Robert Louis Stevenson. He also seemed to be the source of much of Stevenson's knowledge of the legation as recorded in Robert Louis Stevenson, *A Footnote to History: Eight Years of Trouble in Samoa* (New York: Charles Scribner's Sons, 1900), 56–65.

Tupua Tamasese. If the situation on the ground warranted it, Bush was to discreetly inquire into Samoan sentiments regarding a possible alliance with Hawai'i. If Bush found them interested, he was to help the Samoans develop a proposal and forward it to Honolulu before heading to Tonga to repeat the process with King George Tupou.[20]

The choice of Bush and Poor as the senior members of the legation embodied the Hawaiian nationalism that Kalākaua sought to develop, combining a Native Hawaiian nationalist identity and the cosmopolitan na'auao typically associated with Europe and America. Both men were Kānaka, but they were also hapa-Haole, Kānaka Maoli with some Haole ancestry.[21] In choosing Kānaka to lead and staff the legation, Kalākaua was following an informal policy set in place after his world tour, when the all-Haole entourage the mission faction forced upon him raised eyebrows from Japan to Italy. The lack of Kānaka in the king's entourage led some of his hosts to question whether the king remained an independent sovereign or if his kingdom had already fallen under informal American rule. Several Japanese bureaucrats, two Siamese princes, the Khedive of Egypt, and the pope all brought up the question at one time or another. After returning home, the king made certain that Kānaka formed the core of all diplomatic efforts to other non-European/American states and peoples, a move intended both to showcase Kānaka mastery of foreign diplomatic culture and to serve as a reminder of the kingdom's independence.[22]

In 1882, then Minister of Interior Bush also reportedly promoted such a policy, championing John Kapena and John Kaulukou to lead a legation to Japan rather than Gibson's preferred Haole candidates. The kingdom, he argued, wanted Japanese immigration not just for labor, but also to strengthen the population through "amalgamation" with the Japanese. A Kanaka diplomat would have more credibility in making such an appeal than a Haole one, assumedly because the Japanese would perceive a Haole diplomat as representing the interest of planters rather than the kingdom.[23]

For the Sāmoa legation, the choice of Kānaka was of particular relevance, as Kānaka could argue for a personal historical and genealogical

[20] "Ko Samoa Pae Aina," *Ko Hawaii Pae Aina*, December 25, 1886, 2; Walter Murray Gibson to Bush, December 24, 1886, FOEX, HSA; Kuykendall, *The Hawaiian Kingdom, 1874–1893*, 325; Henry Poor, "Journal of the Embassy to Samoa," undated, HHS; John E. Bush to Poor, July 30, 1887, FOEX, HSA.

[21] "Death of H. F. Poor," *Pacific Commercial Advertiser*, November 29, 1899; "John E. Bush Passes Off," *Pacific Commercial Advertiser*, June 29, 1906.

[22] Armstrong, *Around the World with a King*, 47, 126, 187, 208.

[23] "John E. Bush Passes Off," *Pacific Commercial Advertiser*, June 29, 1906.

connection to the Samoan people. Thus Bush and Poor could speak to the Samoans about "our" connections rather than more abstract connections between Kānaka and Samoans. Furthermore, when the legation arrived in 1887, the Kanaka ancestry of Bush and Poor marked continued Native control of Hawai'i as well as the genealogical ties between the legation and their Samoan hosts. Their Haole ancestry, however, could potentially have granted them greater access to the European and American population of Sāmoa, the pālagi, just as it did among the Haole of Honolulu. Their hapa status also allowed them increased access to the small but increasingly influential afakasi community, part-white Samoans such as Malietoa's Under-Secretary of Foreign Affairs William Coe or his sister, "Queen Emma" Coe.

Poor's and Bush's mixed ancestry also physically embodied Kalākaua's vision of Hawaiian na'auao as a bridge between Oceania and Europe, an important part of the legation's appeals to the Samoan people. Furthermore, the two men had mastered skillsets that broadcast the Hawaiian grasp of foreign na'auao. After the death of his father, a teen-aged Bush apprenticed in the printing shop of the *Hawaiian Gazette*, eventually working his way to foreman. In the 1870s, he took on the editorship of the Hawaiian-language paper *Ke Au Okoa*, the first of several papers he would either edit or publish. By 1880, Bush moved to a career in politics and the civil service, serving as the governor of Kaua'i, twice as minister of the interior, and once each as the minister of foreign affairs and minister of finance. He had also been among the planners of the king's jubilee, the massive two-week long celebration of Kalākaua as both Kanaka ruling chief and cosmopolitan king.[24]

Though less prominent a figure than Bush, Poor was by no means unaccomplished. After attending Oahu College,[25] Poor began work as a

---

[24] Gavan Daws, *Shoal of Time: A History of the Hawaiian Islands* (New York: MacMillan, 1968), 282; Abraham Fornander to Katy, September 23, 1886, FDC, BMA. When he returned to Hawai'i after the 1887 coup, Bush also returned to journalism, becoming editor and publisher of *Ka Oiaio*. His editorials and the direction of the paper made him one of the few individuals as hated by Lili'uokalani as he was by the missionary party. He also served as member of the House of Representatives from Ko'olau in 1890. After the overthrow, he and his writing talents returned to the royalist fold, where he and Joseph Nāwahī were among the top targets of the oppressive Republic government. The two were arrested together in 1894, jailed, and treated in an inhumane manner. The government's abuse of the prisoners broke Nāwahī's health. He died several months after his release. Bush's health survived his time in prison, but the experience still effectively ended his career as a prominent voice for the Hawaiian people. "John E. Bush Passes Off," *Pacific Commercial Advertiser*, June 29, 1906.

[25] Later renamed Punahou School.

Bishop & Co. clerk at age fifteen when his father died, later moving to Castle & Cooke. In his mid-twenties the administration selected him as the secretary for Curtis P. 'Iaukea's follow-up to Kalākaua's world tour, attending the coronation of Czar Alexander III, meeting Queen Victoria, and participating in 'Iaukea's push for immigration treaties in Japan and India. Like the king before him, Poor returned with his chest covered in foreign decorations, which he would put on full display in Sāmoa. He then clerked for the Supreme Court before transferring to the Postal Savings Bank, where he was responsible for modernizing their bookkeeping system. By choosing Bush and Poor to head the legation, the Kalākaua administration sent the Samoans two examples of not just the na'auao attained by Kānaka Hawai'i, but also the na'auao available to Samoans under Hawaiian guidance.[26]

TOGETHER IN ONE PAHU: DEVELOPING
THE TREATY

Upon arriving in Sāmoa on January 3, 1887 the legation made it a top priority to develop contacts with the administration of Malietoa Laupepa. On January 5, Bush and Poor attended an event thrown for them by Selu, Malietoa's secretary of state. There they met some of Malietoa's cabinet, including Selu; Le Mamea, the secretary of interior; Lapolu, the secretary of treasury; Fomata, the registrar; and William Coe, the under secretary of foreign affairs. Coe, who was the son of American businessman Jonas Coe and Laupepa's close relative Le'uta, also frequently acted as a translator and guide for the legation, becoming particularly close with Poor and accompanying him throughout Sāmoa. Though few other details remain of the event, Poor did note that the legation was presented with a piece of kapa cloth as a token of esteem and welcome. During this visit the legation requested a meeting with Malietoa.[27]

The meeting occurred on January 7 and was a ritual affair that brought together European and Samoan custom. Despite the heat, which Bush estimated to be about 100 degrees, the Hawaiian party arrived in full European-style diplomatic costume, their chests jingling with foreign and domestic decorations. Upon being introduced, Bush presented Malietoa with a letter of introduction and greetings from Kalākaua. He

[26] "Death of H. F. Poor," *Pacific Commercial Advertiser,* November 29, 1899.
[27] Henry Poor, "Journal of the Embassy to Samoa," BMA.

then gave a short speech in Hawaiian,[28] relaying the Kalākaua's "deep interest ... in the welfare of yourself and the people of Samoa." Upon concluding the speech, Bush presented Malietoa with the Grand Cross of the Royal Order of the Star of Oceania, an order Kalākaua specifically instituted to decorate "the Kings and Chiefs of Polynesia and those who contribute to the welfare and advancement of Polynesian communities." Malietoa responded with a speech of his own in Samoan, acknowledging and reciprocating the friendship of Kalākaua. Coe interpreted the speech into English for the Hawaiian legation, but Bush noted that he could understand many of the words, noting, "the Hawaiian and the Samoan being in many respects alike." Malietoa then entered into conversation with the Hawaiians before a brief kawa ceremony, a traditional means of creating and securing relationships across much of Oceania. After everyone had been offered and drank a cup, the meeting dissolved. The carefully orchestrated combination of European-style and Oceanic diplomacy, medals and uniforms alongside kawa and speeches in Polynesian languages, would remain a staple of Hawaiian-Samoan relations during the legations stay.[29]

A few days later Malietoa's cabinet, though not Malietoa, traveled to Bush's quarters to informally discuss the mission's agenda. The Samoan chiefs voiced a favorable opinion of a possible confederacy, though no commitments were made on either side. The meeting clearly encouraged Bush, who wrote to Kalākaua, "[D]uring the evening's conversation I felt convinced that the King and the Samoan Government were favorable to our visit and the object of my mission. They seem to feel the necessity of being under some power, and that power the Hawaiian Government."[30]

On January 15, the Hawaiian delegation entertained Malietoa and a number of his chiefs with a lavish Hawaiian-style lū'au, exchanging speeches and toasts with their hosts. In the legation's official dispatch, Bush wrote:

Some [chiefs] spoke in the strongest terms of their desire for an alliance or confederation with Hawaii. Subsequent to this a great number of powerful and influential chiefs have called on me and voluntarily expressed their earnest support of

---

[28] It is unclear whether this speech was then translated into English and then into Samoan, or directly into Samoan. The two Samoans who came with the legation would likely have been able to translate directly between the two. The interpreter Kanoa Kauwa may have also been present though no mention is made of who translated the Hawaiians' statements or into which language.

[29] Bush to Kalākaua, January 27, 1887, FOEX, HSA.

[30] Ibid.

an alliance recognizing our superiority as a state, our advanced condition, and the friendly relations of America and European countries.

In a private letter to Kalākaua, he added, "The satisfaction and general good feeling evinced by his Majesty and Government led me to believe that I could, by a little diplomacy, bring about an understanding mutually beneficial to our countries." Bush then set about finding an unofficial channel through which to reach Malietoa for a private interview. Their landlord, the chief Folau, just happened to be a relative of Malietoa and by various friendly gestures Bush convinced Folau and Malietoa's brother, Moli, to secure the desired interview.[31]

On January 20, Malietoa, Coe, Folau, and several chiefs traveled to the legation's headquarters to discuss the possibility of a confederacy. Malietoa explained that all those present were family and could be trusted with whatever the Hawaiians had to tell him. In the legation's journal, Poor recounted:

Bush then stated about the substance of [our] mission, the interest of Kalakaua in the Polynesian States and his desire to aid and assist them, if possible to form a confederacy, that is if it pleased Malietoa to consider such a plan and retain his sovereignty under Kalakaua's direction that [Bush] thought the Hawaiian Government would allow him $5000 or 6000 a year, [to allow him to] maintain the dignity of his office as King.

Furthermore, Bush convinced Malietoa that "such a course would soon make his Government permanent." Bush felt he was on the verge of success, writing:

Everything I said took the King and his advisors very favorably, one of the Taimuas (Nobles) present, advocating the immediate consideration of the matter, and an answer given as soon as possible. The King's answer was as follows: "I am satisfied with everything you have said this evening as being the best and happiest way for us to overcome our present difficulties and pave the way for our future prosperity ... This evening I cannot positively give you my answer, until I present the matter before the Taimuas and Faipules (Nobles and Representatives), but I can say to you, and you may rely upon that assurance, your answer will be favorable."[32]

Malietoa visited Bush once more on January 27. Because any treaty or other type of agreement would need to be approved and signed by the Ta'imua and Faipule councils who acted as the government's legislative

---

[31] Ibid.; Bush, "Dispatch #2," February 2, 1887, FOEX, HSA.
[32] Poor, "Journal of the Embassy to Samoa," BMA; Bush to Kalākaua, January 27, 1887, FOEX, HSA.

body, Malietoa would go to meet with them in nearby Afega. He would send his barge for Bush and Poor on the following Friday, and he made it clear that they should appear in full diplomatic uniform, which "would make a deep and substantial impression." Around this time Bush also suggested that Malietoa allow A. O. Carter, Hawai'i's representative in Washington, to represent Malietoa's government as well. This would be particularly useful for both the Hawaiians and Samoans as Carter was concurrently lobbying for a place in the upcoming conference on the future of Sāmoa. On January 31, Malietoa signed an assortment of letters to Kalākaua, Carter, and President Cleveland, requesting that each allow Carter to act as his representative.[33]

On February 2, Bush and Poor met with the Ta'imua and Faipule to propose and negotiate the agreement of confederation. Bush made a speech outlining the arguments for confederation, but for the most part Malietoa had already gained their support before Bush's arrival in Afega. The majority favored an alliance and agreed to empower Malietoa with the right to draft and sign a treaty of confederation. Others of the assembly, however, put little value in the words of Bush, Kalākaua, or Malietoa; they wanted to see a Hawaiian warship before any decisions were made.[34]

When the various speeches and negotiations were completed, a ceremony was held, raising the flags of the two states side by side, followed by more speeches. An orator speaking on behalf the Ta'imua and Faipule pointed to the flags and stated, "We are especially pleased that today those who were brothers of old are again united." After more kawa and yet another feast Malietoa and representatives from the Ta'imua and Faipule then signed a document of confederation on February 17 and sent it to Honolulu for approval. Staff member Hiram Kaumiali'i included a triumphant note in the next mail: "All have succeeded, Samoa and Hawaii, we are one in this time. The Samoan flag and the Hawaiian are together in one pahu [drum or box]. We have found a home for Hawaii, here in Samoa." Within less than two months of their arrival in Sāmoa, Bush and company had completed the first major step in creating Kalākaua's Polynesian confederacy.[35]

---

[33] Poor, "Journal of the Embassy to Samoa," BMA; Bush to Kalākaua, January 27, 1887, FOEX, HSA; Bush, "Dispatch #7," February 2, 1887, FOEX, HSA.

[34] Bush to Kalākaua, January 27, 1887, FOEX, HSA; Bush, "Dispatch #11," March 7, 1887, FOEX, HSA.

[35] Bush, "Dispatch #11," March 7, 1887, FOEX, HSA; Hiram Kaumiali'i, "Leta Mai Samoa Mai," *Nupepa Kuokoa*, March 19, 1887.

A KINDRED PEOPLE: KINSHIP APPEALS

The willingness of the Malietoa administration to sign on with the Hawaiians can partly be explained by their relative weakness as a government. Though he was the constitutional monarch, Laupepa's position was weakened due to both his lack of military control over Sāmoa and the lack of "kingship" in Fa'a Sāmoa, the Samoan worldview. Loosely defined, ever-shifting, and yet widely understood and respected, Fa'a Sāmoa can be understood as the broad set of political, cultural, and social norms that have unified Sāmoan society for centuries. As Malama Meleisea has argued, however, Fa'a Sāmoa has long stood as a bulwark against centralized governments such as the one Malietoa was trying to develop, privileging the autonomy of regions and villages.[36] Furthermore, the existence of a rival government under Tupua Tamasese weakened Malietoa's government, particularly because of the strong support Tamasese received from his powerful family, Sā Tupua, and from the German element in Sāmoa. Tamasese's "rebellion" put Malietoa Laupepa in a very dangerous position on both a practical and a military level. A man in such a position would have been eager for an alliance.

But the troubles of the Malietoa government cannot completely explain the rapid development of Samoan support for the confederacy. While Malietoa was desperate for help against Germans, the Hawaiians were a relatively unknown entity in Sāmoa. He may have needed allies, but his rapid embrace of the legation and its personnel required something more than desperation. Furthermore, the Hawaiians were eventually able to gain broad support outside of Malietoa's faction, even from within Sā Tupua and Tamasese's inner circle. Part of their success lay in how the Hawaiians did not just present themselves as a nation-state searching for allies, but also as a genealogically connected lāhui seeking to reconnect with and aid their kin. Throughout their time in Sāmoa, the Hawaiians relied heavily on rhetorics of genealogy and kinship central to most Oceanic understandings of identity. The legation, and by proxy the king, argued that historical ties between the two people meant that the alliance was not just proper, but already existed. All the two sides needed to do was acknowledge and build upon the ties created by their ancestors.

Copies of Kalākaua's initial letter to Malietoa, which played a prominent role in early contacts with the Malietoa government, have vanished

[36] Malama Meleisea, *The Making of Modern Samoa: Traditional Authority and Colonial Administration in the History of Western Samoa* (Suva, Fiji: Institute of Pacific Studies, 1987), 20.

from archives in Hawai'i. Kalākaua's letter to King George Tupou of Tonga, however, remains in the Hawai'i State Archive. Considering the similar goals of the legation's visit to Sāmoa and the planned visit to Tonga, the phrasing used in the two letters, and most of the wording, are likely quite similar. In the Tonga letter Kalākaua emphasized the kinship between Hawai'i and Tonga, highlighting "the friendship we have always entertained towards your majesty and the Tongan people, a race so closely allied by blood to the Hawaiians."[37]

During the various meetings that took place between the Hawaiians and the Samoans before the signing of the treaty, both sides continued to reference genealogical ties as an argument in favor of alliance. After the first informal meeting with Malietoa's cabinet, Bush wrote, "[T]hey appear perfectly satisfied that Hawaiians and Samoans are relatives, and that a closer alliance than is accorded to other nations would be proper. This feeling permeates all, the Chiefs and the people." In a speech at the January 15 feast, Bush "dwelt forcibly on the strong resemblance of the two races, and from the similarity of the names of the chiefs [in the genealogies], of their relationship." Even the feast, which the legation planned as a Hawaiian-style lū'au, was an expression of kinship with the Samoans, highlighting shared feasting traditions. Similarly, at the meeting with the Ta'imua and Faipule, Bush prefaced his remarks by alluding to genealogical connections, stating:

I come among you not exactly as a stranger but representing a King and a people closely allied to you by blood, by language, and by similar traditions. Many generations ago the chiefs and people of Hawaii and Samoa visited each other in their great canoes. Some of your chiefs became Kings in Hawaii and our traditions say that our chiefs even were received in Samoa, where a number of them went to seek brides of suitable rank. For many years we have had no communication with you and now we come to renew old friendships and seek new ties among a kindred people.[38]

Like most political speech, one could easily discount such claims of kinship and genealogy as cheap and opportunistic political rhetoric. Indeed without looking at the importance of such ideas in both Hawai'i and Sāmoa, they would seem to be exactly that. The legation's appeals, however, were not just politically expedient, they also reflected a broader

---

[37] Bush to Kalākaua, January 27, 1887, FOEX, HSA; David Kalākaua to George, King of the Tonga Islands, December 23, 1886, ECO, HSA.

[38] Bush to Kalākaua, January 27, 1887, FOEX, HSA; Bush to Taimua and Faipule, FOEX, HSA.

role for both genealogy and thus Ka Wā 'Ōiwi Wale in contemporary Hawaiian politics. The 1872 and 1874 royal elections, for instance, featured major battles over the genealogies of the candidates, particularly between Kalākaua's and Queen Emma's supporters. Samuel Kamakau and others also frequently dueled over genealogical matters in the newspapers, and many genealogies ended up in the newspapers as a way of preserving them.[39]

The use of genealogy in establishing treaties or at least political agreements emerged directly from Ka Wā 'Ōiwi Wale. Alapa'i, the ruling chief of Hawai'i Island, once fought a great battle on O'ahu against Pelei'oholani, the ruling chief of Kaua'i. After a few days, the battle was at a standstill, resulting in nothing but death on either side. Neither chief seeing a benefit in continuing the war, they called for a genealogist, Naili. Naili then related to each their genealogical ties and set up a meeting between the two to find an honorable end to the dispute. Kamakau identified this as a somewhat common solution in such situations, a mutually beneficial invocation of genealogy that demonstrates its centrality within the Kanaka worldview.[40]

Beyond politics, genealogy also formed the basis for traditional Hawaiian cosmology. Epic genealogies like the Kumulipo provide a means of understanding and communicating the history, the ethos, and the mythos of not just the ali'i who traced their lineage through such works, but of the lāhui as a whole. The Kumulipo and similar works also contained accounts of the birthing of the earth, the darkness, humanity, and all the creatures of the earth, sky, and sea, all seen as ancestors and relations of the Kānaka.[41] King Kalākaua's interest in genealogy, both personally and officially, also extended beyond immediate political concerns. In addition to his own personal study of genealogy, the king oversaw the creation of the Papakū'auhau, or Board of Genealogy of the Hawaiian Chiefs, in 1880. The board's stated mission was to collect, unravel, and preserve the genealogies of the ali'i nui to verify chiefly lineages. While these genealogies remained the board's primary focus, by employing a broadly inclusive Oceanic definition of *genealogy* the board

[39] Jonathan Kay Kamakawiwo'ole Osorio, *Lāhui Dismembered: A History of the Hawaiian Nation to 1887* (Honolulu: University of Hawai'i Press, 2002), 152; Puakea Nogelmeier, "Mai Pa'a I Ka Leo: Historical Voices in Hawaiian Primary Materials, Looking Forward and Listening Back," PhD thesis, University of Hawai'i, 2003, 108–118.
[40] Kamakau, *Ruling Chiefs*, 88–89, 72.
[41] Lilikalā Kame'eleihiwa, *Native Land Foreign Desires: Pehea Lā E Pono Ai?* (Honolulu, HI: Bishop Museum Press, 1992), 20–22.

soon became the official means for gathering, examining, and preserving all manner of Hawaiian knowledge. The board continued operating
until 1887 when the post-coup government ended its funding. Another
group, however, the Hale Nauā, a "secret society" formed in 1886, took
up much of the Papakū'auhau's work. In terms of personnel, the transition was an easy one, as many of the members of the board were also
members of Hale Nauā. The president of the board, for instance, was
Princess Po'omaikelani, the sister of Queen Kapi'olani. She was also the
third highest-ranking member of Hale Nauā after her sister and royal
brother-in-law.[42]

Kalākaua also had an interest in Sāmoa and the south in general as
the genealogical homelands of either the Kānaka Maoli as a whole or
of specific chiefly ancestors. In 1879, for instance, he designed the front
entrance of the new 'Iolani Palace to face Kahiki, the ancestral homeland,
specifically southwest toward Sāmoa.[43] Kalākaua also featured several
mo'olelo about Hawai'i and the south Pacific in his *Legends and Myths
of Hawai'i* (1888). Indeed, he set much of the book against the back-
drop of a secondary wave of chiefly migrations from the south, which
over several generations resulted in a merging of "native" and southern
lines within the ranks of the ruling ali'i. By no coincidence, Kalākaua
cited Sāmoa as the specific location where many of these southern chiefs
emigrated.[44]

Kalākaua clearly had an agenda when choosing and collecting these
particular mo'olelo for publication, especially because he composed the
book while developing the confederation. Indeed his specific promotion
of Sāmoa, rather than the less specific Kahiki, as the homeland of both
the god/female-chief Pele and the southern adventurer and Hawai'i Island
ruling chief Pili, emphasized the historical connections underpinning the
confederation. Clearly Kalākaua believed such genealogical connections
between Oceanic peoples, particularly Oceanic ali'i, provided an important foundation for future political alliance.[45]

---

[42] David Kalākaua, "Kalakaua's Medicine Book," notebook, Kalanianaole Collection,
HSA; "Report of the Board of Genealogy to W. M. Gibson, Minister of Foreign Affairs,"
ca. 1882, BMA; Silva, *Aloha Betrayed*, 94–107.

[43] At least symbolically. Technically, the palace faces due southwest, while Sāmoa is
south-southwest.

[44] David Kalākaua, *The Legends and Myths of Hawai'i* (Honolulu, HI: Mutual Publishing,
1990), 69–71, 14–142, 154; Stacy Kamehiro, *The Arts of Kingship: Hawaiian Art and
National Culture of the Kalākaua Era* (Honolulu: University of Hawai'i Press, 2009), 68.

[45] Kalākaua, *The Legends and Myths of Hawai'i*, 69–71, 14–142, 154.

Thus when the Hawaiian Legation in Sāmoa framed their diplomatic appeals within the language of genealogical ties and connections, they were employing a rhetoric that had deep roots both in the Hawaiian past and in contemporary political and cultural battles in Hawai'i. Just as importantly for the success of the legation, such an embrace of genealogy was and continues to be a relatively common feature of many Oceanic cultures, including that of the Samoan people.[46]

On occasion these discussions of genealogy employed, or perhaps merged with, European/American conceptions of racial connections between Hawai'i and Sāmoa, particularly when using the English language. Both the legation and the Samoans sometimes fell back on blood metaphors, which, as Kēhaulani Kauanui has argued, emerge largely from European/American racial discourses. Hawaiian bodily metaphors and terms for close kin usually reference body parts such as the piko (bellybutton) or the ma'i (genitals), which are associated with reproduction. Yet with English providing the early lingua franca between the legation and the Malietoa government, as well as the language most of the legation's documents were recorded in, it is almost inevitable that blood metaphors and discussion of racial connections would find their way into the legation's appeals.[47]

Bush, for instance, explained Kalākaua's interest in the Samoan people in part through his recognition of them as "a kindred race closely allied to the Hawaiians by blood, by language, and by historical traditions." Malietoa echoed these sentiments in his response, which Coe translated as, "It is true that the Hawaiians and Samoans are related by blood and other ties. I have in my possession genealogical records which prove that your kings and people and myself are related." Malietoa sounded a similar sentiment in his first letter to Kalākaua, writing, "By traditions we have learned the truth that your people are of one blood with us." While neither Bush nor Malietoa/Coe relied entirely on "blood" imagery, their words clearly show the influence of European/American racial discourses when discussing kinship in English.[48]

---

[46] Angela Ballara, *Iwi: The Dynamics of Maori Tribal Organization from C. 1769 to C. 1945* (Wellington, NZ: Victoria University Press, 1998), 50; Greg Dening, *Islands and Beaches: Discourse on a Silent Land: Marquesas, 1774–1880* (Carlton: Melbourne University Press, 1980), 34, 74; Richard Phillip Gilson, *Samoa 1830 to 1900: The Politics of a Multi-Cultural Community* (Melbourne: Oxford University Press, 1970), 30.

[47] Kēhaulani Kauanui, *Hawaiian Blood: Colonialism and the Politics of Sovereignty and Indigeneity* (Durham, NC: Duke University Press), 49–52.

[48] Bush, "Address Read to His Majesty Malietoa," trans., January 7, 1887, GRCC, HSA; David Kalākaua to George, King of the Tonga Islands, December 23, 1886, ECO,

Though carrying a very different set of connotations and baggage, racial discourses, like genealogy, still spoke to ways of categorizing peoples as innately tied to or separated from one another. Thus these appeals to race still portrayed Hawaiians and Samoans as intrinsically connected to one another by bonds beyond temporary political necessity. By employing the racial discourses of the time in their bid for an anti-imperial alliance, the Hawaiians and Samoans were also challenging dominant elements of English-language discourses on race in which only "white" races were capable of self-governance let alone international alliances.

THE USES OF ALOHA AND ʻOHANA

Much of the power and importance of genealogy in Oceania stems from the broader import placed on family and kinship in general. A considerable part of the bond between family members in Hawaiian and other Oceanic traditions comes not just from genealogical ties, but from an expectation of aloha (love) based on those ties. As most of the legation's remaining records are in English, including many of the original documents, it is hard to say how often the Hawaiians used the term *aloha* in reference to the Hawaiian/Samoan relationship. Kalākaua's letter to George Tupou references feelings of "friendship" he and the lāhui had for the Tongans, as did Bush's original speech to Malietoa. Yet aloha and friendship are interwoven in Hawaiian thought. The most pervasive translations of "friendship" is *pilialoha*, literally clinging/adhered with aloha. Furthermore, when summarizing the Samoan response to the letter, Bush explicitly refers to it as "the letter of sympathy and love which Your Majesty wrote." The letter may not have contained the actual word, but Bush clearly understood it as an expression of aloha.[49]

On at least three occasions Samoan statesmen affirmed the idea that the relationship between the two kings, and their respective governments, was rooted in alofa, the Samoan equivalent of aloha. In his speech at the signing ceremony, the chief orator of the Taʻimua and Faipule expressed their "greatest thanks for the friendship and alofa you have expressed, which we know to be the voice of your King." In a January 18 letter Malietoa referred to Kalākaua's December 1886 letter as an

HSA; Malietoa Laupepa, "Remarks of King Malietoa in Response to an Address of His Excellency Jno. E. Bush," 1887, GRCC, HSA.
49 Bush to Kalākaua, January 27, 1887, FOEX, HSA; David Kalākaua to George, King of the Tonga Islands, December 23, 1886, ECO, HSA.

acknowledgment that Kalākaua's "love for us is unchanged in the way you remembered me." In a later letter he wrote of his great joy at Bush's presence, and how the envoy acted to "maintain the alofa between the two Governments."[50]

In Hawai'i, Sāmoa, and many other Oceanic cultures, familial connections brought a host of advantages and responsibilities beyond just an expectation of aloha; aloha needed to be acted upon. Family ties and the expectation of aloha between family members played an essential role in maintaining safety and security in everyday life, allowing one access to food, shelter, land, and hospitality in good times and bad. This extended far beyond one's immediate relatives and those one had regular contact with, indeed an important part of the security of this system came from the ability to call upon resources from geographically and genealogically distant parts of one's family in times of trouble. A widely dispersed but still functional family network, for instance, could provide hospitality and safety for those displaced, temporarily or permanently by war, drought, natural disaster, or simple wanderlust. In Sāmoa broadly distributed families also provided a certain degree of protection in wartime, with family on the winning side looking out for the interest of family members on the losing side.[51] As shown in the example of Pelei'oholani and Alapa'i, Hawaiian genealogical appeals could also provide the justification for ending wars.

It should be noted, however, that while Oceanic peoples placed a high value on kinship, by no means did this guarantee harmony between kin. Indeed, the importance of genealogy in determining chiefly mana in much of Eastern Oceania meant that wars and conflicts often occurred between close relatives. Kamehameha, for instance, took control of Kona by slaying his first cousin Kiwala'o. A long-standing conflict between Malietoa Laupepa and his uncle Malietoa Talavou occurred in part because both possessed a valid genealogical claim to the Malietoa title. Among the powerful, kinship was not a guarantee of alliance, rather it was an

---

[50] Bush to Kalākaua, March 11, 1887, FOEX, HSA Malietoa Laupepa to Kalākaua, January 18, 1887, GRCC, HSA (only the English translation is available for this letter); Malietoa Laupepa to Kalākaua, April 20, 1887, GRCC, HSA (available in Samoan and English, *alofa* is used in the original but not the translation).

[51] Malama Meleisea, *The Making of Modern Samoa: Traditional Authority and Colonial Administration in the History of Western Samoa* (Suva, Fiji: Institute of Pacific Studies of the University of the South Pacific, 1997), 28; Mary Kawena Hand and E. S. Craighill, *The Polynesian Family System in Ka'u, Hawai'i* (Honolulu, HI: Mutual Publishing, 1998): 2–3, 5–6.

important value and a resource that could be appealed to in order to create, strengthen, or validate relationships in both mundane and unusual circumstances.

Thus appeals to familial ties and the expectation of aloha provided significant rhetorical tools for both the Hawaiians and Samoans in 1887, allowing them a means for both understanding and developing a confederacy between two nations with relatively little official contact until that point. These genealogical appeals on both sides reflected a genuine feeling of connection and aloha between the two peoples as distant relatives, but it also represented a conscious attempt to create contemporary connections desired on both sides for practical political reasons. The shared genealogical connections between the Kānaka Maoli and Samoans did not create the need or impetus for the confederacy, or else it would have been attempted generations earlier. Rather it created a way to understand and explain the fast tracking of an alliance that both sides desired for political reasons. Furthermore, if they succeeded in creating a fully realized confederacy such genealogical rhetoric would give them a foundation for future mediation within the confederacy.

"VERY FEW LIVE WITH NA'AUAO LIKE OURS": HAWAIIAN EXCEPTIONALISM

While the legation promoted connections between the Lāhui Hawai'i and Lāhui Sāmoa based on ties that stretched deep into their shared Oceanic past, they also emphasized how the more recent past had created distinct differences between the two lāhui in terms of economic and political development. Compared to the nascent Samoan government, the Hawaiian kingdom could boast of superior material wealth, access to diplomatic channels, and political stability. Under their tutelage, the Hawaiians argued, the Samoans would enjoy the same status as their northern kin. This Hawaiian promotion of themselves as more developed than the Samoans stemmed from a broader nationalist belief in Hawaiian exceptionalism based in their mastery of foreign na'auao. By 1887, a combination of Hawai'i's stable central government, geography, and American demand for sugar had allowed Hawai'i to be the best-educated, wealthiest, and most internationally prominent of the Native-led Pacific Island states.

The conquests of Kamehameha the Great between 1782 and 1810, the further unification of Hawai'i and Kaua'i under Ka'ahumanu in 1821, and the constitutional monarchy developed under Kamehameha III in the 1840s allowed Hawai'i to develop a strong centralized state, the first of its kind in Oceania. Except for the brief rebellions of Kekuaokalani in 1819 and George Humehume in 1824, the kingdom maintained a period of internal and external peace that stretched back until 1810, a claim few nations could make at that time. By 1843 the kingdom also achieved international recognition of its sovereignty by the major international powers operating in the Pacific: the United States, France, and the United Kingdom. This recognition was an unprecedented and solitary achievement in Oceania until Western Sāmoa's independence in the 1960s.[52]

In the 1840s, Hawai'i's centralized state also allowed for the creation of a system of government-run public schools, building upon an already considerable foundation left by the privately operated ABCFM mission schools. By the 1880s, Hawaiians were among the most literate peoples in the world, let alone the Pacific. Within the Native professional class and elite, many such as Bush, Poor, and Kalākaua were literate in Hawaiian and English and quite comfortable writing and publishing in either. This would lead to the creation of a small but persistent Kanaka-controlled independent newspaper industry that provided access to local and world news and an outlet for opinion in the Hawaiian language.[53]

Furthermore, the stable government and the kingdom's geography allowed for considerable economic prosperity. The kingdom's location made it an excellent provisioning and wintering stop for the Pacific whaling and fur trades before 1850. After 1850, Hawai'i's benign climate and fertile soil led to the growth of a small sugar industry, which grew exponentially thanks to the American Civil War and the reciprocity treaty negotiated by Kalākaua in 1875. Though the vast majority of the sugar wealth (and a considerable amount of the kingdom's land and water) went into the hands of foreign planters, much still flowed into the government coffers and the economy in general, allowing Hawaiians far greater access to consumer goods than most other Oceanic peoples. Scholars such as Noenoe Silva, Lilikala Kame'eleihiwa, and John Osorio have shown that such "development" came at a high cost to the people of Hawai'i, but without question the Kānaka of the Kalākaua period, especially among the urban Honolulu Kānaka, were wealthier, more literate, more worldly,

---

[52] Silva, *Aloha Betrayed*, 36–37.

[53] Maenette Kape'ahiokalani Padeken Benham, "The Voice 'less' Hawaiian: An Analysis of Educational Policymaking, 1820–1960," *Hawaiian Journal of History* 32 (1998): 123; Helen Geracimos Chapin, *Shaping History: The Role of Newspapers in Hawai'i* (Honolulu: University of Hawai'i Press, 1996), 60–62.

and in their minds far more advanced than their Oceanic kin. Through the confederacy, they promised to train their Samoan and Tongan cousins to achieve the same level of naʻauao as the lāhui Hawaiʻi.[54]

SPREADING THE HAWAIIAN NAʻAUAO

While the Hawaiian government believed, deeply, in the kingdom's exceptionalism, they also understood how that very exceptionalism threatened their continued independence. For Hawaiʻi to remain independent, the kingdom needed other Oceanic peoples to reach the same levels of stability, and more importantly international recognition, that it had. The administration expressed much of this sentiment in their 1883 Diplomatic Protest, stating:

His Hawaiian Majesty's Government speaking for the Hawaiian People, so happily prospering through national independence make earnest appeal to the Government of Great and enlightened States, that they will recognize the inalienable rights of the several races and communities of Polynesia to enjoy opportunities for progress and self-government and will guarantee to them the same admirable political opportunities which have made Hawaii prosperous and happy, and which incite her national spirit to lift up among the Nations in behalf of Sister Islands and Groups of Polynesia.

Though connected to their "Sister Islands and Groups," by geography, culture, and genealogy, the kingdom's naʻauao gave them both a separate status and a responsibility to use that status to push back against imperial aggression.[55]

Following this same logic, the legation made their naʻauao a central component of their appeals to the Samoan elite. In his speeches Bush frequently and openly stated that he, and by proxy Kalākaua, saw the Samoans as undeveloped versions of themselves. On January 15, Bush recalled telling his Samoan audience that:

Their condition today was very much like ours, in many respects, some thirty or forty years ago, and that with forty years the start of them in Christianity and civilization, they could well look to us for friendly advice and advanced ideas in the construction and formation of a stable and liberal government.

---

[54] See, Silva, *Aloha Betrayed*; Osorio, *Lāhui Dismembered*; Kameʻeleihiwa, *Native Land Foreign Desires*.

[55] Walter Murray Gibson, *Report of the Minister of Foreign Affairs*, 1884, Appendix C, FOEX, HSA.

He later expressed similar ideas to the Taʻimua and Faipule:

We have been more fortunate than you in our progress in [illegible] civilization and taking an advanced stand among the civilized nations of the world, and now come to you to extend a helping hand if you desire it … My advice to you is to remain firm and strong and seek to have your country governed by the advanced principles of Modern Civilization and truth and justice will prevail in your favor … My country has fortunately been the exception [among Polynesian countries] and is established and recognized and has become wealthy and prosperous.[56]

The legation also tried to impress the Samoans with material and cultural representations of their assumed superiority, particularly the trappings and formalities of European diplomacy. At the initial meeting, for instance, Bush formally presented Kalākaua's letter while in full diplomatic costume, chest covered in ribbons and medals. Kalākaua, like most royals of his era, had been fond of such decorations and pomp before his world tour, but his voyage had shown him how standard such decorations had become within the social norms of European/American diplomacy. As mentioned earlier, he even created the Royal Order of the Star of Oceania, awarding Bush the Grand Cross and authorizing him to bestow a similar honor upon Malietoa and George Tupou.[57]

Bush's unwieldy title as head of the legation, envoy extraordinaire and minister plenipotentiary, provided yet another sign of Hawaiʻi's diplomatic savvy. With such a designation Bush technically outranked all the other foreign representatives in Apia at the time, none of whom ranked higher than consul. Thus, despite the fact the consuls had more personnel, more money, more influence, and more sheer power than Bush, he still received a degree of social and professional deference from the Americans and the British. Malietoa and other Samoans must have appreciated the importance of such deference being granted to another islander, even a part-white one from halfway across the Pacific. The Germans, however, had little interest in respecting such diplomatic niceties when it came to the Hawaiian legation. They even refused to attend the official British celebration of Victoria's birthday because Envoy Bush received a seat of honor at the festivities above the German consul.[58]

[56] Bush to Kalākaua, January 27, 1887, FOEX, HSA; Bush to Taimua and Faipule, FOEX, HSA.
[57] Bush, "Address Read to His Majesty Malietoa," trans., January 7, 1887, GRCC, HSA; Richard A. Greer, "The Royal Tourist – Kalākaua's Letters Home from Tokio to London," *The Hawaiian Journal of History* 5 (1971): 76–77, 83–84, 99–100.
[58] Greer, "The Royal Tourist," 77; Webb to Gibson, June 25, 1887, FOEX, HSA.

By offering to have Carter represent Malietoa in Washington and Europe, the Hawaiians also gave Malietoa a taste of the diplomatic privilege that Sāmoa might obtain through the confederacy. Carter's status promised access to the halls of power in Europe and America that no Samoan or their representatives had had before, proof of both the naʻauao and the aloha of the Hawaiians. In addition, the displays of diplomatic trappings and the offer of Carter's representation reiterated the message of Hawaiian respect, courtesy, and kinship to the Samoans, sharing their diplomatic status in ways no other nation had.

Equating westernization with progress strengthened the Hawaiian appeal in large part because such ideas were already well established in Sāmoa. Even the connection between Hawaiʻi and foreign knowledge preceded the legation to Sāmoa. Robert Louis Stevenson, who visited Hawaiʻi, Sāmoa, and other parts of the Pacific several years later, wrote that:

In the eyes of Polynesians the little kingdom occupies a place apart. It is there alone that men of their race enjoy most of the advantages and all the pomp of independence; news of Hawaii and descriptions of Honolulu are grateful topics in all parts of the South Seas; and there is no better introduction than a photograph in which the bearer shall be represented in company with Kalakaua.[59]

Thus Malietoa, his supporters, and even his Samoan opponents were already inclined to view the Hawaiians as desirable allies due to their "advancement." Malietoa's language even paralleled that of the legation. He expressed his joy at Hawaiian "advancement," on several occasions, as well as his desire for Sāmoa's advancement under their tutelage. In a letter to Kalākaua, Bush recounted Malietoa's "great pleasure and gratification to hear and to know from [the legation's] appearance of the high culture and advanced civilization of Your Majesty and people." He voiced similar sentiments in a toast at the legation headquarters, saying:

I am satisfied from what I have heard, that your King, my Brother, is enlightened and a highly civilized monarch, and very much esteemed and respected by the monarchs of the world, and that your country, which is so far advanced of ours, that I deem myself fortunate that your King has been considerate in sending to my court a mission with the highest diplomatic honors.[60]

Later that month Malietoa informed Bush, "I shall hereafter ask you to direct us in our affairs and difficulties, and hope you will not hesitate to

---

[59] Stevenson, *A Footnote to History*, 59.
[60] Bush to Kalākaua, January 27, 1887, FOEX, HSA.

give us good and paternal advice. We rely on our Brother, your King, for he is our elder in enlightenment and in knowledge, though we may be his Matua [fathers] in relations." On one level, Malietoa expressed his belief that the Hawaiians were better equipped to deal with the foreign community and the development of a modern government due to their enlightenment and knowledge. At the same time, he reminded Bush of both the kinship bond that required a certain level of fidelity to the Samoans and the Samoans' superior genealogical claims, being the senior line[61]. In declaring Kalākaua his elder in knowledge, Malietoa temporarily waived these claims of genealogical superiority, while not so subtly reminding the Hawaiians such claims still existed.[62]

Malietoa soon began co-opting the na'auao of his Hawaiian allies. When meeting with Bush in late January, he made a point of asking the legation to don their full uniforms when appearing before the Ta'imua and Faipule. As Malietoa had by that time voiced to the Ta'imua and Faipule his own support for the confederacy, Bush now represented Malietoa's na'auao as well as Kalākaua's. Just as the Hawaiians displayed their access to the symbolic power of European diplomacy and material displays for Malietoa, Malietoa now displayed his access for the Ta'imua and Faipule.[63]

The Hawaiians continued to highlight their na'auao in their postsigning efforts as well, and it was essential during these efforts to generate interest beyond Malietoa's inner circle. They were aided by the June 1887 arrival of the HHMS *Kaimiloa*, the tiny training ship at the heart of Kalākaua's plans to develop a Hawaiian navy. Before its arrival, the only significant opposition voiced by the Ta'imua and Faipule was that the Hawaiians, for all their finery and diplomatic recognition, lacked a gunboat. The gunboat was the most important symbol of European and American "progress" in the Pacific and had been for generations. As Bush put it, "[T]he islanders of the South Pacific have learned to have the greatest awe and respect for a war-vessel and [the *Kaimiloa*] will impress them with an idea of the power and ability of the Hawaiian

---

[61] As both groups seemed to understand the Hawaiians as descending from the Samoans in the distant past, the Samoans could thus claim to be the senior line in this relationship. In Oceanic understandings of genealogy, the junior line, in this case the Hawaiian people, are expected to follow and support the senior line, the Sāmoan people. Though more of a guideline than a hard and fast rule, such hierarchical thinking within kin and family groups was strong throughout Eastern Oceania.

[62] Bush to Kalākaua, January 27, 1887, FOEX, HSA.

[63] Ibid.

Government to carry out its plans to assist and protect them." In Sāmoa, as elsewhere in the Pacific, the threat of regularly visiting warships underwrote the position and influence of European/American planters, merchants, and missionaries. The ever-present German warships in Sāmoa allowed the German consul and the local Germans the freedom to disregard and harass the Malietoa government and the Samoan people. The out-gunned, under-powered *Kaimiloa*, despite its many faults, symbolized a developmental distance between the Hawaiians and the Samoans that the Samoans deeply desired to overcome.[64]

For the Kalākaua administration, the political, social, and economic stability of the Hawaiian kingdom was proof of their naʻauao, proof of their capability for self-governance, and proof that they among all the peoples of the Pacific could lead their kin, their fellow islanders, to a future free of the fear of imperial aggression. Many of the Samoan political elite seemed to agree with them, at least based on the eagerness with which many of them became supporters of the confederacy.

In March 1887 the editors of the *Hawaiian Gazette* published a satirical piece mocking Kalākaua, his dreams of a confederacy, and Oceanic peoples in general, portraying the confederacy as the pretentions of a naïve and incompetent savage playing at greatness.[65] The confederacy had become a frequent target of Haole ire in 1887, as the mission faction, defeated in three consecutive elections and denied access to the executive branch, sought to foment rebellion against the king. The author of the March piece, I. Twigg, referred to the confederacy as the "Empire of the Calabash," a term many of Honolulu's Haole population used for the confederacy. The term *Empire of the Calabash* carried a special resonance for the king's Haole opponents. *Empire* called up their vision of a white-supremacist future where European/American empires dominated the world, carrying with it ideas of progress, civilization, and most of all – power. *The calabash*,[66] however, called up a vision of the primitive, archaic Kānaka, sitting together on the floor, eating out of collective calabashes. *The calabash* represented all that was wrong with Native peoples, particularly the fact that they *were* Native peoples.

---

[64] Bush to Kalākaua, January 27, 1887, FOEX, HSA; Bush, "Dispatch #10," February 10, 1887, FOEX, HSA.

[65] I. Twigg, "Hope for the Nation," *Hawaiian Gazette*, March 8, 1887.

[66] In Hawaiʻi, the term *calabash* is typically used for an ʻumeke, or bowl, sometimes made from the calabash gourd, but often carved from solid wood.

Somewhat ironically the 'umeke, the bowl or calabash, provides a perfect metaphor for understanding not just the Hawaiian conception of the confederacy but their success in appealing to the Samoan people as well. To sit around an 'umeke and share a meal was an act of inclusion, of togetherness, of closeness. It represented the boundary between those who were kin or accepted as kin and those who were not welcome. Even today, individuals who are not related by blood or marriage but are seen as family are referred to as "calabash cousins," those who metaphorically eat out of the same 'umeke.

'Umeke were not just practical items, they were significant cultural items as well. The 'umeke of a chief was part of his personal goods, not to be handled by those of low status. 'Umeke belonging to Kamehameha the Great were a key part of the collection of national artifacts preserved by Kalākaua in the national museum. 'Umeke, great and small, were presented to King Kalākaua by his subjects at his coronation, both as holders for other gifts and as objects of prestige and status in and of themselves. 'Umeke, then and now, were family heirlooms, handed down for use as eating bowls, presentation, and their simple artistic beauty. When cracked, the 'umeke were not discarded, but carefully and often beautifully patched so finely that the bare finger cannot feel the seam, the crack and patch increasing the worth of the item due to the care shown in repairing it.

In the Haole mind, the calabash was proof of the uncultured nature of the Hawaiians; for many Hawaiians, it was part of the beauty found *within* their culture, a connection to a shared past, the very thing that tied them together as a lāhui. As the Hawaiians also based a major part of their appeals to the Samoan people on their shared Oceanic past, the 'umeke provided an ironically positive metaphor for the confederacy as a new Oceanic institution. Brought together by the confederacy, the two distant branches of the family might sit together and eat out of the same bowl once again, just as the representatives of the two people ate out of shared dishes on the evening of the Hawaiian-style lū'au held for Malietoa.

The Hawaiians did not come to just share food, however, but to share their na'auao and to hopefully share an Oceanic future free of imperial control. Both the Hawaiians and the Samoans recognized that the recent Hawaiian past had given the Hawaiians significant political advantages that the Samoans lacked, namely a unified government and international recognition. They also recognized the material and economic success of the Hawaiians, in part through the conscious displays of such success on the part of the legation. By putting such advantages on display, the Hawaiians promised the Samoans the opportunity to follow a similar path, to gain what their cousins to the north had gained.

These dual appeals proved successful in Sāmoa. Much to the consternation and confusion of the Haole in Hawai'i, the palagi in Sāmoa, and the Kaiser's government in Germany, the legation was able to draw in the interest and support of Malietoa Laupepa, Mata'afa Iosefo, and numerous other prominent Samoans. As will be seen in the next chapter, they even piqued the interest of Laupepa's enemy, Tupua Tamasese. Not only did the Hawaiian appeals strike a chord with Fa'a Sāmoa, but it also contrasted highly with the actions and words offered by the various empires, who were too unconcerned with the Samoan people to truly aid them but interested enough in Sāmoa to stake their own claims on it.

4

The Hawaiian Model

Imagining the Future of Oceania

Hawaiian appeals to the Malietoa Government in 1887 relied heavily on ideas of kinship and on Hawaiian exceptionalism, with both sets of appeals finding a welcoming audience in Sāmoa. On a fundamental level, however, these dual appeals also reflected the logics at the heart of the confederacy, which were split between the kinship and intimacy of the extended 'ohana and the logics of empire that dominated global politics during that time. While not an explicit attempt at empire building, the confederacy still had the stink of empire upon it – few things in the late nineteenth century did not. At the same time, however, the confederacy promised a Native-driven alternative to empire as the future of Oceania, a transnational politics that operated internally on the logics of Oceanic peoples and externally through the established structures of international diplomacy and law.

This chapter attempts to articulate what the confederacy was, or at least what the Hawaiian legation had begun to imagine it to be, based on the groundwork and preliminary planning they carried out. The Kalākaua administration clearly considered the confederacy to be an anti-imperial one, but such a vague category could include a multitude of different projects. Japan, for instance, would even sell its bold-faced empire building of the 1930s and 1940s as the anti-imperial Greater Asian Co-Prosperity Sphere. The work of the legation on the ground in Sāmoa fleshes out the early planning of the confederacy, allowing for a fuller and more complex understanding of the project.

Malietoa's signing of the treaty so early after the formation of diplomatic ties left the Hawaiian government at a loss as to how the confederacy might operate, internally or externally. They left the research and planning for the official Hawaiian/Samoan relationship in the hands of the legation, who by default became the kingdom's Sāmoa experts. In some ways, the legation was relatively united in their thinking, mistakenly envisioning Sāmoa as an underdeveloped Hawai'i and hoping to remake it in the Hawaiian image. They also quickly moved to stabilize the political situation in Sāmoa, focusing primarily on drumming up support for their ally Malietoa Laupepa as a Hawaiian style mō'ī (king). The legation's personnel soon split, however, in their sympathies toward the Samoans and their understanding of how the relationships between the two peoples should be developed. Where Secretary Poor laid out the conceptual groundwork for Hawaiian political and economic exploitation of the islands, Envoy Bush seemed far more inclined to mould the relationship to accommodate both the Hawaiian na'auao and the fa'a Sāmoa, the Samoan way.

SPREADING THE FA'A HAWAI'I

> They live only in the present, the past and future concern them not, and with their simple habits are a happy and contented race of people. With civilization, education, and law, with their social benefits, it is possible for them to develop a higher type of character and industry and rival their more enlightened brethren in Hawaii.[1]
>
> *Henry Poor*

As late as March 29, 1887, Bush planned on heading to Tonga as soon as the *Kaimiloa* arrived. The longer they remained in Sāmoa, however, the more the Hawaiians realized that the situation was not quite as they had imagined it.[2] Though technically the king of Sāmoa, Malietoa Laupepa lacked any real governmental power. Furthermore, rather than being a "rebel," Tupua Tamasese was a legitimate contender for power in Sāmoa, even without the backing of the Germans. For the confederacy to work, the Hawaiians would need to stabilize Malietoa's standing in Sāmoa by creating a functional government and ending Tamasese's bid for kingship.

Blinded both by their devotion to the Hawaiian model of Oceanic na'auao and their belief that the Samoan people were simply underdeveloped Kānaka Hawai'i, the legation decided that the best course of action would be to remake the "happy and contented" Samoans in the

---

[1] Henry Poor, "The Samoan Islands – A Sketch by Henry Poor," 1887, FOEX, HAS.
[2] John E. Bush, "Dispatch #2," February 2, 1887, FOEX, HSA; Bush, "Dispatch #13," March 29, 1887, FOEX, HSA.

Hawaiian image. The legation had never hidden their intentions, they had even made the Hawaiianization of Sāmoa a cornerstone of their appeals to the Malietoa government and other Samoan leaders. Their early attempts to stabilize the Malietoa government through contemporary Hawaiian understandings of power and rule, however, failed to fully consider the significant differences between Hawaiian and Samoan political tradition. Future failures to do so would likely have led to significant tensions within their relationship, even without the specter of imperial interference.

NATION BUILDING AND MŌ'Ī BUILDING

In June 1887, Bush sent the Hawaiian government a proposal for a centralized government far more in keeping with contemporary Hawaiian politics than with the Fa'a Sāmoa. Bush based the proposal on both the legation's own analysis and "repeated interviews with the Samoan government and foreigners of long residence." The plan called for several influential positions to be appointed by Kalākaua, including an ill-defined position of "Director General ... with prescribed powers of inspection and direction." It also called for Kalākaua to appoint the chief justice of the Supreme Court and the minister of finance.[3]

In many ways, the proposal positioned Sāmoa as something of a client state under Hawaiian guidance. According to Bush, however, the Malietoa government seemed eager to involve Hawai'i in internal Samoan matters, possibly as a way of ensuring Hawaiian commitment to Sāmoa. Bush informed Gibson that the Malietoa government had indicated repeatedly that they would follow Hawai'i's lead on the government reorganization and the confederacy agreement. Bush also indicated that after reviewing earlier drafts of the plan, the Malietoa government had pushed Bush to include the aforementioned positions to be appointed by and directly accountable to the Hawaiian rather than Samoan crown.[4]

Understanding the lack of any real precedent in Sāmoa, Bush argued for a relatively basic central government. Anything else, he argued, probably correctly, would meet widespread dissent and confusion. Though less centralized than the Hawaiian government, the plan still roughly

---

[3] Bush, "Dispatch #22," June 21, 1887, FOEX, HSA; Bush, "Dispatch #23," June 23, 1887, FOEX, HSA.
[4] Bush, "Dispatch #14," April 26, 1887, FOEX, HSA; Bush, "Dispatch #23," June 23, 1887, FOEX, HSA.

followed the Hawaiian model of a constitutional monarchy paired with regional governors responsible for local administration. It kept numerous features from previous Samoan attempts at centralized governments, with Malietoa as the head of state, a cabinet of his selection, and the Ta'imua and Faipule as both a legislature and a national fono (council). Unlike in Hawai'i where governors served at the pleasure of the king, district governors would be appointed through the established customs of each district. Their responsibilities would include a combination of traditional roles and administrative roles under the new government.[5]

The plan also included efforts to develop the infrastructure needed to make such a government effective, specifically the creation of a new national law code, a Supreme Court, and a system of nationally appointed magistrates, tax collectors, and police who would fall under the immediate command of the district governors. Rather than depending on traditional means of recruiting warriors for battle, Malietoa would have a small professional guard under his direct command, "properly officered, uniformed, and drilled, for general purpose and for emergency," similar to the household troops of the Hawaiian monarchs. The Hawaiian plan called for various administrative infrastructure projects, such as jails, courts, a postal system, and customs building, all paid for by loans from the Hawaiian government.[6]

The Hawaiians also sought to help the Malietoa government develop some of the cultural and educational tools needed to develop nationalist sentiment beyond the cultural unification promoted through Fa'a Sāmoa. In a report on Sāmoa, Poor noted that few Samoan children received any education beyond basic training in reading, writing, and the Bible. The only significant exceptions were the wealthier part-Europeans and the students of the religious schools. While he reported positively on the Catholic girls' school, he critiqued the LMS boy's school in Malua for providing too little secular education, which only comprised about one-eighth of the curriculum. As the school trained the vast majority of Sāmoa's village teachers, their poor preparation helped perpetuate the low state of the village schools. The plan to remedy this situation included the extension of the Hawaiian school system into Sāmoa, which Kalākaua proposed in February. In March, Bush informed Gibson that the Samoans welcomed a Hawaiian school and asked Gibson to begin processing

[5] Bush, "Dispatch #23," June 23, 1887, FOEX, HSA.
[6] Ibid.

the request. In May, Gibson informed Bush that two Hawaiian teachers would be coming to Sāmoa in June.[7]

In addition to improving the state of secular education in Sāmoa, the importation of the Hawaiian school system would likely help provide a nationalist education and further indoctrination into accepting a centralized state. Kamehameha IV, Kamehameha V, and Kalākaua all sought to wrest control of the school system from the mission faction, in large part because they understood the power of education as a tool of indoctrination, either for or against the mōʻī. With limited modifications, the Hawaiian school system would instill future generations of Samoan students with their own monarch-centered nationalist education. Furthermore, such schools could portray the confederacy and the Hawaiian kingdom in a beneficial light.

The mōʻī-based nationalism that the schools could help promote would be particularly useful as the bulk of the Hawaiian plan in Sāmoa, like the bulk of the government at home, rested in the office of the monarch. Based on a history of ruling chieftainships, the success of Kamehameha the Great in unifying the islands, and equivalent structures in Europe, the Hawaiian Islands had developed a political culture and a popular nationalist culture focused heavily around the mōʻī. Though Kalākaua lacked the Kamehameha bloodline and even faced considerable genealogically rooted opposition from the supporters of Queen Emma, his cultural policies and initiatives enhanced the centrality of the mōʻī as the center of both the state and the lāhui.[8] Furthermore, the 1864 Constitution that Kalākaua ruled under gave the mōʻī a considerable amount of power, both in terms of the executive branch and his ability to appoint supporters to the house of nobles.[9]

When they arrived in Sāmoa, the Hawaiian legation interpreted the political landscape according to their understanding of *all* "Polynesian" polities as variations of a Hawaiian norm. From the very start, the legation imagined Malietoa as an underdeveloped mōʻī, a belief aided in part by common palagi (white/foreign) misconceptions of Samoan politics

---

[7] Bush, "Dispatch #13," March 29, 1887, FOEX, HSA; Walter M. Gibson to Bush, May 14, 1887, FOEX, HSA; Poor, "The Samoan Islands – A Sketch by Henry Poor," 1887, FOEX, HAS.

[8] See Stacy Kamehiro, *The Arts of Kingship: Hawaiian Art and National Culture of the Kalākaua Era* (Honolulu: University of Hawaiʻi Press, 2009).

[9] Kamehameha V., "Ke Kumukānāwai o ka Makahiki 1864, The Constitution of 1864," Jason Kāpena Achiu Laekahiʻālelo, trans. *Journal of Hawaiian Language Sources* 2 (2003): 28–35.

and the willingness of Malietoa to represent himself as a ruling monarch. In the first letter from Bush to Kalākaua, the only one written entirely in Hawaiian, Bush refers to Malietoa as "Ka Moi Malietoa." He also refers to Tupua Tamasese as a mō'ī in that first letter, though in future English references he refers to Tamasese as either "the rebel chief" or just a "chief." Malietoa, however, remained a "king." Based on their vision of the centrality of the mō'ī, the legation focused their early appeals entirely at Malietoa and his advisors. Even their efforts to reach beyond Malietoa to the Ta'imua and Faipule came at Malietoa's initiative, not their own.[10]

Malietoa, however, was not a mō'ī, and more importantly, Sāmoa was not Hawai'i. For centuries Fa'a Sāmoa had promoted a political principle that Malama Meleisea has termed a "unitary system of dispersed power," unified by culture and identity while diffusing political power. By dispersing power among networks of villages, families, districts, and temporary factions, fa'a Sāmoa allowed Samoans a great deal of autonomy and independence at these levels. Large-scale projects or decisions, including recruitment for warfare, required input, negotiation, and often renegotiation from all interested parties.[11]

The Samoan tendency toward diffusing power and their pride in independence, however, should not be mistaken for a lack of hierarchies. Indeed Samoan society revolved around a series of hierarchal relationships between individuals, families, sections of families, villages, and districts guided by genealogy and historical precedent. Samoans, and especially Samoan men, negotiated these hierarchies through the Matai system, a hierarchy of chiefly and oratory titles including the assumption of the various rights and responsibilities accorded by those titles. While obtaining a specific title required a genealogical tie to the appropriate 'aiga (family), genealogy was not the only factor taken into consideration as multiple individuals might have some genealogical claim on the title. Titles needed to be earned through various means and granted to the prospective matai by those responsible for doing so within the 'aiga. A title made a man or woman into a matai, which allowed for participation in communal decision making. Such participation, however, came at the

---

[10] Bush to Kalākaua, January 3, 1887, Kalanianaole Collection, HSA (Letter in archive is mis-dated, 1886); Bush to Kalākaua, January 27, 1887, FOEX, HSA.
[11] Malama Meleisea, *The Making of Modern Samoa: Traditional Authority and Colonial Administration in the History of Western Samoa* (Suva, Fiji: Institute of Pacific Studies of the University of the South Pacific, 1987), 1–2, 5–6.

cost of increasingly heavy responsibilities owed to the families, villages, and councils associated with their title or titles.[12]

Though all titles marked one's movement into the decision-making community, certain titles marked higher status and influence within that group. The two most powerful of the extended 'aiga, Sā Malietoa and Sā Tupua, held the four most desirable descent-based titles, the Tama'āiga titles. Sā Malietoa controlled the Malietoa title and Sā Tupua controlled the Tupua, Mata'afa, and Tuimaleali'ifano titles.[13] Holders of these four titles could then compete, through war, alliance, and negotiation, to be bestowed with another set of four titles tied to region rather than family. Known individually as *pāpā* or collectively as *Tafa'ifā*, these four titles, Tui Atua, Tui A'ana, Gatoa'itele, and Tamasoali'i, symbolized that the holder had the support of the various polities and councils associated with each title. Though all four titles were centered on Upolu, the role of councils and villages elsewhere in Sāmoa had in conferring such titles meant that in obtaining all four titles one had earned or forced the support of all Sāmoa. For at least a century this had been the pinnacle of political and social achievement within fa'a Sāmoa, but this did not equate to the type of executive authority one would expect of a mō'ī in the Hawaiian sense. Even Malietoa Vainu'upo, who held the Tafa'ifā in the 1830s, expressed neither the desire nor the means to develop centralized rule. As the leader of the mālō, the victorious side in the series of wars that brought him to prominence, he had a certain amount of control over the vanquished. This, however, could not be considered "rule" over such districts as much as the ability to intimidate and persuade them into making certain decisions, particularly regarding titles, ritual, and ceremony.[14]

While the Hawaiians would continue to (mis)understand Samoan politics through the lens of Hawaiian political conventions, they did begin to recognize some incongruities between their vision of Malietoa as a mō'ī and the realities of Fa'a Sāmoa. On February 22, just a few days after the signing of the Confederacy agreement, Bush wrote:

Samoa will be more difficult to govern than Hawaii for feudal customs and rights still exist with traditional jealousies and discords in different provinces. Samoa is

---

[12] R. P. Gilson, *Samoa 1830 to 1900: The Politics of a Multi-Cultural Community* (Melbourne: Oxford University Press, 1970), 23–25; Meleisea, *The Making of Modern Samoa*, 7–8.

[13] Meleisea, *The Making of Modern Samoa*, 33; Tuiatua Tupua Tamasese, "The Riddle in Samoan History: The Relevance of Language, Names, Honorifics, Genealogy, Ritual and Chant to Historical Analysis," *The Journal of Pacific History* 29, no. 1 (1994): 67–68.

[14] Gilson, *Samoa 1830 to 1900*, 58–62.

divided into nine districts or provinces ... Each province has its own feudal chief or governor selected by their own people and he alone they obey: but if he does not suit them they turn him out and put another in. From way back those districts have joined in various combinations against each other.[15]

Though the statement, particularly the allusions to Samoan feudalism, reflect further Hawaiian misunderstandings of Samoan politics and society, it also makes clear that the Hawaiians had begun to understand the disconnect between their imagined version of the Samoan political landscape and what they observed firsthand. Rather than reassessing their interpretation of Sāmoa, however, the Hawaiians sought to reshape Samoan society to fit the Hawaiian model, and to reshape the tamaʻāiga Malietoa Laupepa into a proper mōʻī.

SECURING THE MŌʻĪ

To create a foundation for Malietoa's legitimacy as mōʻī, the legation turned first to his genealogy. Though it took some time, they eventually acquired a "genealogy" of Malietoa, which they sent to Gibson on April 26. Rather than an epic genealogy, such as the *Kumulipo*, what they sent was a brief accounting of Sā Malietoa and the Malietoa title. They obtained this from four councils of orators that, according to Bush, were recognized as the keepers of Sā Malietoa's genealogy: "Lealataua, Leleituau, Salemuliaga, and Taafafalealii-ina." The Hawaiians interpreted the Malietoa genealogy through the lens of nineteenth-century[16] Hawaiian politics, where the primary qualification for ascendancy to the throne had been genealogy. Following contemporary Hawaiian logic, Bush argued that Malietoa's genealogy would "establish Malietoa's right to the satisfaction of the civilized powers." Yet the Malietoa genealogy was just that, the genealogy of the highest chief within Sā Malietoa, not the genealogy of a mōʻī.[17]

The legation also attempted to portray Malietoa as having a "legal" right to rule through an examination of the recent political history of Sāmoa. In a short "Historical Synopsis," Poor summarized the recent political disputes and foreign interventions that had occurred in Sāmoa. His synopsis started in the 1870s, covered the first major attempts to

---

[15] Bush, "Dispatch #8," February 22, 1887, FOEX, HSA.
[16] Genealogy was no guarantee to rule in pre-1800 Hawaiʻi either. Often chiefs of lower rank or sometimes just of junior lines overthrew their genealogical superiors, such as in Kamehameha's defeat of Kīwalaʻō and Umi's defeat of Hākau.
[17] Bush, "Dispatch #17," April 26, 1887, FOEX, HSA; Bush, "Dispatch #19."

create a centralized government, and traced the various shifts in legal authority through which Malietoa Laupepa and the Ta'imua and Faipule claimed their status as the executive and legislative branches of the government. Like the genealogy, Poor's synopsis laid out a case for Malietoa's right to rule, but it did so not on the basis of fa'a Sāmoa, or even genealogy, but on the basis of European-derived legal agreements and earlier, largely unproductive Samoan constitutions.[18]

While the genealogical and legal arguments assured the legation of Laupepa's legitimacy, they, like Malietoa Laupepa, still had to deal with the very real threat of Tupua Tamasese and his German allies. If the Malietoa government should fall to either the Tamasese faction or the Germans, so would the confederacy and plans for a Hawaiian-style Samoan state. In looking to stabilize Malietoa's rule, the legation developed a two-part plan, attacking the rhetorical basis for Tamasese's bid for power and finding a peaceful end to the dispute between Malietoa and Tamasese.

Rhetorically, the embassy sought to deal with Tamasese by discrediting him as both a rebel and a tool of the Germans. Bush, for instance, claimed that "the rebellion in Aana is not an organization of the natives but is directed and supported by the German Consulate and the German firm." The use of the term *rebellion*, which the legation consistently employed to discredit Tamasese and his government, was a clear attempt to delegitimize them according to the values of the nation-state. Bush also attempted to paint Tamasese as a rebel by asserting the genealogical primacy of Sā Malietoa – based primarily on the genealogy provided by Sā Malietoa. This genealogy painted Tupua Tamasese and Sā Tupua to be vassals of Sā Malietoa, leading Bush to claim that their "rank ... as high chiefs is undisputed but [their] pretensions to equality with the Malietoa's is absurd and unwarranted."[19] While this characterization fit into the narrative of Tamasese as a rebel against traditional and legal

---

[18] Henry Poor, "Draft-Historical Synopsis," undated, HHS; Bush, "Dispatch #8," February 22, 1887, FOEX, HSA.

[19] While seeking a closer alliance with another tama'āiga, Mata'afa Iosefo, Bush also sought to cut off any future threat from Mata'afa's status as a holder of a pāpā title by dismissing the Tui Atua title as "a principality or Dukedom, subject to higher authority and that authority has always been with the Malietoa's." He failed to mention that as Tui Atua, and a potential claimant for the title of Malietoa, Mata'afa Iosefo had as strong a claim as Malietoa or Tamasese to the right to create a government. Indeed Mata'afa would eventually be granted a contested claim to the Malietoa title by members of Sā Malietoa and in some accounts even claimed the Tafa'ifa. Bush to Kalākaua, August 15, 1887, GRCC, HSA

authority, it relied on either a gross misunderstanding or misrepresenta-
tion of both faʻa Sāmoa and the relationship between the two families.[20]

The legation also challenged the authenticity of the "rebellion" as a
Samoan project. They vigorously documented German involvement in the
Tamasese government in the hope that Hawaiʻi's diplomatic core might
shame Germany into abiding by earlier promises to support the recognized
government at Afega. Furthermore, they sought to delegitimize Tamasese
as a tool of both the German Empire and the "arrogant, unprincipled,
and ungentlemanly" German copra firm in Sāmoa. For the Hawaiian
government, which was staking its alliance based on explicitly Oceanic,
anti-imperial discourses and sentiment, such characterizations served as
an outright condemnation of the Tamasese government. Tamasese, of
course, also drew support from a relatively broad geographic range within
Sāmoa. The legation, however, consistently glossed over or dismissed
Tamasese's Samoan support to portray him as a cog within an aggressive,
anti-Native German imperial machine. Ironically, such a view of Tamasese
likely matched how the Germans perceived him more than how most
Samoans did.[21]

The Hawaiian reports worked fine for discrediting the Tamasese
government on paper, but this did little to end the actual threat of
the "revolt." While their allies among the Malietoa faction pushed
for a joint military effort to wipe out Tamasese's forces, the legation
shied away from any actual fighting. In part, the desire to do so came
from Gibson's orders to find a peaceful end to the dispute, but it also
signaled recognition of the German desire to turn their financial and
advisory support of Tamasese into direct military intervention. The
Germans claimed that because they had diplomatic relations with
the Tamasese government, and because Tamasese and Malietoa had
agreed to share the government in prior years, any military action
taken by Malietoa or his supporters would be grounds for a military reaction by the Germans. The de facto leader of the Germans
in Sāmoa, J. C. Godeffroy und Sohn[22] agent Theodor Weber, explicitly laid out this argument in a letter to the powerful chief Mataʻafa

---

[20] Bush, "Dispatch #19," May 23, 1887, FOEX, HSA.

[21] Bush, "Dispatch #2," February 2, 1887, FOEX, HSA; Bush, "Dispatch #14," April 26,
1887, FOEX, HSA; Poor to Webb, January 31, 1887, FOEX, HSA.

[22] Godeffroy und Sohn was a German firm with substantial investments in copra plantations in Sāmoa and elsewhere in the Pacific; it also acted as the spearhead of German
Empire within the islands.

Iosefo, as did Tamasese in a letter to the American, German, and British consuls in Apia.[23]

Throughout the legation's stay, the Germans persistently pursued a course of action intended to incite Malietoa's supporters into armed aggression. In May, the Germans brought Tamasese and his supporters into Apia, entertained Tamasese aboard the SMS *Adler*, and raised a new Samoan flag based largely on a German design. In bringing Tamasese and his warriors into Apia, the backyard of Malietoa's government, the Germans clearly intended to provoke Malietoa and his supporters. Knowing he could not retaliate against the Germans directly, they hoped he or his followers would instead take the bait and retaliate against Tamasese.[24]

Poor and Malietoa's translator/nephew William Coe also uncovered another German effort to incite war in Fa'asaleleaga:

> An agent of Mr. Weber's had recently been through the district and sold great numbers of firearms, some in exchange for lands but mostly on credit to be paid for in future with copra on lands. The natives becoming excited by the possession of arms, thirsted for war and were preparing in large numbers to sail over to Upolu and engage the Tamasese party in a fight.[25]

Other than finding a way to profit from both sides of the conflict, Weber was none too subtly setting up a conflict by arming strong Malietoa supporters who resided just across Apolima Strait from Tamasese's capitol at Leulumoega. The German *Adler*, meanwhile, was waiting in port at Apia for an excuse to attack. Combined with other German actions, particularly their continued selling of arms, Bush came to the only reasonable conclusion in his April letter to Kalākaua, condemning "the actions of the German Consul here, who openly allows its subjects to sell firearms and to drill and assist the insurrectionary party ... and thus keep up a state of irritation, which they hope will lead to an open rupture, whereby they may lead to an excuse of forcibly seizing the Group."[26]

The German plans were far from unfeasible, as many of Malietoa's supporters saw little reason to refrain from attacking the Tamasese government. Due to events of the previous year, Tamasese's military capabilities were at a low ebb in early 1887. The Germans, meanwhile, continued

[23] Tupua Tamasese Titimea to Consuls, April 29, 1887, FOEX, HSA; Theodor Weber to Mata'afa, April 28, 1887, FOEX, HSA.
[24] Bush, "Dispatch #22," June 21, 1887, FOEX, HSA.
[25] Bush, "Dispatch #14," April 26, 1887, FOEX, HSA.
[26] Bush to Kalākaua, April 24, 1887, GRCC, HSA.

to flaunt their backing of Tamasese's "rebellion" while snubbing the Malietoa party. Poor wrote that many in Sā Malietoa saw the opportunity and need to obtain the upper hand over Sā Tupua in general, setting up long-term dominance over them. Throughout the months that followed the signing of the confederacy, Bush, Poor, and their Samoan counterpart Coe all spent considerable effort convincing Malietoa's supporters that a diplomatic rather than military solution was the best route forward for Sāmoa and the confederacy. Coe and Poor, for instance, personally helped bring to an end the war agitation in Fa'asaleleaga, while Bush helped persuade a delegation of Malietoa supporters from Manono, Tutuila, and Savai'i to delay any war plans in hopes of a diplomatic solution.[27]

Despite the various factors that seemed to be pushing Sāmoa toward open warfare, the Hawaiian legation succeed in preventing any major fighting during their stay there. Beyond simply delaying armed conflict, the legation actively sought to bring an end to the dispute between Tamasese and Malietoa through peaceful means. They had considerable success in attracting the interest and even support of major figures within Tamasese's inner circle like Patioli, a former member of his cabinet, and prominent members of Sā Tupua like Mata'afa Iosefo, who also held one of the tama'āiga titles.[28]

At the request of Tiai, Tamasese's secretary, the legation even arranged a meeting with Tamasese and several members of his government who had signaled their willingness to suspend the supposed rebellion.[29] When Poor, Coe, and Joseph Strong, the legation's photographer, visited Tamasese's capital at Leulumoega, the Germans moved aggressively to prevent any sort of discussions from taking place. Tamasese was placed under armed guard and physically restrained from meeting with Coe and Poor, but several of Tamasese's cabinet members did manage to meet with the joint Hawaiian/Malietoa delegation. According to the legation's records, they expressed their distrust of the Germans and Weber in particular. Upon learning of the meeting, Tamasese's German advisors placed Coe, Poor, and the cabinet members under arrest to prevent any further

---

[27] Henry Poor, "Extracts from Poor to Webb," April 10, 1887, GRCC, HSA; Henry Poor, "Draft-Historical Synopsis"; Bush to Kalākaua, April 24, 1887, GRCC, HSA; Bush, "Dispatch #14,"; Bush "Dispatch #19."

[28] Bush "Dispatch #19"; Henry Poor to Webb, March 12, 1887, FOEX, HSA.

[29] According to Robert Louis Stevenson, who was Strong's father-in-law, these conditions included a stipend for Tamasese and a home in Honolulu. Robert Louis Stevenson, *A Footnote to History: Eight Years of Trouble in Samoa* (New York: Charles Scribner's Sons, 1900), 61.

discussion from taking place. Realizing they had overstepped their boundaries, imprisoning a diplomatic representative from a friendly nation, the
Germans offered little resistance when the boat crew who had brought
Coe and Poor to Leulumoega broke the prisoners out of custody. Though
they had failed to contact Tamasese, the event showed Tamasese's willingness to entertain the legation's offers as well as German fears that he
might take the Hawaiians up on them.[30]

Despite German attempts to instigate fighting, the desire of many
Malietoa allies to engage Tupua Tamasese on the battlefield, and the legation's attempts fit a tama'āiga-shaped peg into a mō'ī-shaped hole, the
legation was largely successful in their early goals. They prevented open
warfare between Malietoa and Tamasese, increased their base of support
among the Samoan political elite, and developed, alongside the Malietoa
government, a plausible plan for a centralized, constitutional government. A large part of their success came from expanding their dual kinship and progress-based appeals to the Samoan political elite, including
Tamasese. These measures, however, were short-term ones, emergency
fixes to immediate problems. They left largely unanswered the question
of what the long-term Hawaiian/Samoan relationship would look like
within the confederacy. An examination of the way that the legation
understood and interacted with the Samoan people during this time can
provide at least some insight into how the legation and the Hawaiian
government had begun to imagine the nature of the confederacy.

BUSH, POOR, AND THE NATURE
OF THE CONFEDERACY

Though the legation represented the kingdom as a whole, its small size
and relative independence meant that the individual perspectives and
character of its two lead members, Envoy John E. Bush and Secretary
Henry Poor left a considerable impact on the work of the legation. Bush
and Poor shared several similarities. Both men had attained significant
success in their respective private and government careers. Both men
belonged to the growing and increasingly influential hapa-Haole population and were well versed in local and global politics. While Poor had
traveled more broadly thanks to accompanying Curtis 'Iaukea around
the globe, Bush had also traveled. Furthermore, he had served briefly as

---

[30] Bush, "Dispatch #19"; Bush, "Dispatch #21," June 21, 1887, FOEX, HSA; Henry Poor
to Webb, March 12, 1887, FOEX, HSA; Stevenson, *A Footnote to History*, 61.

the kingdom's minister of foreign affairs and his publishing background gave him a very detailed and thorough understanding of the world beyond Hawai'i. Both men also maintained a strong sense of nationalist pride and loyalty to the lāhui, and a commitment to the idea of the confederacy.[31]

After the signing of the treaty, Poor, often accompanied by Strong and Coe, began traveling through different parts of Sāmoa developing the Hawaiian government's knowledge base about Sāmoa. As noted earlier, the Kalākaua administration and the vast majority of the Hawaiian public had a limited understanding of Sāmoa, one of the many problems the legation was tasked with resolving. Poor compiled several reports for the legation, including an account of the recent political history of Sāmoa, a report on general conditions, and copies of various official documents pertinent to the confederacy. During these visits, Poor and Coe also promoted the confederacy among Samoans outside of Apia and acted to quiet the more militant sentiments among Malietoa's supporters.[32]

Bush, meanwhile, focused his efforts largely on developing the Hawaiian diplomatic presence in Sāmoa and nurturing support for the confederacy outside of Apia. He obtained property for and constructed a permanent legation headquarters and as the senior Hawaiian diplomat he spent a great deal of time entertaining Samoan elites from outside Apia. He made two trips to visit Mata'afa, the second time aboard the *Kaimiloa*, hoping to cement Mata'afa's support for the confederacy and obtain his promise to deny resources to Tamasese. He also took the *Kaimiloa* on a visit to the powerful Itu-o-tane region on Savai'i, hoping to drum up support in that region.[33]

While the two remained united on the overall mission of the legation, they did not always see eye to eye, either professionally or personally. Indeed they had significant personal differences, some of which seem to have stemmed from Poor's inappropriately close relationship with Bush's daughter Mollie. Poor even set into play a successful effort to oust Bush

[31] This did not mean they did not have significant political differences within the broader umbrella of Hawaiian nationalism. Bush, for instance, maintained a significant feud with Queen Lili'uokalani during her reign, while Poor remained a supporter of the queen until his death.

[32] Bush, "Dispatch #8," February 22, 1887, FOEX, HSA; Bush, "Dispatch #21," June 21, 1887, FOEX, HAS.

[33] Bush, "Dispatch #12," March 29, 1887, FOEX, HSA; Bush, "Dispatch #22," June 21, 1887, FOEX, HSA; Samuel Maikai, "Lt. Maikai's Logbook," 1887, Monarchy Collection, BMA; Frank Waiau, "Lt Waiau's Logbook (Bishop Copy), 1887," Monarchy Collection, BMA.

as the head of the legation in the waning days of their time in Sāmoa.[34] They also differed significantly regarding the relationship between Ka Wā ʻŌiwi Wale and the future of the kingdom. In general, Bush seemed more inclined to embrace Ka Wā ʻŌiwi Wale, with enough of a familiarity with chiefly genealogies, for instance, to use them in his appeals to the Samoans. He also participated in planning the King's Jubilee, an event that mixed Hawaiian and foreign celebration in the same style as Kalākaua's coronation.[35]

Poor, however, seemed less comfortable with the Hawaiian past. In a letter to his friend and colleague Joseph Webb, Poor expressed views of the Hawaiian past that show a clear discomfort with and indeed loathing for elements of Ka Wā ʻŌiwi Wale. When describing his great sorrow at the news of Princess Likelike's death, for instance, Poor felt the need to comment on rumors the princess had died of fright in the belief that a Native priest was praying for her death. Such rumors seemed particularly strong in the Haole community, and indeed it seems that Poor heard about them through his personal correspondence with Webb. In his reply to Webb he responded:

If it is true as reported that Likelike died of superstitious fear it is still more sad; To think that around such an intelligent mind should still linger any of the

[34] The supposed drunkenness of the legation and Poor's attempt to oust Bush provided much of the fodder for contemporary detractors of the mission as well as historians such as Kuykendall. The legation was hardly a teetotaler affair, indeed Bush's freedom with the legation's gin was a major part of its outreach to various Samoan chiefs, but the level of alcohol abuse seems to have been exaggerated for political reasons. Several anonymous pieces appeared in anti-Kalākaua press accusing the legation of debauchery and ridiculing the confederacy in general. Poor and Coe then forwarded a translated letter purporting to be from Malietoa accusing Bush of drunken debauchery and demanding his withdrawal, with a promise that the original letter in Samoan with Malietoa's signature would be sent later. The original letter was never received in Honolulu, but Coe and Poor's machinations were enough for Gibson to withdraw Bush from the legation and put Poor at its head. Upon news of this, Bush went to Malietoa who then wrote a letter defending Bush's conduct, denying the validity of the letter forwarded by Coe and Poor, and offering Bush a position in his own government. Both Malietoa's letter and Bush's are in George Carter Collection at the HSA. Webb, who went to Sāmoa aboard the Kaimiloa in part to spy on Bush, was surprised that many of the white residents and foreign representatives seemed to have an actual respect for Bush, but noted that his sources said Bush had spent the last months with pulling himself out of an alcoholic stupor. Interestingly, Webb also seems to have relied in part on the German element in Sāmoa. He was the only one among the legation who found the German's to be friendly. George Webb to Gibson, "Dispatch #5," June 21, 1887, FOEX, HSA; Henry Poor to Webb, August 23, 1887, FOEX, HSA; Bush to Kalākaua, August 15, 1887, GRCC, HSA; Malietoa Laupepa to Kalākaua, August 5, 1887, GRCC, HSA; Henry Poor to Brown, August 23, 1887, FOEX, HSA.
[35] Abraham Fornander to Katy, September 23, 1886, FDC, BMA.

heathenish and unreasonable superstitions of the dark ages of Hawaiian life. Will the light of progress, civilization, science and the proud triumphs of the mind over matter never drive away these ghoulish, uncanny and degrading superstitions from the Hawaiian mind?[36]

Poor's unease seems to indicate that such darkness, or at least the fear of such darkness remained alive in at least one Hawaiian mind: his own.

These views of Ka Wā ʻŌiwi Wale seem to have colored Bush's and Poor's respective perceptions of their Samoan hosts as well. While they both believed in the superior naʻauao of the Hawaiian people, the relative value they placed on this superiority differed. Their separate accounts of meeting with Malietoa's inner circle on January 15 bring this difference into sharp relief. In a letter to Kalākaua, Bush recounted giving a speech that placed a heavy emphasis on the kinship between the Kānaka Maoli and Samoans. In a letter to Webb, Poor summarized his own series of toasts and short speeches by writing, "I think you would have been amused at the paternal way in which I addressed these people, but they seemed to like it."[37]

The two also differed in their descriptions of Malietoa, though both explicitly noted Malietoa's choice of clothing. Bush described Malietoa's appearance during their first meeting within a highly complimentary paragraph regarding Malietoa's demeanor and dignity, likening it to Kalākaua's. He then added, "Although he wore but a linen shirt without even a collar on, and a siapo or pau around his waist, his feet without shoes, he still appeared distinguished under such adverse circumstances." Poor, meanwhile, described Malietoa and his cabinet arriving for the feast on the fifteenth in an almost mocking tone, referring to their "[f]ull Samoan costume, i.e. a coarse linen shirt without collar, and a siapo or length of Kapa cloth wound about the loins and hanging about as low as the knee, and bare-footed."[38]

Bush and Poor also seemed to differ in how they viewed their personal connections to, and time among, the Samoans. Bush spent the majority

---

[36] Poor to Webb, March 12, 1887, FOEX, HSA. In 1952 Jennie (Kini) Wilson, wife of former Honolulu Mayor John Wilson, wrote a letter to Eugene Burns regarding his book on Kalākaua. She refuted Burns's claims that such rumors were pervasive, arguing that she was raised around the royal family and never heard such rumors. While Poor's letter proves that the rumors did exist, their circulation seems to have been restricted to certain groups. Burns's sources likely came from the Haole community, who never missed a chance to gossip about Kalākaua and his siblings. Poor's letter was in response to a letter by Webb; thus it seems likely that the Haole community had been Poor's source as well. Jennie Wilson to Eugene Burns, November 26, 1952, General Letters, BMA.

[37] Bush to Kalākaua, January 27, 1887, FOEX, HSA; Poor to Webb, January 31, 1887, FOEX, HSA.

[38] Poor to Webb, January 31, 1887, FOEX, HSA.

of his time with Malietoa and other matai, establishing personal ties with them and picking up a workable grasp of the Samoan language.[39] Poor also made close friends there, but from his remaining letters to Webb, it seems he only did so with Westernized members of the afakasi. He struck up a particularly close relationship with Coe, whose mother was a member of Sā Malietoa and whose father was the prominent American merchant Jonas Coe. He also joked about potential moral dangers posed by the climate and his proximity to the Samoan people. Apia, he wrote to Webb, was so hot he rarely put on his suit and he feared he might soon "degenerate into a Happy 'faa Samoa.'"[40]

The differences between Bush and Poor provide a glimpse into how the delegation was laying the groundwork for two very different types of confederacies. Bush, whose work relied largely on connecting with the Samoans and who seemed to have a more positive connection to the Hawaiian past, also seemed to favor a vision of the confederacy that privileged mutual consent and respect for autonomy. Both would be essential to a confederacy based on Oceanic diplomatic and political cultures in general and Samoan political sentiment in particular. Throughout the early meetings with the Malietoa government, for instance, he carefully avoided the appearance of annexation or the surrender of Samoan sovereignty. When the Taʻimua and Faipule flew the Hawaiian and Samoan flags together, Bush reported that several members suggested that they fly only the Hawaiian flag, as it was the prettier of the two. The suggestion, which likely had a much deeper significance, either as a test or as a bid for an all-out protectorate, took Bush by surprise. He insisted that the two flags remain flying together as equals. According to his own account, Bush was also keen to avoid the appearance of Hawaiian empire in crafting the plans for the new government, only including Kalakaua-appointed positions at the request of the Malietoa government.[41]

Poor represented a mind-set far more prone to disparaging both Ka Wā ʻŌiwi Wale and the supposed lack of Samoan naʻauao. By no coincidence, he was also far more prone to envision the confederacy as having

---

[39] "Samoa Affairs: Everything Quiet at Apia at Latest Accounts," *Pacific Commercial Advertiser,* November 19, 1887.

[40] Bush to Kalākaua, January 27, 1887, FOEX, HSA; Poor to Webb, January 31, 1887, FOEX, HSA.

[41] Bush, "Dispatch #11," March 7, 1887, FOEX, HSA; Bush, "Dispatch #23," June 23, 1887, FOEX, HSA.

minimal Samoan input and numerous similarities to the empires then circling the Pacific. Where Bush sought to avoid the appearance and substance of empire, Poor's letters reflected an openly imperial perspective. In a letter to Webb, hours after landing in Apia, he described Sāmoa as a "very desireable and profitable acquisition to us." In another letter to Webb, Poor wrote, "If Hawaii is to be allowed [by the Powers] to control here – you can have everything your own way. The King and his govt. are so simple and have so little knowledge of govt. that they are willing to accept and adopt any and every plan proposed by the Hawaiian Govt."[42]

The following sections examine the work and the writings that Poor and Bush carried out as part of the legation, examining the differences between the two both in how they viewed Sāmoa and the future relationship.

A POOR SKETCH

While Bush focused primarily on building connections and strengthening support for the confederacy, Poor turned toward the less glamorous but equally important task of data gathering. His reports reflect both a thorough and conscientious effort to report on Sāmoa and a worldview that valued European/American-style modernization, the Hawaiian nation-state, and relatively little else. His short account of recent Samoan history, for instance, relied almost entirely on politics in European-dominated Apia and the dispute between Tupua Tamasese and Malietoa Laupepa over the newly created kingship. Title-based Samoan politics do not figure into his report at all. Poor also authored the centerpiece of the legation's knowledge production efforts, a forty-page document entitled "The Samoan Islands—A Sketch by Henry Poor." Poor's sketch followed the basic format of an encyclopedia article with a heavy dose of editorializing. The article covers, in order: location, geography, population, national features, soil and climate, products, forests, industries and commerce, lands, currency, harbors and roadsteads, foreign communications, the people, political divisions, history, language, religion and education, and government.[43]

Poor's sketch reveals an exploitative mind-set typical of colonial agents throughout the Pacific, envisioning Sāmoa in terms of resources that can

---

[42] Henry Poor to Webb, January 3, 1887, FOEX, HSA; Henry Poor to Webb, March 20, 1887, FOEX, HSA; Henry Poor to Webb, May 7, 1887, FOEX, HSA.
[43] Poor, "Draft-Historical Synopsis"; Poor, "The Samoan Islands – A Sketch by Henry Poor."

be gained and Natives that stand in the way. Pages three through twenty-eight, for instance, focus largely on the exploitable resources of Sāmoa. While an appreciation and understanding of resources are far from exclusive to colonizers, Poor placed a clear emphasis on what could be done to maximize profits around steady, industrially organized exports, not much different from how the Germans viewed Sāmoa. He even gave an approving nod to the German plantations as an example of what the Samoan economy might become. It is not entirely clear if he intended this description only to describe what the Samoans might be able to exploit under Hawaiian "guidance" or if he intended to show what Hawai'i could gain by being the ones to exploit Sāmoa and the Samoan people.[44]

In a private letter, Poor also wrote to Webb that one of the biggest concerns for the future was American dominance of the merchant trade in Sāmoa through the Tutuila route. He noted that Hawaiian companies could compete with the creation of regular steamer service from Apia to Honolulu, "Provisional that the Hawaiians are to rule Samoa." He also noted the potential riches to be gained from smaller nearby islands such as Tokelau, noting to Webb that perhaps Hawai'i should take them as well. In many ways, Poor's "sketch" and his letters to Webb indicate that he saw Sāmoa in the same way many European/Americans saw the rest of the world, as a potential source of wealth that could only be properly developed through foreign initiative. Furthermore, he viewed Hawaiian "rule" over these islands through the confederacy as a sure way to properly exploit those riches with the Hawaiian side of the confederacy gaining the lion's share of the wealth.[45]

Two related colonial memes appear frequently throughout Poor's sketch: the high fertility of Native-held lands and the correspondingly high idleness of Native people. Taking a page straight from the European/American colonial playbook he wrote:

The profuseness of nature in supplying their food and their wants being simple, [Samoan] industries are not many or general, and such of her products as are prepared for trade or personal use amount to but a small percentage of what is possible were the whole population engaged in some industry, to say nothing of the extensive production possible on the great areas of fertile and untilled land.

In most colonial writings, such claims typically led to some sort of argument that only foreign control would allow the land to reach its full

---

[44] Poor, "The Samoan Islands – A Sketch by Henry Poor."
[45] Poor to Webb, May 7, 1887, FOEX, HSA; Poor to Webb, March 23, 1887, FOEX, HSA.

potential because Natives could not or would not. Poor does not disappoint. The laziness of the Samoans, he wrote, meant that they would not work on foreign-owned plantations, thus, "it is necessary for the plantations to import labor." Poor added that Sāmoa only exported one-third of the copra that it should with just their existing trees "owing to the reckless consumption by the natives at their homes and at their feasts; the considerable amount used to make oil for their bodies and their hair; the reckless feeding to pigs and chickens, and the thousands that rot away from sheer indolence to utilize them." With a stunning lack of self-awareness, Poor then expressed the wonders of copra in the European market, where it was manufactured into soaps, candles, and hair oils, while the "refuse" became stock feed or fertilizer.

After finishing his section on Samoan industry, or lack therefore of, Poor turned to the Samoan people, starting with a page and a half on their physical appearance. In a striking effort, he goes on to include nearly every possible stereotype about Oceanic peoples in the space of two paragraphs:

Darwinian theorists may find some argument in the following characteristics: They pick up things with their toes, squat when they meet to talk, and pick out lice from each other[']s head and eat them. In personal character they are far beneath the Hawaiian and lack many of the moral principles. Their greatest failing is petty thieving and deceit. Love, affection, gratitude, morals and justice are but weakly developed in their organization and they are excessively lazy spending most of their time in sleep or play as food is so abundant they have no need to work for it, and each village is a commune where idlers or traders may eat or sleep from house to house ... They live only in the present, the past and future concern them not.

After this list of old colonial favorites, Poor invoked the image of a slavishly devoted Native convert completely brainwashed by the churches. He then noted, almost immediately, "I fear that genuine Christian principles are not very deeply rooted in them as yet." Returning immediately to the slavish spiritual devotion of Samoan Christians, he juxtaposed it with their irreligious habits under their old religion, a "mild" heathenism with "no structure or monuments," of which, "there is now hardly any trace of their previous heathenish beliefs."[46]

While Poor's perspective might be written off as that of a single member of the legation, he did represent far more than just his own views, indeed he represented views that may have been quite common among other

[46] Poor, "The Samoan Islands – A Sketch by Henry Poor."

members of the Kalākaua administration. Other members of the legation certainly expressed similar sentiments, if not with quite the ferocity and regularity that Poor did. In a letter written just a few days after arriving, Hiram Kaumialiʻi noted the properly subdued behavior of Samoan churchgoers, but quickly and pointedly added that even the preachers lacked hats, which no Hawaiian gentleman would have been without in public. He continued, "[T]heir living is a little hemahema [awkward/deficient]. They have no bowls or calabashes, to place the meat and food, they put all the food together in a coconut basket." Even Bush, particularly in the early days of the legation, expressed similar sentiments. In an early letter to Kalākaua, he wrote, "[V]ery few live with naauao like ours. To me their mode of living is like ours when there was no kapu, and [they] are somewhat wild, and their minds are not like that of the Hawaiian nation ... I can truthfully say: 'Hawaii no ka oi.' "[47] Bush also wrote of the effort to find affordable medium-term lodging until appropriations for a permanent legation could be built, complaining that:

There was not a vacant or habitable dwelling to be obtained in Apia. The Government people offered us native houses, but this we could not accept, as the natives here are very curious and do not hesitate or think it rude to come in to your dwelling. Your bedroom is not even sacred to them.

In short, Samoan houses were not habitable, in large part because of the presence of Samoans.[48]

As seen in Bush and Kaumialiʻi's comments, Poor had not developed such negative views of Samoans in a vacuum, but rather from within a Hawaiian nationalist culture that prided itself as much on how it was different from other Oceanic peoples as it did on its roots in Ka Wā ʻŌiwi Wale. Indeed half of the rhetorical basis for the confederacy relied on a belief in Hawaiian superiority, a perspective that almost inevitably would lead to the self-satisfied sense of superiority occasionally expressed by all members of the legation. Had this Hawaiian ethnocentricity held sway and become the dominant lens through which the kingdom viewed the confederacy, it is highly likely that the confederacy would have evolved

---

[47] Bush to Kalākaua, January 3, 1887, FOEX, HSA; Hiram Kaumialiʻi, "He Leta Mai Samoa Mai," *Nupepa Kuokoa*, February 19,1887. The originals of both these letters are in Hawaiian. A translated version of the Bush letter is available at the FOEX, HSA, but the translation presented here is my own, retaining the Hawaiian terms when significant.

[48] Bush to Kalākaua, January 3, 1887, FOEX, HSA; Bush to Kalākaua, January 27, 1887, FOEX, HSA; Hiram Kaumialiʻi, "He Leta Mai Samoa Mai," *Nupepa Kuokoa*, February 19, 1887.

into something far more akin to a Hawaiian attempt at empire than an Oceanic bulwark against it.

ALOHA AMONG CONFEDERATES, DIPLOMACY WITHIN THE 'OHANA/'AIGA

Bush, as seen in the preceding example, was hardly free of nationalist/imperialist sentiment. Such sentiments do not, however, seem to have guided his vision of Sāmoa's present or future with quite the same power they did for Poor. Bush's writings show a different possibility for the future of the confederacy, one rooted less in the logics of empire and more in the logics of kinship. His actions also displayed a desire to work within Samoan concepts of political consent while developing broader support for the confederacy.

After the signing, Bush focused primarily on strengthening support for the confederacy among the Samoan political elite. In keeping with the rhetoric of genealogy and kinship that proved so powerful in their discussions with Malietoa, Bush frequently acted in accordance with Oceanic understandings of relations within families, particularly through an emphasis on generosity. Often this came in the form of small tokens of Hawaiian goodwill and open-handedness. A number of signed notes from Bush to other members of the legation and the *Kaimiloa*'s crew requested that the bearer of the note receive certain items from the ship's stores, such as cash, "[a] felt hat, a good one," bread, and syrup. There is also a note from Coe to Bush, explaining that Malietoa needed $100 and that the queen would be by to pick it up. The cursory nature of the note seems to imply that the issue would not be disputed and that Hawaiian compliance with such a request would be almost reflexive.[49]

Though technically the guests of the Samoans, Bush still displayed Hawaiian generosity and aloha through a heavy emphasis on offering hospitality. The Hawaiians hosted the Malietoa government to a rather extravagant Hawaiian-style feast during their earliest days in Apia, a widely recognized display of both aloha and wealth. Bush, however, felt the building they were renting lacked the space and ambiance for further entertaining and built the new legation headquarters in large part to improve their ability to provide hospitality. Once completed, the legation building became something of a social center where the Hawaiians

---

[49] William Coe to Poor, April 6, 1887, HHS; "Kingdom of Hawaii," 1887, incoming letters-Kaimiloa file, FOEX, HSA.

hosted various prominent Samoans. Visiting delegations wishing to speak with Bush could expect Hawaiian hospitality in Apia, such as the delegation from Manono, Tutuila, and Savaiʻi that came to discuss the confederacy and tensions with Tamasese's supporters in May. Other prominent Samoans living in Apia were frequent visitors to the legation, like the orator Patioli, who resided near the legation in Apia and spent much of his time enjoying the mission's hospitality.[50]

These expressions of generosity and hospitality, of course, were not without political motivation. In loaning or giving money to Malietoa, the legation clearly meant not just to show general Hawaiian generosity, or even Hawaiian generosity to Samoans, but specifically Hawaiian generosity to Malietoa. The same can be said of the hospitality shown toward the delegation from Manono, Tutuila, and Savaiʻi, a collection of chiefs and orators who represented a broad and powerful array of Malietoa's allies from across Sāmoa. The legation also focused their hospitality at potential defectors from the Tamasese faction. Patioli, also known as Lauafi or Maia, had been Tamasese's chief of state until quite recently. He and his daughter, who Poor claimed had been Tamasese's queen, abandoned Tamasese and moved to Apia in large part due to the presence of the Hawaiian legation. While Patioli had left Tamasese's cabinet, he could not officially come out in favor of Malietoa, as "he was indebted to Weber by mortgage on lands. If clear of Weber he would not hesitate to pronounce in favor of Malietoa." In the meantime, however, the new legation building provided him with hospitality and a space to signal his support for the confederacy.[51]

In some cases, diplomacy between Bush and various Samoan leaders moved beyond these broad conceptions of Oceanic kinship and into much more specific uses of kin and kinship networks to conduct diplomacy. The informal January 20 meeting with Malietoa included not just Malietoa's all-male cabinet and the all-male staff of the legation, but female family members of the two main participants, Bush and Malietoa. According to Poor, Malietoa brought along those in his government most closely related to him, including his queen Kui. Poor also specifically noted the presence of both Mrs. Bush and Mollie Bush, Envoy Bush's teenage daughter. In this environment Malietoa declared that all present were family, thus everything that was said could be trusted to remain

---

[50] Bush, "Dispatch #12," March 29, 1887, FOEX, HSA; Bush, "Dispatch #22," June 21, 1887, FOEX, HSA; Poor to Webb, March 12, 1887, FOEX, HSA.
[51] Henry Poor to Webb, March 12, 1887, FOEX, HSA.

private. The presence of female family members seems to have emphasized the familial and thus safe nature of the meeting, and was significant enough for Poor to specifically note as part of the proceedings. Though no doubt in attendance at more public events, the official documents do not mention their participation elsewhere.[52]

Though Western diplomatic traditions left little room for formal female participation and influence, the fact that Bush brought his female family members indicates that he might have perceived their potential as informal representatives of the legation. In part, this may have come from an understanding of gender and politics informed by Hawaiian sensibilities. Nineteenth-century Hawaiian politics included several prominent female figures, often those related by genealogy or marriage to powerful chiefs. Ka'ahumanu, though never formally a ruling monarch, effectively ruled the islands in the decades after Kamehemeha's death in 1819. Kalākaua depended heavily on his sister Lili'uokalani, his wife Kapi'olani, and her sister Po'omaikelani to lead various projects including the Hale Nāua and, in the case of Lili'uokalani, to act as his regent in his absence. He also had to contend with the political opposition of Queen Emma, the widow of Kamehameha IV and a well-connected ali'i nui in her own right. While Bush's wife and daughter lacked the genealogical standing or political background of ali'i wahine like Emma and Lili'uokalani, their presence in the legation still created pathways for diplomacy within Sāmoa. As seen in that "family" meeting, their presence and participation allowed both the Samoans and the Hawaiians to claim an intimate level of connection to one another beyond simple diplomacy.

In at least one other instance, Bush's daughter provided important services to the mission. When visiting Apia, Mata'afa sent his daughter to the legation to give them his greetings and to feel out their interest in meeting with him. His official reasoning was that he had not brought any gifts and was worried the "low opinion" of Mata'afa among Malietoa's allies might have prejudiced the legation against him. Due to his allegiance to Sā Tupua and being a nominal ally of Tupua Tamasese, Mata'afa may have also been wary of meeting directly with Malietoa Laupepa's new allies. Sending a formal delegation of his supporters or going himself had the potential for a loss of face for himself and the legation, or worse, may have unintentionally placed Mata'afa in a direct conflict with either Malietoa or Tamasese. Sending his daughter, however, lessened the potential risk of confrontation and potentially signaled his own willingness

---

[52] Henry Poor, "Journal of the Embassy to Samoa," BMA.

to engage in a kinship-based dialogue with the Hawaiians. Following Mataʻafa's lead, Bush sent his daughter Mollie to carry his reply and negotiate a face-to-face meeting between himself and Mataʻafa.[53]

Finally, at times different actors among both the Hawaiian legation and the various Samoan factions may have tried to strengthen the relationships not by claiming kinship but rather by creating it. According to a personal letter from Poor to Webb, Malietoa had sent a delegation of chiefs to inquire into the possibility of Malietoa marrying Mollie Bush, who rejected the offer. In that same letter, Poor noted that Patioli had established his residence near the legation. In a somewhat derisive tone, Poor noted that the man had "offered" Poor his daughter, while his other daughter, "Tamasese's ex-consort, has become charmed with the guitar music and songs of our baseball dude David and now has him as a paramour." Poor, likely due to his inability or unwillingness to see Samoans as anything more than primitive, unenlightened versions of their Hawaiian cousins, dismissed these events as evidence of the anachronistic and licentious nature of Samoans. Yet both sets of events seem to be relatively clear efforts to create sexual and kinship bonds as a means of strengthening ties between the legation and various Samoan leaders, a diplomatic tool recognized throughout Oceania and indeed globally. It should also be noted that Poor described Malietoa as already married at the time, and as a devoted Protestant the marriage offer seems a somewhat out of character for the king.[54]

The various roles played by women during the legation's stay in Sāmoa show that both the Samoan and Hawaiian men understood women as useful participants in diplomacy, particularly diplomacy between two groups eager to create ties based on kinship and ideas of aloha. The historical and cultural precedents for such female roles in both Sāmoa and Hawaiʻi not only helped to provide a common understanding of the propriety of such female participation, but also emphasized their connections due to their shared understanding of such roles.

At the same time, however, both Mollie and Mrs. Bush were noticeably absent from most of the formal work of the legation, had no official role in the legation, and do not seem to have participated in major events

---

[53] Henry Poor to Webb, March 12, 1887, FOEX, HSA.

[54] Ibid. The personal nature of Poor's letters to Webb and Poor's eagerness to gossip also throw something of a shadow on their reliability, and there is no verification of these claims in any other source. However, due to the potentially embarrassing nature of Mollie's rejection and of David Moehonua's relationship, neither would be likely to make the official records of the legation.

such as the signing of the confederacy. Furthermore, with the exception of the meeting on the seventh, they were largely left out of the official records of the legation and can only be found in Poor's personal letters to Joseph Webb. In the official dispatches, for instance, Bush simply noted that, Mata'afa "sent messengers," leaving out the role of both Mollie and Mata'afa's daughter in coordinating their meetings.[55] This lack of a formal role or recognition of their diplomatic work follows a Western perception of diplomacy, and really all government work, as a strictly male domain. Outside of ali'i nui women such as Emma and Lili'uokalani, whose political voice could not be denied, this understanding of government work as inherently masculine was well entrenched within the Kalākaua administration and was seemingly well entrenched in the legation as well.

HOW THE *KAIMILOA* BEAT THE *ADLER*

Bush's diplomatic efforts extended far outside of Apia. He visited Mata'afa in Atua twice, once before the *Kaimiloa* arrived and once aboard the *Kaimiloa*. He also took the *Kaimiloa* to the Gaga'emauga and Gaga'ifomauga districts on Savai'i, collectively known as the Itu-o-Tane, where Bush visited with local dignitaries from July 11 to July 18. These trips signaled that Bush recognized the need to appeal for support for the confederacy at the level of individual districts and villages. By traveling out to meet and visit with the various chiefs and orators of these districts, Bush displayed Hawaiian respect for these polities or sub-polities and showed that he valued them as allies. Due to the zealousness with which such districts guarded their reputations and independence, such signs of respect were essential for broader support for the confederacy. Indeed, part of Bush's anger at being recalled in July was that the chiefs and orators of the areas he had not yet visited would be offended and perhaps turn their backs on the confederacy. These trips also presented Bush the opportunity to further display Hawaiian generosity and affection, allowing these politically motivated trips to be understood as a show of aloha.[56]

---

[55] Henry Poor to Webb, 12 March 1887, FOEX, HSA; Bush, "Dispatch #8," February 22, 1887, FOEX, HSA.

[56] Bush to Kalākaua, August 15, 1887, FOEX, HSA; George Webb, "Dispatch #6," July 18, 1887, FOEX, HSA; Frank Waiau, "Lt Waiau's Logbook," 1887, BMA; Frank Waiau, "Lt Waiau's Logbook," 1887, FOEX, HAS. There are two copies of Lt. Waiau's Logbook,

During his second visit to Mataʻafa and his trip to the Itu-o-Tane aboard the *Kaimiloa*, Bush had three new tools at his disposal to display the Hawaiians' aloha and generosity: the ship's stores, the ship's band, and the ship itself. Though disparaged in Hawaiʻi and woefully under-gunned compared to the vessels of the Great Powers, many Samoans still admired the *Kaimiloa*. In his June dispatch, Bush wrote:

> The *Kaimiloa* arrived here on the morning of the 15th … Her appearance has excited none but favorable comment in Apia and she and her officers and boy crew have excited special interest among the Samoans, and the native chiefs seem to take a personal pride and interest in her and extend a hearty welcome to her officers. Her appearance has certainly strengthened the position of Hawaii in Samoa and will I think bring the whole of Samoa to our side in peace.

Like the Samoans of Apia, Mataʻafa also seemed to take a personal pride in the *Kaimiloa* when it arrived in Atua, at a place the Hawaiians first identified as "Wainau Bay." Upon coming aboard the ship, Mataʻafa declared that he would rename the bay in their honor, and that it would be thereafter known as "Kaimiloa Bay."[57]

The Samoans could clearly see the difference in size and power between the *Kaimiloa* and the warships of the Great Powers. The German *Adler*, which shadowed the *Kaimiloa* during its time in Sāmoa, was a new, wood-and-steel, composite-hulled vessel that displaced some 1,040 tons. The *Kaimiloa*, meanwhile, was a 171-ton guano trader converted into a gunship in four months. Its crew included many reform school boys sent aboard to learn a trade and to perform as the ship's band. Yet the *Kaimiloa* was still a gunship, and a gunship owned and operated by an Oceanic people, closely related to and now formally allied with the Malietoa government. Even the ship's reform school band, which Haole portrayed as a sign of Kanaka ineptitude, proved a major draw for the *Kaimiloa* in Apia and in other parts of Sāmoa. In Apia, Atua, and at Itu-o-Tane, the band constantly rotated between the ship and shore, providing both entertainment and proof of Hawaiian aloha.[58]

The ship's stores allowed Bush further opportunity to display Hawaiian aloha, presenting his hosts with presents as well as helping supply the

one at HSA and one at Grove Farm. The Grove Farm version has been photocopied and is available at Bishop Museum. The Grove/Bishop Museum copy includes substantial sections in Hawaiian that are not found in the HSA version.

[57] Bush, "Dispatch #22," June 21, 1887, FOEX, HSA; Frank Waiau, "Lt Waiau's Logbook," 1887, BMA.

[58] Bush, "Dispatch #22," June 21, 1887, FOEX, HSA; Kuykendall, *Hawaiian Kingdom*, 334.

festivities ashore. While Bush displayed a relatively open hand with the ship's stores in general, he was particularly generous with the ship's supply of gin. Indeed, throughout their stay the Hawaiians were free with their liquor, including at the feast thrown for Malietoa in January and with their daily visitors at the legation. Poor noted somewhat pointedly, for instance, that Patioli took a strong liking to the legation's open bar policy. Bush's liberality with the Hawaiian liquor caused a great deal of uproar among his detractors. Joseph Webb,[59] who Gibson sent with the *Kaimiloa* to spy on Bush, was disturbed by the sheer volume of gin Bush distributed, complaining that, "Of fourteen cases of gin purchased for the [trip], seven remained on the ship." Lacking Bush's newfound insight into the decentralized nature of Samoan authority, Webb felt that Bush's trips in general were a waste, nothing more than an attempt to "gratify the several chiefs visited by a sight of the ship, and having the band sent ashore to entertain their people."[60]

The long global history of traders, merchants, and other outsiders using alcohol to inebriate and exploit Native peoples brings into question the intent and wisdom of Bush's generosity with his gin. It should be noted, however, that Kalākaua promoted his own efforts to end prohibition in Hawai'i largely by arguing that the kingdom's liquor policies, which exclusively barred Kānaka from purchasing and selling liquor, were discriminatory throwbacks. Bush's liberality with his liquor, which violated similar laws in Sāmoa, seemed to strike a similar chord among many of the prominent Samoans who either hosted or were hosted by the legation. At least that is what one might conclude considering the speed with which the gin disappeared.[61]

Bush's efforts to display Hawaiian aloha become more significant when contrasted with the behavior of the Germans in Sāmoa. While the representatives of both the United States and Great Britain had done their share of exploiting and exasperating the turmoil in Sāmoa, the Germans had the most to gain from and the most interest in weakening Samoan independence. J. C. Godeffroy and Sohn's eviction of the Malietoa government from lands the German company claimed to own at Mulinu'u

---

[59] The same Joseph Webb who Poor regularly corresponded with before the arrival of the *Kaimiloa*.

[60] Bush to Kalākaua, January 21, 1887, FOEX, HSA; Poor to Webb, March 12, 1887, FOEX, HSA; Joseph Webb, "Dispatch 7," July 19, 1887, FOEX, HSA; Joseph Webb to Brown, August 27, 1887, FOEX, HSA.

[61] Kuykendall, *Hawaiian Kingdom*, 257.

provided just one of a number of examples of how the company, backed by the German Navy, routinely antagonized the Samoan people and mocked the very concept of Samoan independence. Appalled by their behavior, Poor described the Germans associated with Godeffroy and Sohn as "more like the ancient Goths and vandals from which they sprung than like modern Christian Gentlemen," an amusing play on European/American claims of Oceanic historic and contemporary savagery.[62]

While the Hawaiian legation and their allies in the Malietoa government were certainly biased against the Germans, they witnessed enough German malfeasance to justify such a bias. Poor reported a crowd of drunken Germans who, after failing to goad the legation into a fight in a hotel restaurant, literally marched into the streets of Apia in a drunken attempt at military drill and began randomly assaulting Samoans. On March 22, the Kaiser's birthday, Poor reported that the Germans and their Samoan employees had rampaged in the streets of Apia before being driven back by a force of Samoans residing in Apia. Such behavior did little to ingratiate the Germans to the Samoan public, especially around Apia. Bush noted as much in a February dispatch:

Their arbitrary, arrogant, and aggressive methods have made them disliked by almost the entire native population as well as by a great majority of foreigners resident here. The native chiefs and people would bitterly deplore German rule and would never be content or prosperous under it but would rapidly be "civilized off the face of the earth."[63]

German disregard for the Samoans even extended to their allies in Tamasese's camp, leading to significant erosion of support for the German-backed Leulumoega government during the legation's stay. On March 12, Poor reported that he had heard several Tamasese's supporters were already losing faith in their German allies after:

[Weber] made a speech to the Tamasese Government giving them every encouragement and making vague promises and undoing it by informing them that $1700 was due his firm for arms and ammunition and a speedy settlement was desirable: that the balance in the treasury (which was in Weber's hands) was already exhausted by previous purchases of arms: advised them all to sell their lands to him (at 25 [cents] per acre) that they might obtain more arms.

Those misguided people are beginning to think that as a man Weber is not all their fancy painted him.

---

[62] Henry Poor to Webb, January 31, 1887, FOEX, HSA.
[63] Bush, "Dispatch #8," 22 February 1887, FOEX, HSA; Poor to Webb, 31 January 1887; Henry Poor to Webb, 23 March 1887, FOEX, HSA.

Poor then noted that Brandeis, the former Godeffroy clerk who Weber sent to "advise" Tamasese, was ready to file a complaint with the German consulate when the Tamasese government decided to only pay him a third of the $150 per month that Weber had negotiated for him. He gleefully added, "[T]he Tamasese Government evidently do not appreciate his services for they think $50 per month is sufficient for a man who was too incompetent to fill a position [at Godeffroy]."[64]

May proved to be particularly disastrous for the Germans. In the beginning of the month, Tamasese's German advisors physically refrained him and briefly imprisoned Poor, Coe, and several of Tamasese's cabinet to prevent even informal meetings between the Tamasese government and the Hawaiians. Later that month, with the Hawaiians stripping away supporters and morale lagging, the Germans initiated a disastrous public relations campaign. On May 28, they presented Tamasese with a new flag at Leulumoega and, according to Bush, convinced one of the orators there to bestow upon him the title Tui Atua. On May 30, they took the provocative step of bringing Tamasese and his chiefs to Apia, where they entertained them aboard the German warship *Adler* under the new flag. While the event clearly showed the Germans' contempt of Malietoa and recognition of Tamasese, it failed in its intended goal of raising morale among Tamasese's supporters. Bush reported:

The visitors expected a salute of cannon for themselves and the new flag, but as the ship has not a saluting battery they became suspicious and disappointed. Tamasese and a few others returned home that morning but the majority staid [sic] on Mulinuu Point where they got into a general quarrel among themselves.

The majority objected to the new flag as being too close a resemblance to the German and were mad that no salute had been fired, and begun to doubt the good faith of the Germans.[65]

The incident served as a catalyst for further discontent. The next day a large faction of Tamasese's supporters from Atua left. They cited among their chief complaints the improper protocols under which Tamasese had received the Tui Atua title over Mata'afa, who had designs on the Tui Atua title and considerably stronger support within the district. Numerous warriors from Itu-o-Tane also left, disgruntled with the entire situation. Tamasese then set out for Falefa in Atua to hold fono (councils), make explanations, and try to induce his former adherents to return. On June 10, the German vice-consul went down to join Tamasese and assist him

---

[64] Poor to Webb, 12 March 1887, FOEX, HSA.
[65] Bush, "Dispatch #22," June 21, 1887, FOEX, has.

in recalling the disaffected warriors, but they both returned on the night of the eleventh having failed in their mission.[66]

By no coincidence, Bush's first trips aboard the *Kaimiloa* in June were to Atua and Itu-o-Tane, regions discontented with Tamasese and his German allies. Seizing upon the Germans' ham-fisted efforts, particularly in attempting to have Tupua Tamasese named Tui Atua, the Hawaiians sought to strengthen their ties to Mata'afa Iosefa by traveling to meet him in Atua, displaying their respect for him as holder of the Mata'afa title and a major power within Atua and Sāmoa in general. If Mata'afa needed further contrast between how the Germans and the Hawaiians perceived their relationships with him, it came during Bush's visit aboard the *Kaimiloa*. The Hawaiians welcomed Mata'afa aboard the ship, toasted him, and impressed him with their generosity and aloha. As noted previously, he responded by renaming the bay after the Hawaiian vessel. Later, as Mata'afa was meeting with the legation on shore, the captain of the *Adler*, which shadowed the Hawaiians into "Kaimiloa Bay," ordered him onboard, interrogated him about the Hawaiian visit, and tried to bully him into supporting Tamasese.[67]

Next, Bush took the *Kaimiloa* out to Safotu, one of the main political centers of the Itu-o-Tane region and the home of a large contingent of Tupua Tamasese's armed supporters, but also one of the centers of discontent with the recent German actions. Bush spent several days ashore, meeting with the chiefs of the region, displaying the *Kaimiloa,* and entertaining his hosts with the Reform School/Navy band.[68] The Hawaiians could not match the Germans in terms of military or economic strength, and the Samoans recognized this. But they clearly outmatched the Germans in terms of alofa.

This was the key to Bush's vision of the confederacy and the way the Hawaiians believed they could secure influence in Sāmoa. Unlike the various empires in the Pacific, who could rely on their military strength to coerce Native polities and colonized peoples through force of arms, the Hawaiians had to rely largely on Samoan trust. The basis of this trust came in proving that the Hawaiians thought of themselves and the Samoans as belonging to one another through genealogy and kinship. Based on his discussions with chiefs from across Sāmoa, Bush wrote in February, "I am convinced that the Hawaiians would, better than a

[66] Ibid.
[67] Stevenson, *A Footnote to History*, 61; Waiau, "Lt Waiau's Logbook," 1887, BMA.
[68] Waiau, "Lt Waiau's Logbook," 1887, BMA.

foreign nation, have the confidence of the Samoans and succeed in raising order out of chaos."[69] Bush's claim of Hawai'i having a chance of success "better than a foreign nation" is rather telling. The exclusion of Hawaiians from the category "foreign," likely indicate Bush's own strong beliefs in the importance of Hawaiian and Samoan kinship. The Kānaka Hawai'i were not foreigners; they were 'ohana.

THINGS FALL APART

Events in Hawai'i, Sāmoa, and Europe, however, set off a series of events that would prevent the Polynesian confederacy from coming to full fruition. First, an attempt by Coe and Poor to have Bush recalled from his position partially succeeded, when Coe's translation of a letter purportedly from Malietoa calling for Bush's withdrawal arrived in Honolulu. The original, however, never arrived, or possibly never existed in the first place. Coe and Poor's machinations were still enough for Gibson to withdraw Bush from the legation and put Poor at its head. Upon hearing this news, Bush went to Malietoa who then wrote a letter defending Bush's conduct, denying the validity of the letter forwarded by Coe and Poor, and offering Bush a position in his own government.[70]

None of this mattered as the fate of the legation and the confederacy had already been sealed. Due to the inconsistencies of maritime postage, word of Bush's recall arrived just a day before word reached Sāmoa that a mission-faction-led coup had forced Kalākaua to sign the Bayonet Constitution, effectively usurping the executive and legislative power of the mō'ī and the lāhui, respectively. One of the new government's first orders of business was to call back the legation and cancel all plans for the confederacy, which had been a focus for Haole anger in the months leading up to the coup. Though Bush remained in Sāmoa as an advisor to Malietoa Laupepa, the confederacy, for all intents and purposes, was dead.

The coup set the stage for a second, more complete coup in 1893, which established informal American imperial rule. Meanwhile in Sāmoa, an 1887 German invasion and the 1889 collusion of the German, British, and American governments led to informal "tri-partite" rule. Over the next decade, both the Samoan and Hawaiian lāhui struggled against the

---

[69] Bush, "Dispatch #8," February 22, 1887, FOEX, HAS.
[70] Bush to Kalākaua, August 15, 1887(#1), FOEX, HSA; Bush to Kalākaua, August 15, 1887(#2), FOEX, HSA.

imperial powers with little success. In 1898, with the Spanish American War expanding America's Pacific empire and a Republican administration back in the White House, Hawai'i fell under direct American imperial rule. In 1899, the United States and Germany split Sāmoa amongst themselves, creating a political separation that persists into the present day between independent Sāmoa and American Sāmoa. The intent of the confederacy had been to avoid such a colonial future, and by that measure it was clearly a failure. It was too little, too late, and frankly, in a time of overwhelming imperial aggression it lacked the sheer gun power needed to keep the empires at bay.

While the confederacy resulted in few long-term impacts, the legation's time in Sāmoa left behind enough of a record to examine how the Hawaiians had begun to imagine the confederacy operating had the overthrow and the German invasion not occurred. Once again the "Empire of the Calabash," which the supporters of the Bayonet revolt had found both ludicrous and threatening, provides a convenient metaphor for how plans for the future confederacy reflected the logics of both empire and calabash. Based on the groundwork laid by the legation, early planning for the confederacy relied on both sets of logics, indeed, the explicit appeals of the confederacy and the initial Hawaiian efforts to stabilize Malietoa retained elements of both. Both sides imagined the emerging relationship as an unequal one, the sort of imbalance that categorized empires far more than it did simple allies.

What this might have meant for the future of the relationship depended largely on how serious the Hawaiians were about their kinship with the Samoans. Following Poor's logics, with an emphasis on exploiting Sāmoa and Samoans, the Hawaiians would have quickly found what the Germans and New Zealand discovered in the twentieth century; imperial bureaucracies do not fare well in Sāmoa. Following Bush's logics, however, the confederacy had the potential to be a radical departure from political trends not just in the Pacific, but worldwide, calling into question the assumed future hegemony of European/Americans and their empires in the Pacific.

Perhaps one of the biggest indicators of the potential such a confederacy held came from its greatest detractors, the Haole elite in Honolulu and the Germans in Apia and Berlin. Acting separately but in indirect support of each other, they acted to end not just the confederacy, but the independence of the governments that supported it. Some of their eagerness to kill the confederacy came from the standard imperial greed that marked so much of the late nineteenth century. The sheer vitriol of both the Germans and the coup leaders, however, hint at something else, perhaps a fear of how the very idea of such trans-Oceanic, Native-driven alliances ran counter to the nationalist and white-supremacist visions of an imperial Pacific through which they defined themselves.

Just as the legation's opponents saw the potential of such trans-Oceanic thinking, so too did the people of Aunu'u, the small island off the coast of Tutuila where deserters from the Kaimiloa *took refuge. Like the confederacy, the event shows the importance and potential of family and kinship as ways of organizing diplomacy in the Pacific. The refugees who fled to Aunu'u did so based on family connections with the people of Aunu'u, calling upon these relationships in times of need like so many had before them. The Kānaka Hawai'i, meanwhile, by staying in Aunu'u and fighting for their hosts, also called on such ties, on Oceanic ideas of friendship, on the cultural similarities between the two peoples, on the premise of connections rooted deep within their shared Oceanic past yet accessible in times of need. Furthermore, by staying in Aunu'u, setting roots there, becoming part of Aunu'u, those sailors, like so many other trans-Oceanic migrants, not only called upon those ideas, but they also renewed them and celebrated them in ways no coup or invasion could ever take away.[71] Trans-Oceanic alliances may not have stopped the rise of empires, but the rise of empires would also be unable to stop the memory, maintenance, and creation of trans-Oceanic ties.*

[71] William Pila Kikuchi, "A Legend of Kaimiloa Hawaiians in American Samoa," *Hawaiian Historical Society Review* (1964): 268–269.

5

"There Is Nothing That Separates Us"

John T. Baker and the Pan-Oceanic Lāhui

PROLOGUE: STEPHEN PUPUHI

On April 23, 1823 the second company of missionaries from the ABCFM arrived in Hawai'i after months at sea. Among the weary company of New Englanders were four Oceanic youths educated at the Foreign Mission School in Cornwall, Connecticut. Three of the youths were Kānaka Maoli, returning to their homeland after substantial stays in New England. The fourth was a Tahitian, Pupuhi, often referred to as "Stephen Popohe" in missionary accounts. As a Tahitian arriving in Hawai'i for the first time, Pupuhi stood at the boundary between foreigner and Native. He had never been to Hawai'i, no known relatives there, and little information on the islands beyond what he had learned from his mission teachers and his Kanaka classmates. The remarkable linguistic and cultural ties between Hawai'i and Tahiti, however, gave Pupuhi an insight into and connection to the Kānaka Maoli that other foreign missionaries, particularly European and American missionaries, lacked.[1]

In addition to his cultural insights into Eastern Oceanic culture, Pupuhi's personal qualities made him a promising missionary. One account from his school days recalled him as having a stature, "above the common size, and uncommonly well-proportioned. His countenance is intelligent and sprightly, and his manners easy and graceful."[2] *Like the handful of Tahitian missionaries who had recently accompanied the British missionary William Ellis to Hawai'i, Pupuhi achieved significant*

---

[1] ABCFM, "Mission at the Sandwich Islands," *Missionary Herald* 19, no. 1 (1823): 11.
[2] Thomas (pseud.), "Infidelity among Christians," *Religious Intelligencer* 12, no. 40 (1823): 634.

popularity among the Kānaka Hawai'i, chiefs and commoners alike. In addition to becoming an advisor to powerful ali'i nui such as Boki, he proved himself to be an accomplished preacher. In 1824, Pupuhi performed the only Hawaiian-language services in Honolulu during an extended absence by Reverend Hiram Bingham. Bingham's fellow American missionaries noted with a mix of approval and confusion that Pupuhi could attract and maintain as large a crowd as Bingham had. By 1825, he had built a thriving congregation in Waikapū, Maui, which he operated largely independent of ABCFM funding.[3]

In 1907, Pupuhi's Hawaiian grandson, John Tamatoa Baker, steamed into Pape'ete, Tahiti aboard the *Mariposa*. Like his grandfather entering Hawai'i, Baker resided in a liminal zone between foreigner and Native, displaying qualities of both, yet not fully captured by the limited definitions of either. A seasoned traveler in his fifties, Baker had been to Europe and the United States several times, but had not yet traveled to any part of the Pacific other than his homeland in Hawai'i. At the same time, Baker was returning to the homeland of his own ancestors, and like his grandfather some eighty years earlier, Baker was entering a land culturally, linguistically, and historically tied to his own.

As the ship pulled into its berth, Baker must have been at least slightly anxious regarding his stay in Tahiti and how he would be received there. He knew he had family in Tahiti, but he did not know how to contact them. He had letters of introduction to prestigious Tahitian families, but no actual friends established in Tahiti and no traveling companion. He arrived as someone who knew he had a place in Tahiti, but no real indication of what that place might be. Before even disembarking the ship, however, whatever worries he might have had about his welcome and his place had been pushed aside. Oceanic networks of travel, kinship, and hospitality quickly swept Baker from the isolation of the solitary traveler and deposited him in the homes and lives of Tahitian nobility, Kanaka expatriates, and finally his own long-lost family.[4]

Baker's visit to his grandfather's Tahitian homeland was just the start of a seven-month voyage through Eastern Oceania, Australia, the Philippines, and Japan. Though a stranger in all of the places he visited,

---

[3] ABCFM, "Mission at the Sandwich Islands," *Missionary Herald* 19, no.1 (1823): 12; ABCFM, "Mission at the Sandwich Islands," *Missionary Herald* 21, no. 49 (1825): 172; ABCFM, *Seventeenth Annual Report of the American Board of Commissioners for Foreign Missions* (Boston: Crocker and Brewer, 1826), 76.

[4] John T. Baker, "Mai Ka Aina Mamao Mai," *Ke Aloha Aina*, August 10, 1907.

Baker's demeanor, musical talents, and standing as the former royal governor of Hawai'i Island earned him a warm welcome in Tahiti, Fiji, Rarotonga, Aotearoa, Sāmoa, and Tonga. Furthermore, ancient and modern networks of Oceanic migration granted Baker relatively easy access into the homes, lives, and affections of his fellow Oceanic peoples. He dined with high chiefs in Tahiti, reunited with his grandfather's family in Papeete, befriended core members of the Young Māori Party in Wellington, entertained Queen Makea Takau Ariki of the Cook Islands, and connected with a string of Kānaka Hawai'i who had made their homes in the south. He visited the thermal attractions of Rotorua and viewed the lava spilling down the slopes of Savai'i. These travels were preserved in a string of letters he wrote to the editors of the Hawaiian-language newspaper *Ke Aloha Aina*, who published them as a recurring column starting in August 1907.

Like most travel literature of the time, Baker's letters not only informed his audience about foreign lands, but also informed them about their relationship to empire and to the peoples and places ruled by empire. In the European/American tradition, travel writers typically wrote from an explicitly imperial perspective, often acting to validate or even celebrate empire. They allowed the reader to gaze upon their empires, future sites of empire, or the empires of others, and thus better understand their expected role as an imperial power.[5]

In the case of Baker's writings, however, the connection between writer and audience came not from their shared perspective and concerns as possessors of empire but from their shared perspectives and concerns as Oceanic subjects of empire. Furthermore, the high regard he held for his own history and culture translated directly into an interest in and respect for the cultures and histories of other Oceanic peoples. As a result, his encounters with and descriptions of other islanders focused heavily on their shared heritage, culture, and struggle in navigating life under empire. Baker's keenness to seek out and celebrate ties between Hawai'i and other parts of Oceania created a vision of the region not as a series of distant places spread amongst various empires, but rather as a network of places intimately tied to Hawai'i and the Lāhui Hawai'i. Through this process of recognizing and reconnecting the lāhui to its Oceanic roots Baker implicitly challenged imperial rhetoric that defined imperial cultures as normative and Hawaiian culture as inherently deviant and anachronistic.

---

[5] Nicholas Thomas, *Colonialism's Culture: Anthropology, Travel, and Government* (Princeton, NJ: Princeton University Press, 1994), 105–107, 125–142.

JOHN TAMATOA BAKER: KANAKA CAPITALIST, POLITICIAN, AND TRAVELER

As noted previously, Baker's journey to the south came partly from his desire to visit the land of his ancestors, specifically the homeland of his grandfather Pupuhi. Pupuhi had married a Kanaka Maoli woman and had several children, one of whom was John's mother Luka. Luka and Adam Baker, an English ship's captain, had two sons, John and Edward. Adam also had another son, Robert Hoapili Baker, with the ali'i wahine Malie Napu'upahoehoe. While his sons were still in their youth, Captain Baker "disappeared" at sea. He returned a few years later with an English bride and a desire to take John and Edward to England for an education. Luka apparently told Adam what he could do with his English wife and English education; both of her sons remained in Hawai'i and attended Lahainaluna.[6]

While at Lahainaluna, John's good looks, intelligence, and personality made him one of the school's most sought-after bachelors. Sometime following his graduation in the 1870s, Baker married the ali'i nui Ululani Lewai, whose small stature and quiet, contemplative demeanor balanced out the towering and often larger-than-life Baker. Ululani was the daughter of Noah Pelei'oholani, a fixture in the courts of the later Kamehamehas. Noah descended not only from his namesake, Pelei'oholani, the famous ruling chief of O'ahu and Kaua'i, but also from the Maui ruling chief Kamehamehanui, the predecessor of Kahekili. Furthermore, Noah's maternal grandfather was George Cox Ke'eaumoku, the son of Nāmāhānā'i Kaleleokalani and Kamehameha's chief advisor, Ke'eaumoku Pāpa'iahiahi.[7]

Despite his rank and influence, Noah had little to offer the young couple in terms of economic support and they struggled financially. To provide for his family when Ululani became pregnant, Baker "shipped" on a three-year contract with hapa-Haole ali'i nui and planter John Cummins in Waimanalo. Ululani, meanwhile, sailed to Maui to give birth among her relatives on her mother's side. The baby, like so many in those times,

---

[6] Rebecca Copp Raymond and Blanche Ralson Martin, *The Baker Clan* (Santa Rosa, CA: Cleek Print, undated), 2–5; Clarice B. Taylor, "Little Tales about Hawaii: J. T. Baker, Model for Kamehameha Statue Pt. 2," *Honolulu Star Bulletin*, September 11, 1951; Taylor, "Little Tales about Hawaii: J. T. Baker, Model for Kamehameha Statue Pt. 3," *Honolulu Star Bulletin*, September 12, 1951.

[7] Taylor, "Little Tales about Hawaii: J. T. Baker, Model for Kamehameha Statue Pt. 4," *Honolulu Star Bulletin*, September 13, 1951.

died weeks after its birth, filling both Ululani and John with great sorrow. It would be the only child the two ever had.[8]

Soon however, Ululani's family connections secured her a place in Kalākaua's court. Ululani quickly found favor in the eyes of the king, who bought out John's contract in 1878 and awarded him a place in the household guard, then under the command of Baker's half-brother Robert. Baker also developed a close personal tie to Kalākaua. In 1879, the king asked Baker, still noted for his physique and handsome face, to pose for photographs in the sacred malo (waistcloth) of Liloa and Kamehameha's feather cape. These photographs became the basis for the famous Kamehameha statue. In 1887, John and Ululani were also among the founding members of Kalākaua's secret society/think tank Hale Nauā, an important component in Kalākaua's post–Bayonet Constitution cultural and political agendas. Baker also served in a number of appointed positions, including captain in the Household Guard (1884), major in the King's Guard (1886), sheriff of Hawai'i Island (1887), governor of Hawai'i Island (1891), and as a member of the Privy Council (1884 until 1891).[9]

During this time, Baker also entered into electoral politics, representing Honolulu in the House of Representatives in 1884 and 1886. He acquired a reputation as a popular speaker at political rallies, including impromptu speeches specifically aimed at stealing crowds away from the anti-Kalākaua Independent and Reform parties.[10] The turmoil, vote suppression, and suffrage restrictions following the mission faction-driven Bayonet Constitution weakened the Native Hawaiian vote and kept Baker and many other pro-Kalākaua legislators out of office in 1887 and 1888. By 1890, Baker managed to return to the legislature along with a cadre of other candidates seeking to restore the old constitution.[11]

---

[8] Taylor, "Little Tales about Hawaii: J. T. Baker, Model for Kamehameha Statue Pt. 5," *Honolulu Star Bulletin*, September 14, 1951.

[9] Frank Karpiel, "Notes and Queries," *Hawaiian Journal of History* 33 (1999): 208–209; Taylor, "Little Tales about Hawaii: J. T. Baker, Model for Kamehameha Statue Pt. 4"; Taylor, "Little Tales about Hawaii: J. T. Baker, Model for Kamehameha Statue Pt. 5"; Taylor, "Little Tales about Hawaii: J.T. Baker, Model for Kamehameha Statue Pt. 6," *Honolulu Star Bulletin* September 15, 1951; Baker, "Former Hawaii Governor, Dies," *Honolulu Star-Bulletin*, September 7, 1921, 1, 3.

[10] "Independent Ticket Meetings," *Pacific Commercial Advertiser*, February 6, 1884; "Local and General," *Pacific Commercial Advertiser*, February 6, 1884, "Political Gatherings on Saturday and Sunday—The Government Endorsed," *Pacific Commercial Advertiser*, January 18, 1886.

[11] Karpiel, "Notes and Queries," 208–209; Robert Colfax Lydecker, *Roster Legislatures of Hawaii, 1841–1918: Constitutions of Monarchy and Republic: Speeches of Sovereigns and President* (Honolulu: Hawaiian Gazette Co., 1918), 178; Taylor, "Little

Though not as prominent in the postoverthrow political battles as Joseph and Emma Nāwahi, John E. Bush, or Robert Wilcox, the Bakers were stout aloha 'āina (patriots) and leaders of the anti-annexation movement on Hawai'i Island.[12] Professor Benjamin Cluff, then president of Brigham Young Academy in Provo, described Baker as one of the leaders of the Hilo royalists. In an article intended to bolster support for annexation, he described Baker as "the most intelligent Royalist I met outside of Honolulu." He then attempted to discredit Baker's allegiances by insinuating Baker was only a royalist out of fear that Kalākaua's ghost would "look down upon him disapprovingly," should he turn against the queen.[13]

Throughout the postoverthrow period, Baker managed to prosper despite the loss of government positions and royal patronage. The foundation of Baker's wealth lay in his lands at Pi'ihonua, Hilo, which Kalākaua had leased to him for a nominal rate. By subletting and developing his Pi'ihonua land, Baker established a steady stream of income as well as capital for various other ventures, most notably a successful ranching operation in Hamakua and South Kohala.[14] The Bakers also remained a fixture in Hawai'i's elite society and leaders of the Kanaka community. While Ululani's geneaology, the couple's wealth, and their former political roles certainly contributed to this popularity, John's outgoing personality also played a considerable role. Long after his death, Hilo residents still

Tales about Hawaii: J. T. Baker, Model for Kamehameha Statue Pt. 8," *Honolulu Star Bulletin*, September 18, 1951; Taylor, "Little Tales about Hawaii: J. T. Baker, Model for Kamehameha Statue Pt. 9," *Honolulu Star Bulletin*, September 19, 1951; Taylor, "Little Tales about Hawaii: J.T. Baker, Model for Kamehameha Statue Pt. 10," *Honolulu Star Bulletin*, September 20, 1951.

12 In 1895, *Ka Makaainana*, John E. Bush's newspaper, reported that "Keone Beka," a political prisoner, had been released from jail, probably following the "Republic's" massive roundup of royalists in response to Wilcox's rebellion, the same roundup that sent Bush and Nāwāhī to jail for several months, and caused Nāwāhī's death. I still have not discovered if this is the same John Baker or more likely his nephew, namesake, and hānai son John T. Baker Jr.

13 Benjamin Cluff, "The Hawaiian Islands and Annexation," *Improvement Era* 1, no. 1 (1897): 445; Obituary of Ululani Baker, "Ke Kiaaina Mrs. Ululani Baker Ua Hala, Aloha No," *Ke Aloha Aina*, October 11, 1902.

14 Hawaii Territorial Legislature, *Journal of the House of Representatives of the Seventh Legislature of the Territory of Hawaii: Regular Session* (1913): 839; Taylor, "Little Tales about Hawaii: J. T. Baker, Model for Kamehameha Statue Pt. 8," *Honolulu Star Bulletin*, September 13, 1951; Taylor, "Little Tales about Hawaii: J. T. Baker, Model for Kamehameha Statue Pt. 9," *Honolulu Star Bulletin*, September 19, 1951; Taylor, "Little Tales about Hawaii: J. T. Baker, Model for Kamehameha Statue Pt. 10," *Honolulu Star Bulletin*, September 20, 1951.

remembered Baker's love for breaking into impromptu song and chant, often carrying his guitar in case he felt the need for accompaniment.[15] Even in Honolulu, John remained a prominent figure, and frequently appeared as a speaker during election season. As the *Star Bulletin* noted, "He never declined an invitation to speak to the voters. He was a noted orator in both the English and Hawaiian languages."[16]

While Baker prospered as an individual, he must have been well aware of the tenuous position of the lāhui as a whole, particularly with regard to the cultural roots that unified and largely defined it. The Hawai'i Baker left in 1907, after all, was far different than the Hawai'i of his youth. When Baker was born in 1852, Hawai'i was a sovereign kingdom, looking ahead to a long future as such under its various treaties and friendly diplomatic relations with Europe and America. In 1907, it had experienced fourteen years under some form of Haole colonial rule and eight years within the American empire. In the 1850s, Hawai'i's economy was based primarily on a mix of subsistence-plus agriculture and a seasonal provisioning trade tied to whaling and shipping. By 1907, Haole-dominated sugar firms controlled the lion's share of the land, water, and economy of the islands. In 1853, the lāhui was still some 71,000 strong. Though far fewer than it had been just a few decades earlier, Kānaka were still the clear numerical majority in the kingdom. By 1907, the population of the lāhui had dropped to nearly 40,000, now only 25 percent of the islands' population.[17]

While imperial influences and rhetoric existed in and had an effect on Hawai'i before the overthrow and annexation, it was not until after annexation that the islands experienced its full brunt. Control of the schools, the government, and a massive chunk of the print media allowed the sugar oligarchs and their allies in the Territorial administration significant influence over culture and society in Hawai'i. The bulk of their efforts promoted Americanization, building a discourse of American cultural superiority and thus the correctness of American imperial rule.

[15] Taylor, "Little Tales about Hawaii: J. T. Baker, Model for Kamehameha Statue Pt. 9," *Honolulu Star Bulletin*, September 19, 1951.

[16] Obituary of John T. Baker, "John T. Baker, Former Hawaii Governor, Dies," *Honolulu Star-Bulletin*, September 7, 1921, 3.

[17] OHA, "The Population of the Hawaiian Islands: 1778–1896," Native Hawaiian Data Book Table 1:1, www.oha.org/databook/databook1996_1998/tab1-01.98.html (accessed October 26, 2010); OHA, "The Population of the Territory and State of Hawai'i: 1900–1990," Native Hawaiian Data Book, Table 1:2, www.oha.org/databook/databook1996_1998/tab1-02.98.html (accessed October 26, 1010). Second number includes hapa and "full-blooded" Hawaiians.

The oligarchs and their Washington-appointed allies made killing the Hawaiian language a major priority, deeming English the official language of government business, including public schooling. Some among the oligarchs and their allies correctly predicted that in doing so they might not only kill the Hawaiian language within a generation or two, but also kill a considerable amount of the Native Hawaiian cultural, political, and social values that remained in the islands.[18]

As a former member of the Kalākaua administration and as someone who grew up within, lived within, and valued Hawaiian culture, such assaults must have been a cause of concern for Baker just as they were for many others within the Kanaka community.[19] Baker was no stranger to the world of cultural politics, after all. As a member of Kalākaua's court, he had experienced a number of kingdom-era cultural projects and confrontations, including Kalākaua's coronation and the mission faction's impotent fury over hula and other expressions of 'Ōiwi Wale culture. As noted previously, the Bakers were also founding members of the Hale Nāua, which sought to shape the kingdom's future through the study and application of both foreign and Kanaka knowledge. As with the coronation and other parts of Kalākaua's cultural agenda, the mission faction and their allies frequently attacked the Hale Nāua as backward, anachronistic, and satanic.[20]

Even after the overthrow and in the face of a government-backed assault on Hawaiian culture, Baker remained openly committed to that culture. His letters back to *Ke Aloha Aina*, for instance, reflected knowledge of and skill in using the mo'olelo (histories/legends), oli (chant), and geography of Hawai'i to connect with an audience literate in Hawaiian culture. Baker also embraced elements of Hawaiian culture in his everyday life, particularly his religious faith, a unique combination of European/American religious trends and 'Ōiwi Wale religious tradition. Unsatisfied with the common Christian options in Hawai'i (Congregationalism, Anglicanism, Catholicism, and to a lesser degree Mormonism), Baker turned to the Christian Science teachings of Mary Baker Eddy. Conveniently there seemed to be little organized Christian

---

[18] Paul Nahoa Lucas, "E Ola Mau Kakou I Ka 'Olelo Makuahine: Hawaiian Language Policy and the Courts," *Hawaiian Journal of History* 34 (2000): 8–10; Robert Stuart MacArthur, D.D., "Native Hawaiian Churches," *The Independent* 47, no. 2447 (1895): 5.

[19] Davianna McGregor, "'Āina Ho'opulapula: Hawaiian Homesteading," *Hawaiian Journal of History* 24 (1990): 4.

[20] Noenoe Silva, *Aloha Betrayed: Native Hawaiian Resistance to American Colonialism* (Durham, NC: Duke University Press, 2004), 114–120.

Science presence on Hawai'i Island, allowing Baker to make creative use of Eddy's teachings and Christianity in general. He remade, for instance, the Christian trinity in a Kanaka image, worshipping the akua (gods) Ku, Hina, and Kaneikawaiola as manifestations of the Christian divine. His discussion of these religious practices in *Ke Aloha Aina* no doubt raised a few eyebrows, but for many within his audience it displayed his continued connection to their shared cultural heritage.[21]

In the rhetoric of those seeking to Americanize Hawai'i, such an embrace of the Hawaiian past was often associated with a backward thinking or provincial worldview, a clear detriment to survival in the modern era. Baker, however, provides a clear counterexample to such rhetoric as he managed to thrive socially and economically while embracing his supposedly anachronistic culture. Furthermore, Baker paired his commitment to the Hawaiian past with a love of travel and a keenness for new experiences. After participating in the lobbying effort against annexation in Washington, D.C., the Bakers toured the eastern United States and Western Europe in 1899, enjoying the experiences available to well-off and well-connected tourists such as themselves.[22]

Their travels together ended, however, in October 1902, when Ululani passed away at the age of fifty-five. Baker fled their beloved Hilo home for his ranch in Hamakua, but even there her death, and the life they had lived together, continued to haunt him. Hoping to find respite in travel, he boarded the steamship *Mariposa* in 1907, accompanied only by his guitar, an engraved cameo of his beloved Ululani, and a desire to connect with the homelands and relatives of his grandfather. In doing so, Baker also found and embraced the cultural, historical, and linguistic connections that tied his own culture to a broader Oceanic culture and provided further validation of the worth and utility of Hawaiian culture.[23]

TAHITI: NETWORKS AND CONNECTIONS

Throughout his voyage and his writings Baker placed a heavy emphasis on the interpersonal networks and connections that migration and travel had created across Oceania. In doing so, he created a vision of the rest

---

[21] Baker, "Mai ka Aina Mamao Mai," *Ke Aloha Aina*, November 31, 1907.

[22] Obituary of Ululani Baker, "Ke Kiaaina Mrs. Ululani Baker Ua Hala, Aloha No," *Ke Aloha Aina*; Obituary of John T. Baker, "John T. Baker, Former Hawaii Governor, Dies," *Honolulu Star-Bulletin*, September 7, 1921, 3.

[23] Obituary of Ululani Baker, "Ke Kiaaina Mrs. Ululani Baker Ua Hala, Aloha No," *Ke Aloha Aina*.

of Oceania not as a series of distant and foreign places, but as a place tied to Hawai'i on an intimate level. Nowhere were these trans-Oceanic networks more important to him or his narrative than in Tahiti. Upon his arrival Baker found comfort in two very different social circles connected to migratory networks between Hawai'i and Tahiti. The first was the circle of ari'i (chiefs) connected to the Salmon clan. One of the family, Ninito Salmon, traveled to Hawai'i in the 1850s and married into the prominent hapa-Haole Sumner family, moving back and forth between Hawai'i and Tahiti through much of her adult life. Ninito and other prominent Tahitians, such as her cousin Princess Manaiula Tehuiarii, who also married into the Sumner family, established a strong social connection between the Hawaiian and Tahitian elite. As a result, prominent Tahitians, including the Salmons, occasionally visited Hawai'i and joined in the Honolulu social scene either temporarily or permanently. While Baker was in Tahiti, another member of the Salmon clan, Ari'i Pa'ea, was making quite a stir in Honolulu due to his long-distance courtship of Queen Lili'uokalani.[24]

Baker's entry to the Tahitian elite came from yet another Salmon, who Baker identifies only as the *keiki mu'umu'u*, or maimed child. Several years earlier the anonymous keiki had come to Hawai'i, and apparently the two had met. Recognizing Baker's name on the passenger manifest, the keiki welcomed him as he got off the ship and introduced Baker to Tati Salmon, the clan's British-educated patriarch and a high ari'i of Papara. Baker spent the day with the Salmons, watching a Catholic procession and sharing several meals with the family.[25]

That evening he entertained them Hawaiian style, playing his guitar (likely a steel guitar) and singing various Hawaiian mele including Kalākaua-era songs such as "Hawai'i Pono'ī" and "Aloha 'Oe." He also sang several songs connecting Hawai'i and Tahiti, noting that "it was appropriate to release the wind gourd of Laaomaomao," in reference to the Tahitian companion of the legendary Hawaiian chief Moikeha. His Tahitian hosts, Baker reported, were enthralled with his singing, but even more so with his instrument. Tati's youngest sister, Alexandrina Manihinihi Salmon, also entertained Baker with a lū'au, after some

[24] Zeno (pseud.), "Romantic Career of the Venerable John K. Sumner," *Pacific Commercial Advertiser* (1903): 2; John Renken Kaha'i Topolinski, "Nancy Sumner, Hawaiian Courtlady," *Hawaiian Journal of History* 15 (1981): 50–58; "Col. Baker Met Prince Salmon," *Hawaiian Gazette*, 14 January 1908, 5.

[25] Baker, "Mai Ka Aina Mamao Mai," *Ke Aloha Aina*, August 10, 1907.

awkwardness getting in touch with each other and confusion over a letter of introduction.[26]

The Salmons would host Baker once more on July 14, when he was one of only two nonfamily attendees at a birthday party thrown for one of Tati's children. His dining companion at this event was Pa'ea, the Salmon who was then attempting to woo Lili'uokalani. Baker described him as a tall handsome man and in a later interview he reported that Pa'ea had asked him many questions about Lili'uokalani, particularly regarding her wealth, property, and age. Baker found the questions odd, but not as odd as Salmon's claims that he intended to marry her. He did not feel it was his place to write to Hawai'i with his impressions of the man until he was in Japan and heard of Pa'ea's somewhat disgraceful behavior in San Francisco and Hawai'i. He assured his interviewer that the Salmons were a very respectable family, adding, "I suppose in every family there is one to make a fool of himself."[27]

The second social circle Baker fell into in Tahiti was one much farther down the social ladder, but no less important in tying Tahiti and Hawai'i together. Just as Ninito Salmon, Pupuhi, and other Tahitian immigrants had settled in Hawai'i during the course of the nineteenth century, a number of Kānaka Maoli had also settled in Tahiti. Within days of arriving Baker met up with Mokuahi, a native of Kohala, Hawai'i, then living on Moorea. Though he had been abroad for so long that he forgot much of the Hawaiian language, Mokuahi still remembered his education in Hilo under the ABCFM missionary Reverend Lyman. Mokuahi introduced Baker to Liwai, whose mother's family was from Hilo and whose relatives still resided there. Like Mokuahi he had lived in Tahiti for decades, having left Hawai'i at the death of Kamehameha III (1854), and had become hemahema (awkward) in his native tongue.[28]

After an evening spent reminiscing about mutual acquaintances and singing songs celebrating different Hawaiian lands, Liwai invited Baker

[26] Baker, "Mai Ka Aina Mamao Mai," *Ke Aloha Aina*, August 10, 1907; Baker, "Mai Ka Aina Mamao Mai," *Ke Aloha Aina*, August 31, 1907; "Col. Baker's Grand Time in the South Seas," *Hawaiian Gazette*, January 31, 1908. Baker had thought his friend, James Boyd, had sent the letter to the keiki of Tati Salman, but in reality it had gone directly to Manihinihi. Baker was waiting for the keiki to introduce him to Manihinihi who was waiting for Baker to come and introduce himself as Boyd's letter said he was interested in doing. Baker finally contacted her after a serendipitous encounter with her husband, resulting in her sending for Baker and demanding that he come and see her at once.

[27] Baker, "Mai Ka Aina Mamao Mai," *Ke Aloha Aina*, September 21, 1907; "Col. Baker Met Prince Salmon," *Hawaiian Gazette*, January 14, 1908, 5.

[28] Baker, "Mai Ka Aina Mamao Mai," *Ke Aloha Aina*, August 10, 1907.

to his home. There Liwai's Maohi[29] friends and family hosted Baker, plying him with food and asking him questions about Hawai'i. Baker again turned to his guitar and Hawaiian repertoire to add to the celebrations, much to the joy of his audience, who claimed they had never heard such music before. His Maohi hosts sang Baker "an old Polapola [Borabora] song," a bawdy song similar to the kolohe (naughty/rambunctious) music Kānaka often sang amongst themselves, leading Baker to comment, "They really believe that I am a Polapola and this is my birthplace."[30]

Though Hawai'i had a particularly strong history of immigration to and from Tahiti, Baker ran into Kānaka in other places as well. In addition to meeting a Kanaka named Alapai in Rarotonga, Baker also learned from Queen Makea Takau Ariki that so many Kānaka had visited or immigrated to Rarotonga in the past that the voices of part-Kānaka echoed throughout her land. In Sāmoa he met a former Hilo resident named "Coaster" and a man from Ni'ihau named Kaomea. Even in distant Aotearoa, where far fewer Kānaka had ever visited, let alone immigrated, he found connections to Hawai'i, including an elderly Pākeha (white) woman in search of news of her family in Hilo. When Māori politician Maui Pomare discussed an earlier visit to Hawai'i, he and Baker found that the two had several mutual acquaintances in Honolulu. In Gisborne, a newspaper interviewer also asked Baker about Prince Kūhiō, who had visited a few years earlier.[31]

Baker's persistence in pointing out the existence of networks of travel and migration between Hawai'i and other parts of Oceania invited his Hawaiian audience to look to Oceania, rather than the American empire, as a geographic lens for understanding how the lāhui fit into both the region and the globe. In imperial European/American travel writing on the Pacific, the presentation of Tahiti and other islands as strange and

[29] The term *Maohi*, a cognate of the Hawaiian Māoli and Māori in Te Reo Māori, is used in the society islands and nearby areas to refer to the indigenous peoples of those islands.

[30] Baker, "Mai Ka Aina Mamao Mai," *Ke Aloha Aina*, August 10, 1907; Baker, "Mai Ka Aina Mamao Mai," August 17, 1907. Following more recent conventions this paper will refer to Society Islanders by the broad term *Maohi*, rather than by their island of origin. Baker follows a Hawaiian convention of the time, recognizing the islands by their names but refers to most Maohi people and traits as "Polapola," or Boraboran, after the island of Borabora.

[31] Baker, "Mai ka Aina Mamao Mai," *Ke Aloha Aina*, September 21, 1907; Baker, "Mai ka Aina Mamao Mai," *Ke Aloha Aina*, September 28, 1907; Baker, "Mai ka Aina Mamao Mai," *Ke Aloha Aina*, November 9, 1907; Baker, "Mai ka Aina Mamao Mai," *Ke Aloha Aina*, November 16, 1907; "He Manuhiri No Hawaii," *Te Pipiwharauroa*, interview with John T. Baker, trans. Paul Meredith, September 1907.

mysterious lands have a clear appeal, namely creating a mental and emotional separation between the colonial subject matter and the imperial readership. In contrast, presenting Tahiti as the land where Kailianu's son Liwai lives does the opposite, emotionally connecting the Hawai'i readership to Tahiti on a human level. The incorporation of those Kānaka Maoli into Tahitian society and the creation of large Maohi/Maoli families brought the two even closer together, calling upon the importance of extended relations in the Kanaka consciousness.

The same can be said for Baker's accounts of searching out his own Maohi relatives, a quest that consumed a considerable amount of his time on Tahiti. Despite several false starts and dead ends that led him back and forth across the island, Baker eventually located a relative of his grandfather in Pape'ete. She presented Baker with mats, kapa, and other household goods, a sign of their closeness and the openness of her home to her Hawaiian kin. She also showed him a book containing his grandfather's genealogy and told him what lands his grandfather and his family came from. When news reached other members of the family that Pupuhi's grandson was in Tahiti, the right to host him became a matter of dispute. Another female family member soon confronted Baker's host, apparently contesting her right to host him over other members of the family. Awkward as the situation seemed to be, at least there was no question of Baker remaining a stranger in Tahiti.[32]

ALOHA 'AINA: LAND CLAIMS

Baker's columns in *Ke Aloha Aina* also displayed a strong connection to the lands of Oceania as an extension of his connection to the lands of Hawai'i, frequently using comparisons to well-known lands in Hawai'i as a way to describe the lands of other lāhui. Like his descriptions of human networks, Baker's attempts to connect these lands to Hawai'i worked on both an intellectual and emotional level. Baker was far from immune to the emotional effects of the similarities between Hawaiian and other Oceanic lands, being frequently swept up by landscapes so tantalizingly similar yet so geographically far from his own home.

Off the coast of Savai'i, for instance, Baker witnessed the eruption of Matavanu, a volcano in the same Itu-o-Tane districts that Envoy John E. Bush had visited some twenty years earlier. Watching the lava trailing

---

[32] Baker, "Mai ka Aina Mamao Mai," *Ke Aloha Aina*, September 7, 1907.

down to the ocean, pouring over the cliffs, and into the sea, he noted, "This is a worthwhile name for this island, Savaii-Hawaii. Tears come to my eyes as a I looked out, it was like looking at Hilo, the hill Halai stands there, like the fiery veil on top of Mokuaweoweo and Kilauea, this is how the fire burns here." The reminder of Hawai'i Island brought back a flood of memories and loneliness to Baker. Aboard the ship, looking out at the lava flows, Baker reminisced:

[I am] reminded of Waimea, and I thought of the two of us covered in the fog and on seeing the forests of Mahiki … to deposit the bones of the one I love … and I begin to sing, softly, with a sleeping spirit, with loving tears:

> How will this cold end, that we two meet and pulse within,
> Oh you and I, oh the embrace of the cold,
> Oh to see these things that I see.

I unfastened my watch with the image [of Ululani] and searched the uplands. I know some stupid things I have done, oh the love, forgetting the good thoughts. I looked to the mountains and the fog was done, and the banks of clouds were bunching below the forest like the uplands of Kapaukea and Kukuikomo. I thought of the places I went with this most loving and beloved woman.[33]

In other cases, Baker's use of Hawaiian lands as stand-ins for Oceanic ones seemed largely a matter of convenience. In his initial description of Papeete, for instance, he told his readers: "If you think of the view from Hakalau to Papeekeo [on the Hamakua coast], then it is like the island of Hawai'i, progressing through the districts until you arrive at Hilo Bay. There is a lagoon to the south like Keahua … It is hot like Kawaihae, if not Kona perhaps, and the living is like Lahaina in all ways." Baker also described the isthmus of Taravao as similar to "Kamaomao [Maui], broad, desolate [of people], and green with growth." Tonga had "the placing of Niihau, spread out," but with the agricultural abundance of Puna. The island of "Nuapou," likely Niuafo'ou, the northernmost island of the Kingdom of Tonga, was like Kaho'olawe, a small island isolated from the sea by cliffs, but like Puna on top, "the coconuts and the hills, at one place it is like going to Makuu, at another Kamalii and the trip on the smooth lava of Malama." The Fijian archipelago he described as "[m]ountainous lands, like Keanae on Maui."[34]

---

[33] Baker, "Mai Ka Aina Mamao Mai," *Ke Aloha Aina*, November 24, 1907.
[34] Baker, "Mai Ka Aina Mamao Mai," *Ke Aloha Aina*, August 10, 1907; Baker, "Mai Ka Aina Mamao Mai," *Ke Aloha Aina*, August 24, 1907; Baker, "Mai Ka Aina Mamao Mai," *Ke Aloha Aina*, November 16, 1907.

Baker also used Hawaiian places to help his reader understand the cultural significance rather than physical features of a place. Whakarapa[35] Aotearoa, for instance, was a place of major cultural significance to many of the Māori in that area, noted as one of the first places that their ancestors landed their canoes. Baker equated it geographically and culturally with Kualoa, Oʻahu, to give his readers a sense of the cultural importance and mana of the place, calling it the piko of the land. Further reinforcing the importance of both places to their respective people, he recounted a moʻolelo about Kahahana's surrender of Kualoa to Kahekili and Kahahana's resulting loss of the entire island of Oʻahu.[36]

In connecting the lands he visited to the lands of Hawaiʻi, Baker implicitly called upon his readers' sense of aloha ʻāina. While aloha ʻāina can and often is directly translated as patriotism, its fuller meaning includes a sense of the spiritual and often genealogical connection Kānaka developed to the lands of Hawaiʻi in general, as well as to specific places. This aloha ʻāina was not something foreign occupation could displace as easily as it could displace a government. In Hawaiian society, the continuity provided by ʻāina in stories such as the one he retold about Kualoa served to connect the present and the past through the continuity of the land; as long as the land was there, the history of the lāhui remained vital and relevant. At the same time that history reiterated the deep spiritual and cultural connections between the land and the lāhui; as long as the lāhui remembered their history, their aloha ʻāina would remain vital and relevant as well. In using Hawaiian lands as a rhetorical stand in for other Oceanic lands Baker transferred some of this aloha ʻāina to those other lands, making them more "real" in his and his readers' hearts just as the physical descriptions made them more real in their minds.

"THERE IS NO LITTLE THING ONE FAILS TO RECOGNIZE": TRACES OF AN OCEANIC PAST

Throughout the journey, Baker eagerly observed and reported on numerous similarities that hinted of a shared past and shared origins between the lāhui Hawaiʻi and the rest of Oceania. He frequently noted, for instance, the physical similarities between Kānaka Hawaiʻi and other islanders, a commonly used if not-always-reliable marker of shared ancestry. On

---

[35] Modern-day Pangaru.
[36] Baker, "Mai Ka Aina Mamao Mai," *Ke Aloha Aina,* November 31, 1907; Baker, "Mai Ka Aina Mamao Mai," *Ke Aloha Aina,* December 7, 1907.

multiple occasions, for instance, Baker wrote of being mistaken for a Māori by other Māori. On one particular occasion, he struck up a conversation with a Māori gentleman who looked the same as a friend of Baker's, Kalawa of Puna. Coincidentally, the men both happened to be ministers, much to Baker's amusement.[37] More importantly, however, Baker also sought out, participated in, and reported on numerous experiences that highlighted the cultural evidence of ancient and recent connections between Hawai'i and other parts of Oceania. In doing so Baker not only reminded his readers of this past, but also of the importance of Hawaiian culture as a connection to the other parts of Oceania and to the Hawaiian place within a larger pan-Oceanic lāhui.

I KA ʻŌLELO NŌ KE OLA: IN THE LANGUAGE IS LIFE

Baker's trip occurred during a period in which both the Territory and the oligarchy sought to devalue the Hawaiian language as anachronistic and lacking utility in an age of Europhone empires.[38] Many within the lāhui understood this, correctly, as not simply an attack on the language, but an assault on the people who depended heavily on that language to define themselves and their culture. As Baker traveled, he found that his understanding and use of the Hawaiian language retained significant practical and cultural value throughout Eastern Oceania. Rather than an anchor tying him to a supposedly dead past, the Hawaiian language allowed him to connect with peoples and cultures thousands of miles from home on a far deeper level than he would as a strictly English speaker.

In Tahiti, for instance, he frequently communicated with people through a mix of Tahitian and Hawaiian. Indeed the two were so easily intelligible that Baker's letters to *Ke Aloha Aina* contained untranslated or partially translated statements in Tahitian, including the bawdy Boraboran song taught to him by Liwai's family.[39] Enough movement had occurred between Hawai'i and Tahiti for Baker to have likely known his Hawaiian would serve him well in his grandfather's homeland, but he was quite

---

[37] Baker, "Mai Ka Aina Mamao Mai," *Ke Aloha Aina,* November 2, 1907; "Col. Baker's Grand Time in the South Seas," *Hawaiian Gazette,* January 31, 1908.

[38] Maenette Kapeʻahiokalani Padeken Benham, "The Voice 'less' Hawaiian: An Analysis of Educational Policymaking, 1820–1960," *Hawaiian Journal of History* 32 (1998): 130; Lucas, "E Ola Mau Kakou I Ka ʻOlelo Makuahine," 8–10.

[39] Tomo ana i ta maro tutui, Inu ana i ta pia a rote, O ole na'u i tii atu-e, Ua ta tane i here mai no, To hinaalo ia'u nei.

surprised to discover that it served him equally well in Aotearoa. On the train ride leaving Auckland, for instance, he began speaking with his fellow passengers much as he had with the Maohi, with them speaking in Te Reo and he in 'Olelo Hawai'i.[40]

Enough difference remained that at times Baker's understanding was imperfect. He was unable, for instance, to understand chanting at times, such as when his female relatives were contesting for the right to host him, or when welcomed at a marae in Aotearoa.[41] Room also remained for the occasional embarrassing misunderstanding. At one point, Baker went to eat with a group of Maohi friends in Tahiti. Arriving after the others were already seated, they told him to take off his hat and coat and have a seat, then gestured toward him and repeated, "Tamaa, Tamaa." Thinking they were telling him to remove his shoes, kama'a, he did so, only to find they were telling him to try some of the tamaa, a fish dish. Though somewhat embarrassed, Baker had the good humor to include the incident in his letter. While this showed a difference between the languages, it also shows Baker's comfort and familiarity with Tahitian and the degree to which that mutual intelligibility accompanied a cultural and social comfort in moving from a Hawaiian context to a Tahitian one.[42]

While the mutual intelligibility of the two languages was significant, the slight difference between Te Reo Māori and 'Olelo Hawai'i also served Baker in marking him specifically as being from Hawai'i, which many Māori of the era believed to be Hawaiki, the northern lands from where the Māori had come. Though in his Gisborne interview Baker argued that Kānaka Maoli and Māori likely had shared roots in the central Pacific, Baker was still willing to let Hawaiki's place in the Māori worldview smooth his passage into the Māori community.[43] Upon arriving in Auckland, a Māori gentleman greeted him and extended out his Aroha, to which Baker replied with "Aloha." The reply struck the man as peculiar, prompting him to ask where Baker was from. Upon learning that he was a visitor from Hawai'i, the man befriended him and excitedly introduced him to Auckland's Maori and Pakeha elite. At Whakarewarewa, Baker again found these dynamics to work in his favor, noting that as he

---

[40] "Col. Baker's Grand Time in the South Seas," *Hawaiian Gazette*, January 31, 1908; Baker, "Mai Ka Aina Mamao Mai," *Ke Aloha Aina*, August 17, 1907.

[41] Baker, "Mai Ka Aina Mamao Mai," *Ke Aloha Aina*, September 7, 1907; Baker, "Mai Ka Aina Mamao Mai," *Ke Aloha Aina*, October 26, 1907.

[42] Baker, "Mai Ka Aina Mamao Mai," *Ke Aloha Aina*, August 17, 1907.

[43] "He Manuhiri No Hawaii," *Te Pipiwharauroa*, interview with John T. Baker, trans. Paul Meredith, September 1907.

walked around the area, many Māori "spoke Maori to me; and I replied I am a Hawaiian, and they came and gave me their aloha, with the words, 'From Hawai'i are the bones of the kupuna.'" This initial conversation led to three days of Baker being hosted by local Māori communities eager to see the Manuhiri no Hawaiki, the stranger from Hawai'i.[44]

In sharing these linguistic connections with his Hawaiian-language audience in Hawai'i, Baker also shared the importance of 'Ōlelo Hawai'i both as a link to other Oceanic peoples and as a specific marker of Kanaka identity. Where the English-only schools and administrators argued that the Hawaiian language, and by extension Hawaiian people, had no place in an American modernity, Baker's accounts implied that they both continued to serve a significant role in an Oceanic one.

AN OPEN BOWL AND AN OPEN GOURD

Baker made some of his strongest and most persistent arguments for cultural similarities with a broader pan-Oceanic lāhui around understandings of hospitality and generosity. As a traveler, it should be no surprise that Baker placed a high value on generosity and hospitality, but his articles make it clear that he celebrated these as explicitly Oceanic values that Native Hawaiians shared with the Māori, Maohi, Samoans, Tongans, and Fijians. The openness and warmness with which other Oceanic peoples welcomed him into their homes and the gifts that they heaped upon him reminded Baker of similarly defining traits among his own people, and he explicitly stated this both to his readers and to his hosts. Furthermore, Baker experienced a great deal of hospitality not just as a guest, but specifically as a Kanaka guest, noting that many of the people he visited extended particularly strong welcomes to him due to their shared cultural and historical ties rooted deep in the Oceanic past.

Baker's accounts from Tahiti, for instance, are full of examples of the hospitality he received through the networks mentioned previously, including the Salmons, Liwai's Maohi family, and Baker's own relatives. In addition to the general spirit of hospitality, the details of the hospitality he received reflected a specific style of hospitality Baker and his audience typically associated with Hawaiian culture. In his interview in the *Gazette*, he described the event he attended as a guest of Princess Teri'i Manihinihi as a lū'au, noting, "I've forgotten their word for it, but

---

[44] "Col. Baker's Grand Time in the South Seas," *Hawaiian Gazette*, January 31, 1908; Baker, "Mai Ka Aina Mamao Mai," *Ke Aloha Aina*, October 19, 1907.

it was a luau all the same." Even many of the foods were the same, taro, fish, banana, and breadfruit, noting, "all the things we have, they have."[45]

When feasting with Liwai's Maohi neighbors and family in Tahiti, he made more explicit arguments about the similarities between Hawaiian and Tahitian hospitality, noting:

> These are a good people, like us Hawaiians, an open bowl and an open gourd. The following was supplied: raw fish, yams, some ahi poke, taibero, taro, sweet potato, banana, breadfruit, coconut, chicken and pig, above us the table and below the people, the table was covered in hau leaves. [It was] much like our parties/meals, standing and offering the bottle before eating, saying, here is the food, it has been prepared ... eat and drink without unease, and talk together with our happiness on meeting together ... Aohe wehena mai kakou [nothing separates us].

The lū'au thrown by Princess Manihinihi, his meals with the Salmon's, and Baker's meals with Liwai's relations also included another component that Kānaka would find both familiar and integral to proper hospitality, exchanges of music and song to create a proper atmosphere.[46]

Baker's emphasis on Oceanic hospitality remained prominent in his visits to other lands as well. When discussing the Māori he had met in and around Auckland, Baker commented on their similarities to Kānaka Hawai'i:

> A pleasant people, full of aloha ... [they are] no different from us, the generosity, the dissoluteness, the hospitality, the care of some people, and the reckless spending of some, these complain and sit collected in one place to chat day and night, some are well supplied and truly well off, and some are destitute and some people are drunks, men and women.

While obviously some of the things Baker found familiar about the Māori were negatives often associated with colonized peoples, he again emphasized hospitality and generosity as shared positive features of Kānaka Hawai'i and other islanders.[47]

His Māori hosts also presented Baker with gifts nearly everywhere he went, which Baker took care to highlight as examples of a shared sense of generosity. The Māori community at Rotorua gave him numerous gifts and the sister of Maui Pomare presented him with a watch chain made of

---

[45] "Col. Baker's Grand Time in the South Seas," *Hawaiian Gazette*, January 31, 1908; Baker, "Mai Ka Aina Mamao Mai," *Ke Aloha Aina*, August 10, 1907.

[46] Baker, "Mai Ka Aina Mamao Mai," *Ke Aloha Aina*, August 10, 1907; Baker, "Mai Ka Aina Mamao Mai," *Ke Aloha Aina*, August 17, 1907.

[47] Baker, "Mai Ka Aina Mamao Mai," *Ke Aloha Aina*, October 19, 1907.

gold and pounamu (greenstone). Hiremi Te Wake of Whakarapa presented him with a pounamu of his ancestors and members of his family even offered Baker land if he wished to settle among them. At Parengarenga, Māori rancher and storekeeper Ngawini Yates not only presented Baker with gifts, including a pounamu inherited from her ancestors, but also instructed other members of the community to do so as well. In an interview Baker gave upon returning to Hawaiʻi, Baker noted that a number of other Māori had given him gifts in Auckland. He told the interviewer:

It was embarrassing on one occasion, for I was presented with three beautiful pieces of New Zealand greenstone. They were family heirlooms and were of unknown age. I refused to take them saying that it was too much but they insisted, saying that I was the first man from the old home of their ancestors that they had ever seen and that I must take the stones.[48]

Baker spent relatively little time in Tonga and noted little about the Tongan people other than their physical beauty and a general disregard for headwear, but he did note that they were like the Hawaiian people and the other "red-skinned" people of the Pacific, in being "loving, welcoming, and friendly." Among the Samoans, he noted several differences between them and the Kānaka Hawaiʻi, but was struck by how similar they were in their pleasantness and generosity. He said the same of the Fijians, writing that they were a pleasant people, particularly in contrast with a perceived "unfriendliness" among the Indo-Fijian population.[49]

Baker's perception of Indo-Fijians as less friendly than the indigenous Fijian population may have been partly based on a better cultural understanding of other Oceanic peoples, but it may have also been due to a phenomenon Baker witnessed throughout his journey, namely a heightened level of generosity, hospitality, and aloha *between* Oceanic peoples. Liwai's Maohi relations, for instance, embraced him so wholeheartedly because they thought of him as one of their own, perhaps for his Tahitian ancestry, but also perhaps as a Kānaka Hawaiʻi. The Māori embraced him as not just as a visitor, or even as kin, but according to a specific belief that Hawaiʻi was the Hawaiki that they originated from. They embraced

---

[48] Baker, "Mai Ka Aina Mamao Mai," *Ke Aloha Aina*, November 9, 1907; Baker, "Mai Ka Aina Mamao Mai," *Ke Aloha Aina*, December 7, 1907; Baker, "Mai Ka Aina Mamao Mai," *Ke Aloha Aina*, October 26, 1907; "Col. Baker's Grand Time in the South Seas," *Hawaiian Gazette*, January 31, 1908.

[49] Baker, "Mai Ka Aina Mamao Mai," *Ke Aloha Aina*, December 14, 1907; Baker, "Mai Ka Aina Mamao Mai," *Ke Aloha Aina*, November 16, 1907.

him as the iwi[50] of their ancestors, and thus deserving of an especially warm welcome.[51]

Some of the gifts Baker received in Aotearoa, such as the pounamu, also emphasized the connections and ties between Hawai'i and other parts of Oceania. Though the Māori people viewed pounamu as a valuable gift in general, in some ways it also proved a well-suited gift for this Manuhiri mai Hawaiki, this stranger from Hawai'i. According to some traditions, a man from Hawaiki, Ngahue, went to Aotearoa, where he found pounamu. Taking a large chunk back with him he fashioned axes with which he built one of the fleets of canoes that brought the Māori to Aotearoa. Thus they not only gave him items of value, but items whose very existence was often associated with visitors from Hawaiki and established ties between those lands and Aotearoa.[52]

A prominent Māori woman in Rotorua, who Baker identified only as the sister of the chief "Laniwili," gave Baker her piupiu skirt, often associated with haka, declaring "[Y]ou are one of our people, what are you to me? You are a brother of mine." She also gave him a kalo and an 'uala (sweet potato), two of the most important crops in Eastern Oceania in general and the most important staples of Hawai'i and Aotearoa, respectively. She then asked him to one day return the gift with a slip of kalo and leaves from an 'uala vine from Hawai'i. Though such a cycle of gift giving may have had little practical or economic value, its symbolic and cultural value would be inherently clear within both Māori and Hawaiian culture.[53]

This idea of a greater expectation of hospitality between Oceanic peoples emerged again in Tonga, when Baker sought to meet with King George Tupou II. Baker overheard some Haole from the ship referring to the Tongans as a lazy people, "and because of this talk I was hurt," as he understood their comments about Tongans to be an insult to a kindred people and thus to himself. The incident inspired Baker to seek out some Oceanic solidarity, and if possible to show up his fellow travelers. He

---

[50] *Iwi*: bones, the most cherished part of the body, where the *mana* resided. In Maori, it is also a word for clan/"tribe."

[51] Baker, "Mai Ka Aina Mamao Mai," *Ke Aloha Aina*, August 17, 1907; Baker, "Mai Ka Aina Mamao Mai," *Ke Aloha Aina*, October 19, 1907.

[52] John Mitchell and Hillary Mitchell, *Te Tau Ihu O Te Waka: A History of Maori of Nelson and Marlborough* (Wellington, NZ: Huia Publishers, 2004), 22.

[53] Baker, "Mai Ka Aina Mamao Mai," *Ke Aloha Aina*, October 26, 1907. There is no record of whether Baker ever sent such gifts back, though Baker in general was known for his honesty and of being a man of his word. It also seems out of character for him to violate the aloha and generosity of his hosts by not returning the gifts.

declared that he would seek an audience with the king. His fellow tourists mocked his claims, noting that even though Baker was a prominent individual, they had been informed the king simply did not see tourists. Baker replied, "In your going to see [him], [the desire is based] not in the aloha, but, to sightsee and spectate, [but] mine is in the aloha, he will see my skin and blood as my calling card, for they are close to his." The king did indeed meet with Baker, presenting him with an autographed picture and the grounds for silencing the Haole visitors. Baker attributed his meeting with the Tongan King not to his status as a former member of Kalākaua's court, though this likely helped, but as a Kanaka, bonded to the Tongans by kinship, history, and culture.[54]

THE HAKA MEETS THE HULA AT ROTORUA

Baker also emphasized similarities between specific Hawaiian cultural traditions and those of his hosts throughout Oceania, with a particular emphasis on dance and music. Other Oceanic peoples also frequently asked Baker questions about the way of life in Hawai'i and to provide demonstrations of Hawaiian culture, again with an emphasis on dance and music. Baker the tourist and observer quickly became Baker the cultural ambassador, a role he reveled in throughout his trip. Baker's accounts of the ensuing musical and dance exchanges again validated Kanaka culture, this time not only as part of a broader Oceanic culture but also something valued and applauded by the other peoples of Oceania.

Nowhere did this prove truer than Baker's short time among the Māori community around Lake Rotorua, which started with Baker arriving as a tourist but leaving as something of a local celebrity. Following the established tourist routes, Baker came for the attractions centered on the area's geothermal activity, including geysers, hot springs, and mud pools. Upon arriving at Rotorua, Baker wrote that he and about fifteen others went to the nearby village of Whakarewarewa to see "the hula of the Maori people," already an established part of the region's tourist circuit. There he described a "Hula Poe," a women's haka performed with poi, small lightweight bags twirled as a show of dexterity and struck as percussive accompaniment. Though he enjoyed their hula, he noted with a mix of cultural bias and the critical eye of a fellow practitioner: "They have not caught Hawai'i in the excellence, they are in the middle, they are not

---

[54] Baker, "Mai Ka Aina Mamao Mai," *Ke Aloha Aina*, November 16, 1907.

like, perhaps, the niniu [dizzy spinning] Molokai or the poahi [spinning]
Lanai."[55]

While Baker was walking around Whakarewarewa, the Māori dancers began to speak to him in Te Reo, and they reacted with some great
surprise when he replied that he was not a Māori but a Kānaka Hawai'i.
They greeted him with great aloha, for as they told him, "From Hawaii
are the bones of the ancestors." Following on this idea of kinship and
similarity, Baker reported that:

> Their faces are like ours, the face is heavy, and thus are theirs, and when a song
> sung to them in the aloha, then they are crying the tears of the old people, man
> and woman, the posture of the body is like ours ... In the bearing of the bodies
> and the faces we are very alike, there is no little thing that one fails to recognize.

The dancers then insisted that he dance and sing for them in the Hawaiian
style, a task he was always eager to undertake.[56]

The next day Baker went to nearby Rotomahana, another lake, and
spent the day witnessing more geothermal wonders before returning to
the hotel around 5:30 PM. While he was out, news of the Hawaiian visitor traveled through the Māori community around Rotorua. No sooner
had he returned to his hotel when a messenger fetched him and took him
to a structure on the lakeside, which he described as a government-built
community center covered in carvings of "men and women with their
tongues hanging out." He noted that the Māori were fond of wood carving, putting him in mind of a famous ali'i, Luali'i, who was known for
his obsession with carving images into all manner of wooden implements.
"They are not satisfied without engraving the face from the forehead and
the cheeks, to the lips and the nose," he wrote, "It is truly ugly for us to
look at, to them [the images] are pretty."[57]

As with the evening before at Whakarewarewa, the Māori women
again performed a "Hula Poe," though this time the men also danced
what Baker described as the "Hula Hakalewalewa [Whakarewarewa],
a hula for rising the anger and preparing for war ... a way of instilling
fear, unleashing the tongue of this one and that one, and flaring the eyes."
After the hula, the Māori told him of their happiness in meeting with "the
alii of the bones of their kupuna, [stating] that we are the same, them and
the people of the Hawaiian Islands, and to come and see them and so
forth." They then requested that Baker show them "the Hawaiian ways,"

[55] Baker, "Mai Ka Aina Mamao Mai," *Ke Aloha Aina*, October 19, 1907.
[56] Ibid.
[57] Baker, "Mai Ka Aina Mamao Mai," *Ke Aloha Aina*, October 26, 1907.

and he again danced and sang for them, answering their questions about Hawai'i and returning their aloha. He did not return to the hotel until midnight.[58]

As the next day was a Sunday, Baker went down to the shore to pray before breakfasting with the local Māori on foods cooked with geothermal heat, including fresh-water crayfish that Baker described as similar to the Hawaiian 'ōpae 'oeha'a. While breakfasting, he heard the popular story of the lovers Hinemoa and Tutanekai, who were separated by her parents but united by the music of his flute. He retold the entire story for his Hawaiian audience, providing yet another way for them to connect with and find ties to his Māori hosts. He also commented on its close resemblance to the mo'olelo of Ka'ililauokekoa and Kauakahiali'i, which shared the theme of a young ali'i wahine who follows the call of her lover's flute.[59]

After attending an Anglican service along the lakeshore, he headed, by invitation, to what Baker identified as the compound of "Laniwili," an elderly ariki (important/paramount chief). A Māori woman welcomed Baker with a chant, and while he could not quite understand the words, he understood the meaning and intent. He described the chant as being "like what we were accustomed to when the rulers traveled around the island, and in the places they visited the people crowded and called their name." Remembering his beloved patron Kalākaua, Baker began to tear up somewhat, though he remained still until the chanting was completed, then moved forward and greeted each of the sixty or so people there before entering the nearby meetinghouse.[60]

Baker identified the house as being "of the old style ... 73 years old, clean and pretty inside."[61] He described the various carvings, noting again the Māori love for woodcarving and the skill of the carvings. He also relished the general atmosphere of the house, reflecting, "I think in the old times, in our buildings, the ea [air/sovereignty/life] was sweet, and that is how it is here." For the third night in a row, hula and haka were exchanged. Different groups of Māori danced, with the women performing a dance Baker described as having "nothing fun or pretty about

[58] Ibid.
[59] Ibid.
[60] Ibid. Based on the circumstantial evidence I suspect that *church* and *meeting house* were in Ohinemutu, but I cannot say for certain.
[61] If Baker was in Ohinemutu, he may have been at Tamatekapua meeting house at Te Papaiouru Marae. Tamatekapua was built in 1873 rather than being seventy-three years old.

it, flaring the eyes and sticking out the tongue." Though not entirely in agreement with Māori performance aesthetics, Baker understood the importance of showing his appreciation for the dancing: "[T]he good and pono [balanced/correct] thing to do is clap and cry out applause, with many pleasant words, because [if one lets out] a laugh, these people are listening." More men's and women's dances followed, the women with tattooed lips Baker described as "deep blue, a thing of beauty."[62]

During speeches by Laniwili, his sister, and his grandson, his Māori hosts again stated their happiness at meeting with a Kānaka Hawai'i, and a prominent Kānaka at that, declaring their love for their ancestors and the land they had come from. Baker then spoke, accepting their hospitality and thanking them for it, both sides affirming it as "a gift given completely, with no thought of tomorrow." As everyone sat down for the feast that had been prepared, Baker's Māori hosts again insisted on seeing and hearing the music and hula of Hawai'i, which Baker gladly obliged to, recalling that his audience "all died in the happiness and fun." It was at this point that the sister of Laniwili presented him with her piupiu, a kalo, and a 'uala/kumara as mentioned in the previous section.[63]

Similar incidents of dance-and-music-based cultural exchange also occurred in Tahiti and Rarotonga. Baker described the Tahitian dancing he witnessed, specifically at the Salmons and the celebration at Liwai's house, as different than the Hawaiian. He wrote of the Maohi, "They are a skilled people at the hula, with a style like the hula kui, with their legs moving fast and rapidly shifting them." Like the Māori, the Maohi also encouraged him to dance and sing, asking him if the Hawaiian hula was the same as theirs, and if not, what was the Hawaiian style. Once again Baker's performance and their interest in Hawaiian style and forms transformed the event into a cultural exchange, pulling the participants closer together despite the significant differences in their performances.[64]

Contemporary Hawaiian music, sometimes as an accompaniment to dance and sometimes not, provided a similar medium or cultural exchange. In Tahiti Baker relied heavily on his guitar to provide accompaniment while singing. In some cases, his hosts returned the sentiment with their own music, including the bawdy Boraboran song in Tahiti. Thus, this music, like the hula, was not only an expression of Baker's own love for Hawaiian music, but an attempt to use that music to connect to other

[62] Baker, "Mai Ka Aina Mamao Mai," *Ke Aloha Aina*, October 26, 1907.
[63] Ibid.
[64] Baker, "Mai Ka Aina Mamao Mai," *Ke Aloha Aina*, August 17, 1907.

islanders and to create cultural bonds that built upon the shared values of hospitality, generosity, and leʻaleʻa (pleasure seeking). This included learning their songs, like the Borabora song and at least one Māori song that he played a number of times for his Māori hosts.[65]

In addition to allowing him to participate in these exchanges, Baker's understanding of and participation in hula and mele also shaped his descriptions, allowing him to understand these events not as a spectator but as an informed practitioner. His descriptions of Māori dancing, for instance, focused specifically on details that differentiated Māori and Hawaiian dance, from the flaring of the eyes and unleashing of the tongues, to the way that the women's arms moved during the dance. He also noted the existence of a parting chant and dance, as in Hawaiʻi. Similarly, upon learning that Baker was a Kanaka Hawaiʻi, the Māori performers were not just excited to meet him, but also wished to see and hear Hawaiian dance and music. Like Baker they were interested in witnessing a new form of a shared art, turning the event from a tourist spectacle to an exchange between practitioners.[66] It is not known, however, if like Baker, they secretly assured themselves of the superiority of their own styles, and thus the superiority of their own culture within the broader family of Oceanic cultures.[67]

On a relatively simple level, these exchanges verified for Baker, his hosts, and his readers the Oceanic understandings of art and culture that underpinned dance and music from Honolulu to Wellington. But these different forms of Oceanic dance were not just variations of a shared art form, they were variations of an art that had deep cultural significance throughout Oceania. Kānaka Hawaiʻi, for instance, traditionally used hula to celebrate and honor gods, aliʻi, heroes, places, and events. It provided entertainment, but it also preserved knowledge that marked and maintained regional, familial, and factional identities. It was an art form appreciated for its beauty, but one that also created, maintained, and sometimes bridged the boundaries between the sacred and the profane.

[65] Baker, "Mai Ka Aina Mamao Mai, *Ke Aloha Aina*, August 10, 1907; Baker, "Mai Ka Aina Mamao Mai," *Ke Aloha Aina*, August 17, 1907; "Colonel Baker's Grand Time in the South Seas," *Hawaiian Gazette*, January 31, 1908.

[66] Later exchanges around Polynesian dance led to innovation in dance around the Pacific. Other Hawaiians, for instance, later picked up Māori poi balls and Kiribati grass skirts as props for hula, while Hawaiian gestures and music have had an impact on dance styles around the Pacific.

[67] Baker, "Mai Ka Aina Mamao Mai," *Ke Aloha Aina*, October 19, 1907;" Baker, "Mai Ka Aina Mamao Mai," *Ke Aloha Aina*, October 26, 1907.

By 1908, hula also had a long history as a focus for cultural preservation in the face of colonial logics and projects. After the overthrow of the kapu system and the ascension of hula-hating neo-Calvinist theology, many early to mid-nineteenth-century Kānaka used hula to mark their independence from the missionaries, particularly in the courts of Boki, Liliha, and the young Kamehameha III. The tradition continued in the "private" funerary performances of the later Kamehamehas and the full-scale revival under Kalākaua and Liliʻuokalani. Indeed the incorporation of hula into Kalākaua's coronation ceremonies proved to be a major political and cultural turning point in his reign, signifying a public dismissal of the mission faction's anti-Native moralizing. As a member of Kalākaua's court and the Hale Nāua, Baker had been at the heart of both the battles over hula and the rejuvenation of the art under the patronage of the mōʻī. Though commonly thought of as war dances by non-Māori, haka played a similarly diverse role in Māori culture, welcoming guests to marae, preserving cultural knowledge and values, and marking shared ancestral identities. It also marked a practice that both Māori and Pākeha (white settlers) recognized as a distinct cultural boundary between the two.[68]

Baker's conduct during these cultural exchanges also seemed to help pull him in closer to his hosts, allowing them to recognize him as a variation of themselves at the same time he was recognizing them as a variation of himself. Though unfamiliar with local customs and languages, he was familiar enough with Eastern Oceanic ideas of propriety and respect to comprehend the general mood and improvise his specific actions, recognizing and honoring elders and persons of mana, knowing when to laugh, when to cry out, and when to remain silent and respectful. Furthermore, he was generous with his time, person, and aloha, expressing himself properly as a guest rather than as a consumer of tourist spectacle.

But, perhaps most importantly he was generous with his expansive knowledge of Hawaiian song, hula, moʻolelo, and genealogy. In the exchanges of dance, music, and aloha that Baker participated in he showed both sets of audiences, his hosts and his readers, the pan-Oceanic cultural foundations upon which their diverse art forms were built. At the same time, as a practitioner he was able to explain and display the differences between Kānaka Maoli, Maohi, and Māori dance, highlighting some of

---

[68] Silva, *Aloha Betrayed*, 108–120; Noenoe Silva, "Kanawai E Hoʻopau I Na Hula Kuolo Hawaiʻi: The Political Economy of Banning the Hula," *Hawaiian Journal of History* 34 (2000): 29–31; Samuel Kamakau, *Ruling Chiefs of Hawaii* (Honolulu, HI: Kamehameha Schools Press, 1992), 276–288, 290–291, 297–300.

the diversity and creativity to be found across Oceania – while gleefully declaring the superiority of the Hawaiian forms. These exchanges and his reporting on them allowed Baker, his hosts, and his readers to understand their shared cultural roots, the roots that made them who they were, not just as Māoli, Māori, and Maohi, but as elements of a broader pan-Oceanic lāhui.

When Baker made his way back to Hawai'i in 1908, relatively little had changed since he had left. The islands remained under foreign political occupation and the lāhui remained economically outpowered and under cultural assault from a territorial regime that threatened their language, history, and collective identity. Under US occupation, Hawaiians were presented with the choice, either be part of a dying lāhui relegated to the past or embrace a new American identity.

While his trip and his writings did little to directly combat the American occupation, it did provide an alternative conception of the place of the lāhui in the broader world, one as useful today as it was then. They were not small, isolated remnants of the past nor were they simply Americans. Rather they were part of a larger, geographically spread, culturally diverse, and still thriving Oceanic lāhui linked by language, culture, travel, and ancestry. Indeed the very characteristics that Europeans and Americans had long used to dismiss the lāhui as archaic proved to be the links that connected them to other modern lāhui of Oceania. Their generosity, hula, bodies, language, mo'olelo, and aloha 'āina were not things to be hidden or snuffed out, but rather they were the heart of who the Kānaka Hawai'i were and the proof of their links to Oceania.

As Stephen Pupuhi gradually adjusted to his life in Hawai'i, he could not have guessed that one day his grandson would travel through Oceania as an impromptu ambassador of the Hawaiian people. He could, however, have guessed the importance of Hawaiian language and culture in such an enterprise. Like Baker in Tahiti, Tonga, and Aotearoa, Pupuhi had found his own Oceanic roots to be both useful and meaningful in Hawai'i. Apparently he also found life among the Hawaiian people to be familiar and appealing, settling there and starting a family with a Kanaka Maoli woman, a family that remains part of the Lāhui Hawai'i to this day. Like his well-traveled grandson, there must have been many moments when Pupuhi looked out at his flock, his neighbors, and his family and thought to himself, "a'ohe wehena mai kakou," there is nothing that separates us.

6

Maka'āinana or Servants of the Dollar?

Oceanic and Capitalist Values

In 1902, the US House of Representatives carried out an investigation in Hawai'i regarding the transition from independent nation to territory. When a call went out for written and oral testimony, the people of Hawai'i, Kānaka and non-Kānaka alike, seized the opportunity to be heard directly by the federal government. Considering the lack of any real measure of democratic input into the imperial regime, this was a rare opportunity. While the testimonies contain a clear Kanaka unhappiness with the American imperial presence, Kānaka focused primarily on negotiating the realities of life under empire. Ali'i nui, planter, and proud royalist John Cummins may have captured the overall sentiment the best when he wrote:

The action of the Congress of the United States in annexing the islands is not and never will be approved by the Hawaiian people in general ... You have made us American citizens against our will; we now propose to make the best of the situation.[1]

The specifics of *how* the lāhui might "make the best of the situation," remained a matter of some debate, with many inside and outside of the lāhui promoting their visions of the correct path forward. For John Tamatoa Baker, rancher, landlord, and entrepreneur, the best path lay in retaining the cultural and political cohesion of the lāhui while seeking individual success through capitalism, specifically small-scale agricultural capitalism. His voyage allowed Baker to expand his vision out to other lāhui within Oceania, and he took every opportunity to encourage his

---

[1] CPIPR, *Hawaiian Investigation: Pt 3, Exhibits, Memorials, Petitions, and Letters* (Washington, D.C.: Government Printing Office, 1902), 114–115.

hosts and his readers to follow his own path and achieve comfort and independence through agricultural entrepreneurship. This pursuit of individual economic success, he believed, would develop a socioeconomic base of small, independent, landowning farmers, an Oceanic yeomanry that would strengthen and empower themselves and their lāhui despite the yoke of imperial rule.

This embrace of the yeoman farmer as the foundation of the Hawaiian/Oceanic future was hardly unique to Baker. The idea had been popular in certain circles in Hawai'i since the 1830s, when American missionaries proposed it as a form of na'auao needed to revive the population. The missionaries were simply putting a Hawaiian gloss on the long-standing American lionization of the yeoman farmer – which ironically depended on and provided a justification for the mass dispossession of land from indigenous peoples. Within a few decades of their arrival, the missionaries, their allies in the government, and their former students at Baker's alma mater, Lahainaluna, attempted to create the legal infrastructure for their envisioned Kanaka yeomanry through the Māhele, a transition from a traditional Hawaiian land tenure system to Western-style private property. By no coincidence, this also provided the first step in creating the legal infrastructure for non-Native landownership, something else eagerly encouraged by the missionaries and other members of the foreign community. More than half a century later, support for small-hold farming in Hawai'i surged again in the decades before and after Baker's voyage, with a particularly heavy focus on homesteading efforts.[2]

Baker's account of his voyage, however, also brings to light a fundamental clash between the capitalist values that he espoused and those of the broad pan-Oceanic lāhui that he had begun to envision. Specifically, the two value systems disagreed sharply around culturally defined limits of economic desire. By the turn of the nineteenth century, the capitalist urge to acquire had reached something of a fever pitch in the United States and other parts of the industrial world. Within the capitalist worldview, no real upper limit on either wealth or the desire to acquire wealth existed. There was no point beyond which wealth acquisition was no longer needed or even desired, a moral, cultural, or even personal cap on economic desire. The lack of such a limit and the willingness

[2] Ralph S. Kuykendall, *The Hawaiian Kingdom: 1778–1854 Foundation and Transformation* (Honolulu: University of Hawai'i Press, 1968), 273–274; Lilikala Kame'eleihiwa, *Native Land and Foreign Desire: Pehea Lā E Pono Ai* (Honolulu, HI: Museum Press, 1992), 201–208; Davianna Pōmaika'i McGregor, "'Āina Ho'opulapula: Hawaiian Homesteading," *Hawaiian Journal of History* 24 (1990): 6–7.

to pursue unlimited wealth had brought about an age of powerful and unprecedented corporate giants such as United Steel and Standard Oil. Indeed the American economy, and a great deal of the world's economy, depended on the belief that neither wealth acquisition nor consumption would ever or could ever be capped. Greed, in essence, was the engine that drove the entire modern economy. Were that greed removed, capped, or even constrained, the world markets would be thrown into absolute disorder.

Yet many people, both in Hawai'i and elsewhere, recoiled against this sort of limitless desire and greed with horror and distaste. Lacking the economic motivations provided by capitalism, this sort of greed could only serve to fracture relationships and stability within the society. Most agricultural communities, particularly those engaged in subsistence and subsistence-plus agriculture, would likely place a high value on mutual support and personal connections, both of which would be threatened by a focus on acquisition. Even in the United States the Populist movement of the 1890s was inspired in part by recognition of the disaster that unfettered capitalism and greed could and often did unleash on rural communities and society.

Like many other rural areas of the world, Hawai'i was in a liminal state, being a part of the capitalist world that both celebrated and fed off greed while living in a culture that historically eschewed it. One of the terms used for desire, was *ake*, literally "the liver," where desire was believed to be held. Ake or akenui, great desire, reflected Hawaiian views of the bodily manifestations of emotion, with desire being felt as burning and aching in the liver. Akenui was not necessarily a bad thing, but akenui after wealth needed an upper boundary to avoid destruction of the individual and the community. One way of understanding this upper boundary of desire was the point of being lawa, satisfied, sufficient, or adequate. When asked if one would like more food for instance, Hawaiians might refuse by saying they were already *lawa*, satisfied, not *piha*, full.

A famous example of the power of the idea of lawa can be seen in the famous mele aloha 'āina, "Kaulana Nā Pua," which was written by Elaine Prendergrast for the Royal Hawaiian Band, who refused to sign an oath of loyalty to the coup government after the overthrow, costing them their employment. The most famous section of that mele goes:

> A'ole mākou a'e minamina
> I ka pu'ukālā a ke aupuni.
> Ua lawa mākou i ka pōhaku,
> I ka 'ai kamaha'o o ka 'āina.

> We do not value
> The government's sums of money.
> We are satisfied with the stones,
> Astonishing food of the land.

Money, the desire for money, was not the prime concern for the band, rather it was their independence and loyalty to the monarchy. Instead of signing the oath and collecting a regular paycheck, the band members were instead lawa, satisfied with what could be taken from the land, even the stones. Akenui after the dollar would stymie their independence and their political voice, which could only be retained by seeking to be lawa rather than to acquire blindly and persistently.[3]

In his attempts to exhort other islanders to embrace his vision of Oceanic capitalism, Baker was at times forced to acknowledge the limits and even dangers of the capitalism he promoted. The struggle for Baker, and many others in Oceania, was how to keep sight of the importance of lawa while succeeding in a world driven by limitless akenui. The most important incident occurred early in his voyage on the isthmus of Taravao in Tahiti, were the local people critiqued capitalism, and Baker, for a value system that placed no upper limits on desire. As he traveled through the Pacific and witnessed the operation of empire throughout the Eastern Pacific, Baker transformed these Tahitian/Oceanic critiques of capitalism and the importance of lawa into a broader critique of empire and imperial cultures, casting them as inherently flawed and dangerous due to their failure to understand and value such a limit.

THE GOSPEL OF THE OCEANIC YEOMAN

In September 1907, Baker traveled to the Hokianga river area in the north of Aotearoa. On his first full day in the Hokianga region he wandered by a sawmill and struck up a conversation with some local Māori men. Once again Baker's speechmaking and Hawaiian roots allowed him to make a quick transition from tourist to impromptu cultural ambassador. He soon attracted a crowd of Māori passersby, interested in meeting and talking to "[a] Hawaiian, from the land of the ancestors." According to Baker, the crowd pressed him to describe the Hawaiian way of life and his experiences traveling Oceania.[4]

---

[3] Samuel Elbert and Noelani Mahoe, *Na Mele o Hawai'i Nei: 101 Hawaiian Songs* (Honolulu: University of Hawai'i Press, 1970), 62–64.
[4] John T. Baker, "Mai Ka Aina Mamao Mai," *Ke Aloha Aina*, November 31, 1907.

Never one to miss an opportunity, Baker launched into an impromptu speech promoting a vision of Native yeomen as the best route forward for the various Oceanic lāhui. He began with his observations of land development on the North Island, "If land is farmed and cleared, then it belongs to a Haole, and if it is cultivated in pieces, with chunks of forest remaining, then it is a Maori's. That's how we are in Hawaii." Encouraged by the knowing laughter of the Māori crowd, Baker continued. "And what is the reason we don't farm our lands?" The crowd replied, "For the lack of money." Baker pushed further, "So you wait to get the money and then farm, but where is that money coming from?" The crowd responded that they did not know, that this was the problem.[5]

Baker pushed on, laying out a vision for success in the Pākeha-dominated economy:

If I don't have money and I don't know the place to get it, then here is the correct path. The man and woman awaken early in the morning and the woman cooks the two of them some breakfast while the man goes and clears some land ... wipe the eyes with the hands, eat till full, go to the job of the Haole. Return in the evening and return to the garden, then go back and bathe and eat. If perhaps you do this and the year passes, the land will be cleared and the plants will be planted. Then you can harvest the fruits of the goodness of your weariness.

Baker did not record the general response to his speech, though his plan seemed long on sweaty ambition and short on workability. Impressed by Baker's speech, a man from the crowd, a "hapa-Haole" like Baker, invited him to visit his nearby home at "Waharapa." This man, who Baker called "Tuwake," was most likely Heremia Te Wake of Whakarapa,[6] a successful farmer and a leader of the Te Rarawa Iwi.[7]

Baker spent two nights as a guest of Te Wake, bonding over their shared economic outlook and status, describing Te Wake as "a rich and well situated man, like John Baker." Like Baker, who looked after his own affairs as well as those of his deceased brother Edward, Te Wake was "a head of family, and some of the people who he heads are devoted to this place, a loving and proper man." Baker was particularly impressed with the obvious signs of Te Wake's wealth, including "some large houses, good homes and well provisioned, and lacking nothing for life." More important than this display of wealth was the agricultural enterprise that was the source of Te Wake's wealth, which Baker described as 4,800 acres

---

[5] Ibid.
[6] Now known as Pangaru.
[7] Baker, "Mai Ka Aina Mamao Mai," *Ke Aloha Aina*, December 7, 1907.

of land and a considerable number of pigs, sheep, and cattle. Baker also described the lands of Whakarapa as being as culturally significant as they were fruitful. "This was where his chiefs lived in the old times, and a place where chiefs were born, like the stories of Kualoa, the belly button of the island of Oahu, a center post. The canoes of all the high chiefs would come there and were tethered above, and the chiefly people humbled themselves." After a few days, Baker took his leave of Te Wake, who gave him several pieces of kaori gum and pounamu (carved greenstone).[8]

Baker's sawmill speech and his time with Te Wake fit well into a larger pattern of promoting and celebrating small-scale agricultural entrepreneurship among Oceanic peoples. In Tahiti he frequently pressed his Maohi hosts as to why they did not pursue more market-centered agricultural development. With the quality of the Tahitian soil and the favorable climate, Baker argued that the Maohi could turn over a considerable profit with hard work and the right crops. The same was true in Rarotonga, where he noted that considerable money could be made in copra production. "If you have 10,000 trees, a dollar a tree, $10,000 a year. But I saw no Native working this way, and the Haole that have gotten land, it is filled with coconut and planted. Many are the lands of the [Cook Islands Māori] left forested, like our [Hawaiian] lands."[9]

Baker even saw fit to encourage Tahitian high chief/planter Tati Salmon to greater involvement in agricultural entrepreneurship, noting that he and other prominent members of his family had undeveloped lands well suited for copra production. Baker may not have realized that Tati and his family had already engaged in significant agricultural enterprises throughout the region and acquired significant debts in doing so. Though Baker did not record Tati's response to his prodding, the issue was likely a sensitive one for the Salmon patriarch.[10]

While clearly influenced by the popular celebration of the smallhold farmer in both Hawai'i and the United States, Baker also supported Native agricultural entrepreneurship due to his own economic successes, particularly his ranching endeavors on the Big Island and leasing lots to smallhold sugar planters in the Hilo area. Between these different efforts, Baker had achieved a level of economic stability and comfort that

[8] Ibid.; Baker, "Mai Ka Aina Mamao Mai" *Ke Aloha Aina*, November 31, 1907.
[9] Baker, "Mai Ka Aina Mamao Mai," *Ke Aloha Aina*, August 24, 1907; Baker, "Mai Ka Aina Mamao Mai," *Ke Aloha Aina*, September 28, 1907.
[10] Claus Gossler, "The Social and Economic Fall of the Salmon/Brander Clan of Tahiti," *The Journal of Pacific History* 40, no. 2 (2005): 199–200; Baker, "Mai Ka Aina Mamao Mai," *Ke Aloha Aina*, September 28, 1907.

relatively few other Kānaka had achieved under capitalism. In addition to providing material comfort, Baker also knew that the pursuit of wealth in twentieth-century Hawaiʻi was a matter of power and to a certain degree independence from the economic might of the planter/missionary oligarchy. Baker's wealth had allowed him, for instance, to remain a prominent anti-annexation leader throughout the postoverthrow era without the fear of economic ruin faced by less economically independent leaders, such as Joseph Nāwahī and John E. Bush. As he traveled across the Pacific, Baker could see that what was true in Hawaiʻi was true throughout the rest of the Pacific; in an ocean controlled by capitalist empires, wealth was a well-established key to power. For a lāhui with little capital, few mineral resources, and little chance of competing in manufacturing, only agriculture offered any hope of acquiring that wealth.[11]

LAND AND POWER UNDER EMPIRE

In Baker's mind, small-scale capitalist agriculture also offered a means to ameliorate or even reverse the rampant problem of Native land dispossession in Hawaiʻi. While imperial land policies affected many of the peoples of the Pacific, the settler-controlled administrations of Hawaiʻi and New Zealand had proven particularly motivated and efficient at the removal of lands from Native control. Like many other Kānaka, Baker acknowledged land dispossession as one of the greatest, if not the greatest, threat to the lāhui, telling the Māori language newspaper *Te Pipiwharauroa*, "Our biggest problem is that we have no land, the Europeans have acquired it all. We are very concerned that we have no land."[12]

Baker was hardly alone in his concerns. As noted elsewhere, the Māhele of the 1840s had created the legal infrastructure for private ownership of land, quickly followed by laws allowing noncitizens to purchase land. Petitions and other evidence point to some concern over this process, especially among the makaʻāinana, who were worried that foreigners would soon control the government and the land. With the creation of the sugar industry in the 1850s and the boom in sugar prices during the US Civil War, more and more of the land did indeed come under control

---

[11] Benjamin Cluff, "The Hawaiian Islands and Annexation," *Improvement Era* 1, no. 1 (1897): 444–445.

[12] "He Manuhiri No Hawaii," *Te Pipiwharauroa*, interview with John T. Baker, trans. Paul Meredith, September 1907.

of foreigners and naturalized citizens. The greatest masses of land outside of Haole control during the 1880s were the government lands; the crown lands, which were controlled by the ruling sovereign; and the extensive holdings of Bernice Pauahi Bishop, who had inherited the estates of most of the major ali'i of the Kamehameha line.

With Pauahi's death in 1884, her vast holdings largely went into a trust whose beneficiaries were the children of Hawai'i, but whose trustees were named from the same circle of missionary families who would provide the leadership for the 1887 Bayonet Revolt and the 1893 overthrow. Those two events also placed the government lands and crown lands under control of the same mission/sugar oligarchy who ruled Hawai'i until the 1950s. Though prohibited from selling large amounts of government lands by the 1900 Organic Act, the oligarchy still managed to use their control over these lands to great effect. They "swapped," for instance, 40,000 acres of government land on Lāna'i for a few hundred acres of undevelopable forest preserve on O'ahu.[13] Control of government lands also granted the oligarchy the ablity to reward themselves and their followers with favorable leases on highly productive agricultural lands while keeping those lands away from any who might oppose their control.

By the start of the territorial period, land purchases by the Haole elite and the oligarchies' blatant abuse of land policies to benefit themselves had greatly decreased Kanaka access to new agricultural land outside of a handful of elites such as Baker and Samuel Parker. Attempts to remediate the situation proved largely fruitless until passage of the Hawaiian Homesteads Act of 1920, which arguably benefitted the oligarchs and other large land concerns more than it did the Hawaiian people.[14] For the lāhui Hawai'i, whose culture often celebrated and was fed by connections and ties to the lands, losing control over land also presented a clear risk to that culture. The government and crown lands contained many wahi pana, culturally significant locations celebrated in mo'olelo, hula, and oli and central to the relationship between the lāhui and the Hawaiian past.[15] Loss of control of these areas further accentuated the cultural threat the lāhui found itself under in the early years of American rule.

Considering the costs of losing control over the lands of Hawai'i, it should be no surprise that Baker put a high premium on retention and

[13] Jon M. Van Dyke, *Who Owns the Crown Lands of Hawai'i?* (Honolulu: University of Hawai'i Press, 2008), 222.
[14] Davianna Pōmaika'i McGregor, "'Āina Ho'opulapula: Hawaiian Homesteading" *Hawaiian Journal of History* 24 (1990): 19, 27–29, 33–34.
[15] Van Dyke, *Who Owns the Crown Lands*, map inserts following page 68.

acquisition of land. He noted approvingly of Maohi control of land in Taravao, Tahiti. As will be discussed later in this chapter, part of that retention of control came from Maohi unwillingness to sell or mortgage their lands and jeopardize their livelihood. At the same time, Baker noted somewhat approvingly, part of that control came to the lack of a feasible means of doing so. "Their lands," he wrote, "none of them sell though they rent. They cannot sell because it is not administered. If you sell to someone and someone else does not agree, you are headed towards a fight."[16]

When interviewed in Gisborne, Baker used the lack of Kanaka-held land in Hawai'i as a cautionary tale for the Māori, but noted hopefully that "you the Maori people are a well-off people as you retain your lands." He then urged the readers of *Te Pipiwharauroa*, "Hold on and retain your homes, do not sell one inch of your land." In Tahiti, he argued, many Europeans pursued marriages with chiefly women in pursuit of lands. In New Zealand, he claimed, "Maori marry Maori so that the land remains with the Maori." Considering the amount of Māori land Pākeha had confiscated, bought, married into, and otherwise obtained in the decades leading up to his visit, Baker may have held an overly optimistic understanding of Māori landownership. Nonetheless, the interview still illustrated his deep belief in the importance of landownership for the strength of the various Oceanic lāhui as well as their potential for agricultural success.[17]

Baker also argued that when properly applied, the pursuit of agricultural capitalism in Hawai'i and elsewhere could provide a path to greater land retention. The model he laid out for the Māori crowd at the sawmill, for instance, envisioned hard work as both the means to gain wealth from the land as well as the means to prevent the selling of land for simple profit. At the same time, access to land and the ability to increase landholdings through agricultural capitalism were essential components of the type of small-scale agricultural pursuits Baker promoted.

Control over land and the unwillingness to sell it had certainly been essential to Baker's own success. As a reward for his work in the court of Kalākaua and to help support Ululani, one of a dwindling number of ali'i nui left in the islands, Kalākaua had leased him a significant amount of land at Pi'ihonua, Hilo. Through his own agricultural efforts and

---

[16] Baker, "Mai Ka Aina Mamao Mai," *Ke Aloha Aina*, August 24, 1907.
[17] "He Manuhiri No Hawaii," *Te Pipiwharauroa*, interview with John T. Baker, trans. Paul Meredith, September 1907.

through subleases, Baker acquired the capital for various other land purchases, including his large and prosperous ranch in the Hamakua area.
When speaking to some traveling companions in New Zealand, Baker
explained his unwillingness to sell land as the heart of his economic success, describing his rents and profits off the land as:

The fruit supporting me for these six months, that is the fruit I harvest, with
moderate consumption. I have been asked to cut the tree and harvest the
fruit, but I do not think that is right ... If I sell this land and the rental [con-
tracts], and earn a hundred dollars, for what? Here at most, probably just to
end one source of rot [to deal with a debt], but this is a waste ... Leave the
fruit till it is mature. I pick [only] the fruit that are mature, and thus I measure consumption, and this is [all] I eat ... I eat the fruit and the seed I plant
again, I start the fruit again, and eat the ones I grew as seedlings from the
earlier plants.[18]

Falling in line with Baker's vision of self-reliant Native agriculture,
this metaphor emphasized living within one's means, avoiding debt, and
the relationship between Oceanic peoples and the land, each sustaining
and caring for the other. His measured consumption of "fruit" allowed
him to avoid the "rot" of debt, which could force him to sell the fruits
that sustained him. Cutting the trees would provide short-term profit,
but would also end the long-term security that possession of the land
ensured. Furthermore, his measured consumption allowed him to save up
for future investment, to "plant the seeds" for future consumption.

Baker's embrace of Te Wake as a kindred spirit stemmed not only
from their mutual economic success, but also from their shared economic
philosophy. Te Wake's papers and the memories of his daughter, Dame
Whina Cooper, show a man much like Baker in his thinking regarding
land sales. Despite earlier land sales as a means of acquiring capital, as he
aged he grew strictly opposed to the sale of land. He instructed his heirs,
for instance, that the sale of land led only to the suffering of future generations, while also arguing that money could always be made by one willing to put their sweat into the land.[19] The fact that Te Wake's agricultural
efforts allowed him to hold onto and preserve culturally important lands
made his efforts even more meaningful and provided further support for
Baker's belief that the preservation of the lāhui required ownership and
control over land.

[18] Baker, "Mai Ka Aina Mamao Mai," *Ke Aloha Aina*, November 31, 1907.
[19] Michael King, *Whina: A Biography of Whina Cooper* (Auckland: Hodder and Stoughton, 1983), 43.

The way Baker and Te Wake understood land sits at an interesting middle ground between capitalist and shared Māori and Kanaka understandings of land. Avoiding the sale of land for short-term profit rather than as a source of potential long-term income certainly made sense in a capitalist mind-set, and indeed it still does. But the importance that Baker and Te Wake placed in land extended past prudent management, and it seems unlikely either man would sell land at that stage of their life even to invest in other ways that might be just as if not more profitable. Throughout Eastern Oceania, after all, land was not just the thing that fed people, it was, as one of Baker's Tahitian companions put it, "the foundation of the kamaaina [child-of-the-land or commoner]." Land was political power, it was mana, it was the root of the community and the culture. As Te Wake and Baker had both seen during their lives, the loss of indigenous culture, power, and stability followed close behind the loss of land.[20]

ECONOMIC DIVERSITY AND INDEPENDENCE

With the eye, and the desires, of a successful agricultural entrepreneur, Baker remained constantly on the alert for new agricultural opportunities for both himself and the lāhui. Small-scale vanilla production in Tahiti piqued Baker's interest, as it seemed to contrast both with traditional subsistence agriculture and with the plantation economy of Hawai'i. Baker often investigated different kinds of land use, such as sheepherding in Australia, flax production in Aotearoa, and copra throughout the Pacific, all of which he perceived as potential agricultural industries for Hawai'i. In Australia he also noted the importance of developing park lands to nurture the budding Pacific tourist trade, writing to his Hawaiian readers, "If all the wahi pana of our land were transferred to park lands, there would be none as beautiful." He went on to note that such parklands could become a draw to boost local economies as well as direct sources of revenue. In Hawai'i, he noted, "There are none of these types of tourist places that the visitors go to with a desire to see and throw around a few dimes, [with] a few activities for them to have and a place for the common man to spend their time." Though it remained unsaid, this would also provide some security for wahi pana, preventing them from development by the sugar and pineapple industries.[21]

---

[20] Baker, "Mai Ka Aina Mamao Mai," *Ke Aloha Aina*, August 24, 1907.
[21] "Mai Ka Aina Mamao Mai," *Ke Aloha Aina*, August 17, 1907; "Mai Ka Aina Mamao Mai," *Ke Aloha Aina*, December 28, 1907.

Baker's interest in economic diversity again emerged from his own economic experience, which included ranching, agricultural rents, and other small ventures. In later years he also pursued opening a creamery, obtained the first permit to produce gas in Hilo, and floated a scheme in Kohala to develop pineapple production on homesteading land.[22] This constant search for new money-making activities allowed Baker not only to generate more income, but it also provided a measure of insulation from the volatile sugar industry, which had the potential to create as many bankruptcies as it did millionaires. By its nature, sugar was a capital-intensive crop. Comparing it to vanilla, Baker argued that sugar required restrictively high amounts of start-up capital for the cuttings, planting, pulling, milling, and refining before any profit could be realized. Small farmers had to borrow money to plant cane, which meant putting their land up for collateral and living just a bad crop away from losing it.[23]

Furthermore, once cane is cut it must be milled within a day or two before it begins to spoil. As noted by Ray Stannard Baker in his 1911 exposé of the Hawaiian sugar industry, small farmers lacked the ability to mill their own cane and could not transport it further than a day's travel as the plantations controlled all or nearly all of the railways and wharfs. As a result, small planters often sold their crops to mills owned either by large planters or the Big Five sugar factors, who could name their price for the cut cane because no other options were available. This not only increased the economic power of the oligarchy, and their profits, but it also increased their political power. For a small farmer raising cane, upsetting the oligarchy was a sure, slow, and painful method of economic suicide.[24] Living in Hilo, Baker had seen how sole reliance on sugar had left small-hold farmers at the mercy of the vagaries of the industry and their wealthy neighbors, and he seemed to consider it a trap for the small landowner.

In Baker's mind, vanilla, as grown in Tahiti, held far more promise for small-scale Oceanic farmers. Though labor intensive it required minimal

[22] "Hilo May Have a Creamery Plant," *The Hawaiian Gazette*, October 20, 1911; Fifth Legislature of the Territory of Hawaii, *Journal of the Senate of the Fifth Legislature of the Territory of Hawaii: Regular Session* (1909): 303; Clarice B. Taylor, "Little Tales about Hawaii: J. T. Baker, Model for Kamehameha Statue Pt. 8," *Honolulu Star Bulletin*, September 18, 1951.

[23] Baker, "Mai ka Aina Mamao Mai," *Ke Aloha Aina*, August 17, 1907.

[24] Ray Stannard Baker, "Wonderful Hawaii: A World Experimentation Station, Part II: The Land and the Landless," *American Magazine* 73, no. 2 (1911): 206–207.

financial investment, needing only forestlands, knowledge, and cuttings, which could be had cheap, unlike cane cuttings. As with copra, Tahitians could grow small quantities of vanilla and exchange the dried beans for cash or goods from local stores and traders, who collected and resold them in bulk. Vanilla held less promise for wealth than cane, but it also held far less risk, requiring considerable more sweat investment than capital.[25]

WEALTH AND VALUES

Baker eagerly promoted not just a general vision of an Oceanic yeomanry, but also a set of capitalist values he saw as essential to that vision. In presenting capitalism in this manner, he, like the missionaries and others before him, cast capitalism not just as an economic system but as a component of na'auao, enlightenment. Rather than pulling islanders into the light of Christ's kingdom, however, he hoped to pull them into the light of economic success and through that success a measure of independence and stability.

Typical of promoters of capitalism, Baker preached the value of hard work as the key ingredient in economic success. He directly pressed his fellow Oceanians to work harder in the quest for agricultural wealth, substituting sweat for capital whenever possible or necessary. Often he did so through unfavorable comparisons with white settlers, for instance, commenting on how the Pākeha's lands along the Hokianga were cleared of forest while those of the Māori, like those of the Kānaka at home, were not. While he admitted that a lack of capital was a problem, he still insisted that hard work and perseverance would provide all that the prospective Oceanic farmer needed to get ahead.[26]

Baker was quick to judge those he perceived as unwilling to provide the hard work demanded by agricultural capitalism. While acknowledging that the land provided the people of Tahiti with abundant resources, he still felt the need to mention the "laziness" of the Tahitian Maohi in both in his interview with *Te Pipiwharauroa* and in his letters home. He dismissed the people of Rarotonga as lazy and useless, employing the Hawaiian saying, "O moe loa kane, o nana wale wahine," the man is a great sleeper, the woman just gazes about. He was noticeably less

---

[25] Baker, "Mai ka Aina Mamao Mai," *Ke Aloha Aina*, August 17, 1907.
[26] Baker, "Mai ka Aina Mamao Mai," *Ke Aloha Aina*, November 31, 1907.

aggressive in his comments about Tati Salmon though he did seem disappointed that much of his land remained uncleared.[27]

Baker was also keen to point out the importance of avoiding unnecessary expenditures and debt. In his interview with *Te Pipiwharauroa,* Baker was asked if he had any words for the Māori people, and he included a fair amount of economic advice. In addition to encouraging the Māori readership to hold onto their lands, he also urged them to "[m]ake sure you plug the holes in your bank accounts … You must not go into debt; avoid debt as you would the devil." Similarly, Baker also warned the Māori readers, "Do not speculate or gamble; do not be hasty to be rich."[28]

In opposition to the perceived lack of proper capitalist values among other Kānaka and other Oceanians, Baker frequently presented his own economic success as proof of the importance and effectiveness of embracing capitalist values. In his interview with *Te Pipiwharauroa* he presented his life as a rags to riches story centered on hard work and avoiding unneeded expenses. Based on his interview, the article described him with the following:

He started with nothing. There are two reasons why he has obtained means: firstly, through hard work; secondly, through plugging the holes in his pocket. When he first started working little was his wage yet he tried his hand at everything. He was not afraid to try anything. He was not afraid to work even though he did not get much from his hard work at the start. Yet there was money in raising chickens. He suppressed his wants, allocating money for the more important things, like saving to buy a piece of Government land, rather than spending money on clothes. The holes of his pockets were plugged. As he did not drink alcohol, that hole was plugged, and that money was saved for more substantial things. The man who smokes a pipe burns a hole in his pocket, if he ceases smoking his pipe, it is a hole that can be plugged.[29]

Like many who achieve economic or political success, Baker's reflections on his own success and his promotion of individual-oriented values such as hard work and "plugging the holes" obscured the role of luck, connections, and systemic inequalities in capitalist success. While hard work and conservative spending habits were important components in Baker's success,

[27] Baker, "Mai Ka Aina Mamao Mai," *Ke Aloha Aina,* September 28, 1907; "He Manuhiri No Hawaii," *Te Pipiwharauroa,* interview with John T. Baker, trans. Paul Meredith, September 1907; Claus Gossler, "The Social and Economic Fall of the Salmon/Brander Clan of Tahiti," *The Journal of Pacific History* 40, no. 2 (2005): 199–200.

[28] "He Manuhiri No Hawaii," *Te Pipiwharauroa,* interview with John T. Baker, trans. Paul Meredith, September 1907.

[29] Ibid.

he failed to mention the role that his marriage to an ali'i nui and his ensuing connections to the court of Kalākaua had played. Indeed his economic empire grew out of the long-term leases of crown lands at Pi'ihonua granted to him by King Kalākaua. Furthermore, it should be noted that like Envoy Bush and Secretary Poor, Baker may have also benefitted from his status as a hapa-Haole, both in his dealings with the Haole-dominated business community and during his time as a civil servant.

Many less-influential Kānaka of the era were finding out that hard work and wise spending meant little in the face of government policies that favored the oligarchy and the harsh realities of twentieth-century agricultural capitalism. Future Honolulu Mayor Johnny Wilson, for instance, often pointed to his own family's failed agricultural efforts in the lush valley of Pelekune, where hard work and wise spending were meaningless without a means of transporting crops to profitable markets. While large, well-connected planters could cobble together public and private resources to assure cheap transport of sugar, small farmers could not do the same to get their food crops to the Honolulu market.[30]

While Baker explicitly promoted hard work and "plugging the holes," his writings and actions also show an implicit promotion of other essential capitalist values, particularly the normalization and even celebration of capitalist desire. In Taravao, Tahiti, for instance, he questioned local Maohi as to why they *failed* to akenui, to greatly desire, after the dollar. In his mind such akenui was not just desirable but a contemporary human norm that other Oceanic peoples too often failed to conform to. He, however, had little trouble conforming to this norm. While an appreciation for the security of crop diversity drove his constant look for new economic opportunities for the lāhui, Baker's writings show that he was also driven by his own deep and often tangible desire to accumulate wealth. When discussing the potential wealth to be derived from developing flax production in Hawai'i, he reflected, "[A]uwe! My pocket is sore with thoughts of seeing a little ripe and proper fruit again. Many are the fruit for the one who does not stop and savor offal."[31]

When discussing the potential wealth to be had off the lands of the Salmons and their royal relations, Baker noted longingly:

This is a large family, three daughters, three sons, sitting as ruling chiefs with no thought of the great wealth available in the land. If a child of Hawaii thinks to

---

[30] Bob Krauss, *Johnny Wilson: First Hawaiian Democrat* (Honolulu: University of Hawai'i Press, 1994), 175.

[31] Baker, "Mai Ka Aina Mamao Mai," *Ke Aloha Aina*, December 7, 1907.

*come here and marry one of these people and work the land and get the wealth
before them, perhaps that is where their thoughts are. Two daughters of [Queen]
Pomare are here unmarried by the young men. If in my younger days, I would
take this breadfruit, it is a low hanging one, using the fruit picker for Hawaii. It
is just out of range of the hands.*

Baker's akenui not only included the desire to pick such fruits, but also a
more general desire that the fruit *must* be picked by someone, preferably
a Kanaka Hawai'i if the Tahitians refused to do so. For Baker, the accu-
mulation of wealth was not simply a means to an end, but an end unto
itself, a desire that expressed itself through physical longings. In Baker's
mind, the failure to make money when opportunity presented itself was a
moral failure, a perspective that generations of Haole had used to justify
their efforts to pick the fruits of Hawai'i regardless of the cost to the
Kānaka Hawai'i.[32]

Similarly, Baker's promotion of "plugging the holes," seemed to extend
past simple financial prudence and into an embrace of stinginess. He
would acquire a reputation as a "stingy alii" that remained even after his
death.[33] While many Hawaiians might have bristled at such a description,
Baker seems to have embraced it. He teasingly described his friend Te
Wake, for instance, as, "A man who takes care [of his wealth] and even
firmer [pa'a] in his stinginess [kuli] than I am, and he lived well supplied.
His wealth is from his stinginess [kulipa'a]." The terms Baker used to
describe himself and Te Wake in this last passage, *kuli* and *kulipa'a*, provide insight into how the capitalist values Baker promoted as economic
virtues conflicted with the Oceanic values he embraced at other times
during his journey. *Kuli* meaning "deafness" and *kulipa'a* meaning "solid
deafness," referring to one who turns a deaf ear to appeals for aid or
generosity.[34]

Furthermore, Baker frequently measured other islanders, as individuals and groups, not just by their desire and ability to accumulate wealth,
but also by their conspicuous displays of wealth. He placed considerable
value in his own appearance, dressing as he felt a man of his economic
status should, fully outfitted in European and American fashion. In Tahiti
he donned formal late-Victorian attire, including tails and gloves, when

[32] Baker, "Mai Ka Aina Mamao Mai," *Ke Aloha Aina*, September 28, 1907.
[33] Clarice B. Taylor, "Little Tales about Hawaii: J.T. Baker, Model for Kamehameha Statue
Pt. 10," *Honolulu Star Bulletin*, September 20, 1951.
[34] Baker, "Mai Ka Aina Mamao Mai," *Ke Aloha Aina*, November 31, 1907; Mary Kawena
Pukui and Samuel H. Elbert, *Hawaiian Dictionary* (Honolulu: University of Hawai'i
Press, 1986), 180.

meeting the French governor in the stifling equatorial heat. He wrote that the manners and costume were sure to impress, as they were the same he used when received by President McKinley in Washington.[35]

He also commented upon the less "complete" attire of other islanders, typically with a certain air of cultural and social superiority. Indeed, he frequently employed attire, particularly Western attire, as a measure of the na'auao, or enlightenment, of a particular people. In Tonga he wrote that the manner of living was like that of Puna, except that the Tongan men went around with a cloth wrapped around their waists instead of pants, thus Puna was superior. When arriving in Papeete, he noted that some men walked around with a loincloth, similar to that of Kānaka Hawai'i in previous times. In Fiji after being pressed by a Haole man as to whether he thought Kānaka were superior to other island peoples, he replied that they were superior in part because no one went around without hats.[36]

Baker's equating of wealth with personal worth might be best seen in his favorable interactions with other members of the Oceanic economic elite. While Baker never describes Te Wake's age, appearance, or even his family, he does describe Te Wake's wealth in some detail. Baker described his compound, for instance, as multiple large structures, "a bit of a haphazard style, but, one of wealth." Clearly the wealth mattered far more than the style; the wealthy can always afford a touch of eccentricity. He was also quite impressed with the landholdings and livestock of Ngawini Yates', another prominent and wealthy Māori entrepreneur he met in the North of Aotearoa.[37]

Baker's tendency to be drawn to others who shared his economic status and eagerness to display it led him to a chance encounter with Dr. Maui Pomare, future New Zealand MP and a member of the Young Māori Party. Having spotted two well-dressed young men of mixed Māori and European descent walking down a street in Wellington, Baker stopped a little further up the street and waited for them to pass by. One of the two men split off while the other continued toward where Baker was standing. He and Baker briefly examined each other before Baker, outgoing

---

[35] Baker, "Mai Ka Aina Mamao Mai," *Ke Aloha Aina*, September 21, 1907; Baker, "Mai Ka Aina Mamao Mai," *Ke Aloha Aina*, September 28, 1907.

[36] Baker, "Mai Ka Aina Mamao Mai," *Ke Aloha Aina*, August 10, 1907; Baker, "Mai Ka Aina Mamao Mai," *Ke Aloha Aina*, November 16, 1907; Baker, "Mai Ka Aina Mamao Mai," *Ke Aloha Aina*, December 14, 1907.

[37] Baker, "Mai Ka Aina Mamao Mai," *Ke Aloha Aina*, November 9, 1907.

as always, smiled and introduced himself as a Kanaka Hawai'i, already quite aware of the doors this opened among many within the Māori community. The young man gave Baker his Aroha, and for once it was Baker who was surprised, as the young man explained he had recently been to Honolulu and knew W. O. Kamika (mission scion and overthrow participant W. O. Smith) and Keone Wilikina (future mayor Johnny Wilson). The young man then introduced himself as Maui Pomare, who Baker had been hoping to meet after a discussion with James Caroll, the first Māori to hold the position of minister of Native affairs.[38]

The two headed to Pomare's office where Baker learned that Pomare, though only thirty-two, was the head of the Māori Board of Health and had some thirty-seven doctors working under him, including two other Māori. As Pomare explained, the board focused on "the reorganization of domestic life and caring for the health of the current generation," including the promotion of European-style housing and furnishing, and thus the economic activity needed to purchase such things. Pomare credited such efforts with an increase of 5,000 individuals among the Māori population. With a still dwindling Native Hawaiian population at home, such a claim clearly interested Baker, buoying his hopes for his own lāhui as well as for Pomare's. Pomare later revealed that a key part of his plans included the suppression of alcohol, much to the teetotaler Baker's approval.[39]

While Baker was highly impressed with Pomare's position and commitment to his people, he was equally impressed with Pomare's displays of and comfort with the material wealth that defined success and power in that era. As noted earlier, his initial interaction with Pomare came about largely due to Pomare's well-heeled appearance. When Baker visited Pomare's home, he noted approvingly that it was a large and beautiful house in a European style. He was also quite impressed with Pomare's white groomsman and white cook, the only time he commented on servants of any race during his voyage. Pomare's wife and children were off on a vacation, but his sister acted as the hostess. The two men continued their discussions after dinner, following Victorian custom by retiring to the homo-social space of the smoking room although neither man smoked nor drank. Pomare's mastery and ownership of upper- and middle-class

---

[38] Baker, "Mai Ka Aina Mamao Mai," *Ke Aloha Aina*, December 14, 1907.
[39] Baker, "Mai Ka Aina Mamao Mai," *Ke Aloha Aina*, December 14, 1907; Derek A. Dow, "'Pruned of Its Dangers': The Tohunga Suppression Act of 1907," *Health and History* 3 (2001): 51.

European/American social spaces impressed Baker almost as much as his mastery over the human propensity for the vices associated with them.[40]

As seen in the gendered descriptions of his evening with Pomare, Baker's vision of Oceanic economic success not only celebrated contemporary capitalist consumption patterns, but contemporary capitalist gender norms as well. Pomare's education and labor had allowed him social and economic success outside of the home, which in turn allowed him to present himself as patriarch and master within the home. Pomare's labor supported the household while female domestic and social labor, either in the form of his absent wife, white cook, or sister, supported his role as the patriarch of the family. This male consumption of female labor, indeed male monopoly over female labor, had also become the norm in Hawai'i, not just from the soft influence of middle-class capitalist culture, but also the introduced legal system and the influence of the American missionaries.

Baker's vision of landholding among the future yeomanry also relied heavily on these nineteenth-century visions of a patriarchal nuclear family as the basis for society. Baker's vision of a hypothetical Māori farmer clearing out *his* lands along the Hokianaga, relies on the narrative of successful male farmers achieving wealth and independence through their own hard work and primarily for the benefit of their immediate family. In keeping with the nineteenth-century capitalist vision of how the world should work, the hypothetical Māori wife's work is entirely domestic, carried out in support of her husband rather than providing economic support for the family. Baker's espousal of such a vision shows not only the success the missionaries and their early allies had in spreading such norms, but also the willingness of many among the Kanaka elite to promote these norms as a means for Kānaka further down the social and economic ladder to find economic success and stability. Even Baker however, had to give credit to women like Ngawini Yates, whose marriage may have strengthened her economic standing but who had plentiful resources and business acumen of her own. Indeed she had been running her family's businesses on her own since her husband's death in 1900.

The control of female domestic labor was not the only way Baker envisioned women as essential to male advancement. His own success, after all, was launched by his marriage to an ali'i nui. Baker's success through marriage was hardly unusual, and indeed he promoted such male advancement through marriage elsewhere. His longing description of

[40] Baker, "Mai Ka Aina Mamao Mai," *Ke Aloha Aina*, December 14, 1907.

the undeveloped lands and unmarried daughters of the Salmon clan, for instance, focused on how "a child of Hawaiʻi," specifically a male child, could obtain such "fruit" for their own gain. Again, he presented women not as potential yeowomen and landowners, but rather as a means for enterprising males to gain access to land through marriage. The emphasis on hard male work not only hides the importance of women in the success of Baker, but it also maintains the illusion that hard work and determination alone were enough for economic mobility.

POROʻI'S CRITIQUE: AKENUI AND LAWA

Baker's vision of Oceanic yeomen elevating their collective lāhui relied heavily on a belief that the strength of the lāhui lay in the individual, specifically the male individual, rather than in the ties that held the individual members together. At the sawmill on the Hokianga, for instance, Baker did not focus on the possibilities for collective capitalism among the different hapū and iwi, a form of capitalism that Hazel Petrie has shown to be quite widespread and successful during the nineteenth century.[41] Instead he focused on the individual male farmer, supported by female domestic labor, as the path to success. This elevation of the individual is central to the rhetoric of modern capitalism. The values Baker promoted, intentionally or unintentionally, also placed considerable emphasis on the individual. An ethic of hard, self-motived agricultural work, "plugging the holes in one's pockets," and nurturing economic desire all depend largely on shaping and policing the needs and desires of the individual rather than the collective. At times, however, Baker's interactions with and admiration of other Oceanic people led to a direct conflict with his individualist and procapitalist vision.

In late June 1907, Baker traveled to Taravao, Tahiti, with Poroʻi, an ariʻi with ties to the area. Baker noted Taravao's lushness and expressed a mix of concern and disdain over the lack of agricultural development. There were a few coconut plantations, but these were largely under white direction. The local Maohi, however, grew traditional and foreign food crops for subsistence, along with some small cash crops, mostly vanilla and copra, to provide any wants or needs beyond what they could produce themselves. Despite the availability of land and markets, Baker

---

[41] Hazel Petrie, *Chiefs of Industry: Māori Tribal Enterprise in Early Colonial New Zealand* (Auckland: Auckland University Press, 2006).

noted that the people of Taravao, and many Maohi in general, had little interest in expanding their entanglements with the cash economy, either as planters or as labor. He wrote of them:

They do not akenui [greatly desire] for the dollar and they will not work for wages ... [For them] the foundation of the kamaaina [children of the land] is not to labor [for others], because they are the land, the land is theirs to work, to plant, and to take for sale for a few dimes and please the body. They are lawa [sufficient/ satisfied] in things to eat.

Noting the happy and satisfied lives of the Taravao Maohi, Baker immediately began to press Poroʻi not just on why the Maohi did not develop more land, but also on their perceived failure to adopt a proper capitalist sense of desire. He pointedly asked, "Why do you not akenui the dollar to get all manner of goods?" assuming that akenui, that driving desire, to be not just normal but downright necessary.[42]

For many within Oceania – though clearly not Baker – this akenui for the dollar had a clear potential for social disruption, driving the individual to acquire at the cost of a balanced life and one's ties to the people around them. Channeling such sentiment, Poroʻi replied:

You [Hawaiians] have many dollars and progress ... and are you not slaves and servants for the dollars? Perhaps you do not rest, perhaps your lands go to the Haole in the akenui of yours for the dollar ... For us here, ours is a life of comfort.

God provided us and perhaps you as well, with the banana, growing and flowering year round, the taro growing for you to fetch as you can, here is the yam, and there is the breadfruit, three different types, and all these types of plants mature sometime [during the year]. Therefore, why overburden and ruin your body for the dollar, for what reason? It is lawa [sufficient/satisfactory] to have some convenient money.[43]

The discussion continued in a later English language interview Baker gave to the *Hawaiian Gazette*. He elaborated that he told Poroʻi that if they worked as labor or on cash crops the Maohi could make more money. Poroʻi, however, replied that if they did so, "Where would we get our food?" Baker responded that if they worked more, they could always buy food. Poroʻi laughed, telling Baker, "Oh yes, we would work for some white man and get money for our work, then we could hand back the money to the white man for food."[44]

[42] Baker, "Mai Ka Aina Mamao Mai," *Ke Aloha Aina*, August 24, 1907.
[43] Ibid.
[44] "Col. Baker's Grand Time in the South Seas," *Hawaiian Gazette*, January 31, 1908, 3.

This discussion with Poro'i forced Baker to confront the conflicts between the pan-Oceanic value systems that he envisioned as validating Hawaiian culture and the capitalist values he was promoting as the economic salvation of Oceanic peoples. Poro'i's comments on the Hawaiian situation, presenting them as largely landless and left as servants and slaves to the dollar must have struck Baker particularly strongly. He concluded his account of the discussion with, "I believe he was right."

A career politician, a devoted royalist, and a former leader in the anti-annexation movement, Baker was more than aware of the tenuous position his people now faced, subjects of a foreign empire that entrusted the islands to a kleptocratic oligarchy. Portraying this general turn of events as the result of Hawaiian akenui for the dollar lent considerable force to Poro'i's words. Akenui may have been essential for the pursuit of capitalist fortunes, but in Poro'i's words it presented a clear threat to the well-being of the individual or lāhui who embraced it.

Poro'i went further, presenting akenui and Baker's embrace of it as a departure from the independent and arguably freer way of life embraced by the people of Taravao. His fellow Maohi, he argued, avoided the dangers of becoming servants and slaves to the dollar by recognizing and valuing a culturally defined and promoted upper limit on desire, which Baker reported as *lawa*, sufficient or satisfied. The Maohi did not eschew consumer goods and the market economy, indeed they gladly engaged it for those needs and wants they could not provide by themselves. In recognizing an upper limit to that desire, however, they avoided risking their lands, breadfruit, taro, yams, and bananas, all the things that made them the kama'āina.

Poro'i continued by recounting a brief parable about a man who lived inside of a large overturned barrel. As word of this man's unusual living situation spread, it reached a local ali'i. Concerned, the ali'i came to investigate. Seeing that the man lacked a proper home, the ali'i assumed it was for lack of means to improve his lot. Determined to help the man, the ali'i stood at the opening of the barrel and greeted him, then called out "What can I do for you? I will hire you to work for me." The man in the barrel replied, "E ke alii e, may you live long, all that I want to ask for from you is that you remove yourself from the mouth of the barrel, as you are blocking the radiance of the sun. This is my desire." Poro'i noted that this seemed to be the problem with the lāhui Hawai'i, whose desire for money blocked "the glory of relaxing and seeing the Lord. You are in the darkness, [with] the worship of this other god, the dollar, your god, that is where all your thought is. But, perhaps this way is coming to us here, God is the one that knows, this is his role."[45]

Poroʻi's parable shares enough parallels with the story of Diogenes the Cynic's meeting with Alexander the Great to assume that Poroʻi or someone else had read this account and recast it in a Tahitian setting.[46] Like Poroʻi, Diogenes questioned the pursuit of wealth as a worthwhile human endeavor, part of his larger philosophical questioning of the norms of Greek culture and society. Poroʻi, however, reshaped the story to critique capitalist akenui as a violation and threat to the norms of Maohi culture and society. His Maohi Diogenes illustrates the importance of recognizing an upper limit for desire, allowing the individual and the community to live comfortably without the disorder caused by akenui after the dollar.

Poroʻi's heavy use of Christian language also called upon the significant cultural strength of Christianity in the Pacific to reinforce the importance of lawa. By the early 1900s, the peoples of Oceania had largely converted to Christianity, and Christianity had been the dominant religion in Tahiti for the better part of a century. Poroʻi's appeals to Christianity would have been a natural and powerful rhetorical choice that would also have been well understood by Baker and his Kanaka readership at home. Indeed few in Baker's audience would need to be reminded of Christianity's frequent injunctions against the blind pursuit of wealth or have trouble understanding Poroʻi's implicit argument that the Maohi recognition of a point of sufficiency demonstrated proper Christian values as well as Oceanic ones. Rather than being deviants within the capitalist value system as Baker initially posited them, Poroʻi recast the Maohi of Taravao as the standard bearers of both Christian and Oceanic norms.

Poroʻi's synthesis of Greek Cynicism, Christianity, and Maohi cultural values took the wind out of Baker's pro-akenui sail. As Baker put it in the *Gazette* interview, "He shut me up," a somewhat unusual situation for the talkative and quick-witted Baker. Soon enough, however, Baker recovered and launched into his own speech, one far more in line with Poroʻi's thinking than Baker's normal capitalist mind-set. He thanked Poroʻi for his words and noted that the way of life in Hawaiʻi had once been quite similar to that of Taravao. He recounted his memories of his grandparents' lifestyle some forty-five years earlier, recalling it as similarly lawa.

[45] Baker, "Mai Ka Aina Mamao Mai," *Ke Aloha Aina*, August 24, 1907.
[46] After conquering Cornith, Alexander supposedly went out to meet Diogenes, intrigued by his philosophy and well-known antics. Finding Diogenes sleeping in a massive wine barrel, Alexander asked him if there was anything Alexander could do for or give Diogenes. Diogenes supposedly replied, "You could move over, you're blocking my sun."

They supplied themselves with enough food to live comfortably and did not seek after more than they needed. No one could mistake them for slaves to the dollar, for they lived as a "free and truly religious people." He noted that his grandmother had raised him for much of his childhood and would pray with him every night, asking the Lord, "Do not give him great wealth elevating him till he forgets you, nor so little wealth that he becomes a thief."[47]

Baker's use of the term *lawa* to describe both the sufficient lifestyle of his grandparents and that of the Maohi of Taravao hints at not just sufficiency in terms of material goods, but also a set of skills and knowledge that today might be associated with the concept of self-sufficiency. In the Hawaiian language, *lawa* also means sufficient in the sense of capability, sufficient in skill and knowledge to be able to competently perform a task. In this case, he seems to have implied a bit of both. The Maohi, like his grandparents, could provide for themselves because they were sufficiently skilled in subsistence-plus agriculture to do so, something many Kānaka Maoli of Baker's time lacked. At the same time, their willingness to recognize the point of sufficiency, lawa, as an upper limit to desire, allowed them to minimize the economic and cultural dangers many Hawaiians had experienced in the decades since then, namely the loss of land, food sovereignty, and economic independence.

Poro'i's words forced Baker to reevaluate, if not completely internalize, Kanaka critiques of capitalism he, as a successful capitalist, normally pushed aside. As seen in his recounting of his grandmother's prayer and his positive memories of his grandparent's lifestyle, Baker was quite aware of Kanaka and Christian critiques of greed similar to those made by Poro'i. As an entrepreneur, landlord, and well-heeled world traveler, however, he seems to have fallen into the habit of dismissing such critiques as unsuited for the modern world. His tongue-in-cheek description of himself and Tu Wake as *kulipa'a*, for instance, signaled an awareness of such Hawaiian critiques of greed, but it also signaled that Baker's deafness typically extended to the threat such capitalist thinking posed to the Oceanic value systems he held so dear.

Baker's growing sense of Hawaiian culture as part of a shared Oceanic culture opened the way for him to view these anticapitalist critiques as part of a larger Oceanic value system, one harder for him to shunt aside

[47] "Col. Baker's Grand Time in the South Seas," *Hawaiian Gazette*, January 31, 1908; Baker, "Mai Ka Aina Mamao Mai," *Ke Aloha Aina*, August 24, 1907; Baker, "Mai Ka Aina Mamao Mai," *Ke Aloha Aina*, August 31, 1907.

than an isolated Hawaiian system. Presented in this way, these critiques of the deviance and danger of greed even forced Baker, however briefly, to reconsider his own relationship with economic wealth. Surrounded by Maohi in the land of his grandfather, Baker could see for himself that such value systems remained feasible, indeed they were preferable for the pursuit of a well-maintained and considerably more independent lifestyle such as that enjoyed by the people of Taravao.

Baker's time with Poro'i and the Maohi of Taravao certainly left a deep impression on him. In addition to his account of it in *Ke Aloha* Aina, it was one of only a handful of events Baker discussed in his English-language interview with the *Hawaiian Gazette*, where he purposefully presented Poro'i's discourse of lawa as superior to his own promotion of akenui. He also repeated the story of his grandmother's prayer for the Māori newspaper *Te Pipiwhorua*.[48] Touched as he was by the incident and by the memory of his grandmother's words, too much of Baker's identity and sense of self incorporated the values and ways of capitalism for him to abandon the pursuit of the dollar. The lawa living of his grand-parents and the people of Taravao ran directly counter to Baker's own visions about how the lāhui Hawai'i and by extension the other peoples of the Pacific might "make the best of the situation," namely through an embrace of small-scale agricultural capitalism. Lawa was important, but under imperial rule Natives needed wealth if they were to retain any power at all.

The incident did seem to have an impact, albeit a short-term one, on the sartorially inclined Baker's views of the importance of elite Western fashion. Soon after the discussion with Poro'i, the fashion conscious Baker uncharacteristically described the simple clothing of the local Maohi as follows, "[T]he men wear white clothes, white coat, no shirt, and an undershirt ... The women pretty clothes but no shoes. These islands are pleasant and calm. We [Hawaiians] really are slaves and servants to the dollar of the Haole and the toil of work."[49]

In Tonga several months later, Baker had fallen back into his comfort-able consumerist mind-set, noting critically that the women lacked hats. He commented on their failure to desire Western fashion and material culture, only to be rebutted by a Tongan woman whose rhetoric closely

---

[48] "Col. Baker's Grand Time in the South Seas," *Hawaiian Gazette*, January 31, 1908. "He Manuhiri No Hawaii," *Te Pipiwharauroa*, interview with John T. Baker, trans. Paul Meredith, September 1907.

[49] Baker, "Mai Ka Aina Mamao Mai," *Ke Aloha Aina*, August 31, 1907.

matched Poro'i's. God had already given each Tongan woman a head of hair to guard their heads from the sun, she explained, so "it is a waste of time to chase after [the fashion of] some Haole woman." The woman's appeal to a sense of lawa appealed to Baker, forcing him to reconsider the virtues of Tongan hatless-ness.[50]

Despite the incident at Taravao and his clear sympathy with Poro'i's perspective at that moment, Baker seemed either unwilling or unable to fully grapple with how these capitalist values he incorporated in his own life and promoted at nearly every turn threatened the pan-Oceanic cultural traits that Baker embraced and celebrated throughout his journey. Such traits and the associated values focused not on individuals, but rather on the connections and ties between individuals. Baker portrayed the exchange of dance and music he participated in and the hospitality and the generosity he received as collective expressions of identity among Oceanic peoples. Each of these relied in one way or another on sharing as a means of developing and maintaining connections between individuals, typically at a direct cost to the individual in terms of wealth, time, and energy. An intense focus on the wealth and desires of the individual, plugging the holes in one's pocket, and relentless labor in the pursuit of the dollar, might detract from the willingness to display such generosity and the cultural resources needed to participate in hula, haka, or the musical exchanges he enjoyed so thoroughly throughout his journey. Furthermore, as Poro'i pointed out, it threatened the land, the very basis of the maka'aināna and for living a lawa lifestyle.

Baker's journey and writings allowed him to promote and strengthen both his vision of a collective-focused Hawaiian cultural future and an individual-focused Hawaiian economic future. Yet his writings also display, with just as much clarity, the potential for and even the inevitability of conflict between these two visions of the Hawaiian/Oceanic future. While Baker attempted to portray himself as a model for the proper values of an Oceanic entrepreneurial yeoman, his reputation as a "stingy alii," his admitted kulipa'a, and his constant akenui also provide clear lessons on the dangers of this model. In some ways Baker balanced these urges, partly through an outgoing personality and partly through the cultural expectations of hospitality and sociability. While remembered as a stingy ali'i, he was also remembered as an excellent host, and as seen throughout his journey and elsewhere in his life Baker was always willing to share his thoughts, time, music, and aloha – but not his wealth.

---

[50] Baker, "Mai Ka Aina Mamao Mai," *Ke Aloha Aina*, November 16, 1907.

Admittedly, this conflict between a collective-oriented Oceanic culture and an individual-oriented imperial/Western capitalist perspective is hardly a new concept, indeed it is well-worn enough to have moved beyond familiar and into the realm of a lazy anthropological cliché.[51] Yet in Baker's writings, the conflict between these two value systems remains not just relevant, but essential to understanding the costs for Oceanic peoples trying to "make the best of the situation."

LAWA AND THE CRITIQUE OF EMPIRE

Despite the clear impact his time at Taravao had on Baker, he remained steadfast in his embrace of capitalist values and his vision of agricultural entrepreneurship. Considering how Baker understood his own economic success as an extension of his embrace of capitalist values, even Baker's momentary questioning of them is surprising enough. The conversation with Poroʻi, however, also provided Baker with some of the impetus and perspective to develop a broader critique of the various empires then occupying and colonizing Oceania as well as the logics driving and rationalizing those actions.

Even at Taravao Baker had quickly recognized that Poroʻi's championing of lawa over akenui raised possibilities that extended beyond economics. After recounting his grandmother's critique of greed, Baker launched into a closely related critique of empire, or at least of imperial desires and actors. The problem in Hawaiʻi, he told his new Taravao friends and his Hawaiian readers, was that the Kānaka had been led astray by their teachers, the missionaries, who then abused Kanaka trust for their own profit. They asked the chiefs for lands and then hoarded the wealth they received from those lands. They told the Kānaka to stop caring for their weapons of war, then snatched the islands by arms after the Kānaka who knew the ways of war had all passed away.[52]

Baker focused on the reasoning and values that motivated these imperial actors in Hawaiʻi, noting, "How strange they are! They do evil and we watch. The things they did have been done with hatred. We have thought about it and these actions have a source, and in our thinking and seeing, [it is] an evil source. We have no desire to have such a source, and we think they are like the fire." Though he did not state directly what

[51] Cases can certainly be made for individualistic values within Polynesian culture and collective values among the most capitalistic of Western empires.

[52] Baker, "Mai Ka Aina Mamao Mai," *Ke Aloha Aina*, August 31, 1907.

this evil source is, akenui after the dollar seems to be a fair assumption considering their earlier conversation. Even if that was not the case, however, Baker made it clear that he felt this source to be an essential cultural difference that separated the lāhui Hawaiʻi from the Haole, a difference rooted in opposing understandings of wealth. "Many are the Haole," he claimed, "that come to us when destitute, cared for by Kanaka. Eat together, sleep together, and after these Haole get rich, these Haole are never seen again." This lack of gratitude and the inability to return generosity with generosity was a familiar Kanaka complaint, one that many Kānaka saw as a fundamental ethical or moral flaw common among the Haole.[53]

Despite this lack of gratitude, however, the lāhui persevered, refusing to turn their backs on generosity as a cornerstone of their identity. Thus they also refused to turn their backs on the Haole who continued to arrive, expecting the Kānaka of the present to care for them just as the Kānaka of the past had cared for the ones who had come before. "Auwe," Baker sighed, "that is how we are."[54] After establishing this difference between the generosity of the lāhui Hawaiʻi and the lack of reciprocity on the part of various colonial actors in Hawaiʻi, Baker then sought to highlight the ties between the lāhui Hawaiʻi and the lāhui Tahiti. "You are truly good," he said to them, "and thus also are we [Hawaiians], thus we [Tahitians and Hawaiians] are one people, in our talking, in the way of eating, the living, the actions, all the things I have seen in the style of hosting, there is no separation between us; our [Hawaiian] way is thus, a heart like yours, full of love." The conversation that had begun with Baker's somewhat myopic promotion of akenui had now transitioned to a broad critique of the mindless and ungrateful akenui of imperial actors, positioning them as a dangerous deviation from Oceanic norms of hospitality and sharing.[55]

Life under empire, however, threatened both the Kānaka and pan-Oceanic culture Baker envisioned. As seen with Baker, the Lāhui Hawaiʻi's attempts to "make the best" of an undesirable situation put them at risk of intentionally or unintentionally accepting and furthering the logics and values of empire. By creating projects and institutions that limit opportunities for success, power, and even survival to those who assimilate imperial logics and values, colonialism can often turn

---

53 Ibid.
54 Ibid.
55 Ibid.

a population of unwilling subjects into proponents of empire within the space of a few generations. In following such a path, the territorial administration of Hawai'i was hardly unique, but they were quite proficient at it.

Even John Baker, antiannexation leader, aloha 'āina, and die-hard supporter of the Kalākaua family, supported and reinforced the capitalist ethics at the heart of American empire in part because the American occupation had supported his success as a capitalist. His embrace of capitalist values certainly predates the American occupation of Hawai'i, indeed his keen economic drive had been a significant part of his own kingdom-era success. The overthrow and the subsequent American occupation, however, encouraged him to embrace such values even tighter, as they were now the only perceivable path forward under the new system. If the American empire had a heart, it would certainly be warmed by the sight of a Hawaiian royalist and patriot traveling through Oceania and promoting the economic values that had helped fuel the growth of the empire.

This focus on making the best of life under empire leaves relatively little room for resisting empire, or even critiquing it beyond specific actors or projects. While John Cummins and many other Hawaiians may have been displeased with annexation, the hundreds of pages of testimony and evidence they presented before the US House investigation in 1902 typically addressed the specifics of the American administration of Hawai'i rather than the American occupation of Hawai'i. Many of them, like Cummins, John E. Bush, and Robert Wilcox, had fought annexation and no doubt still desired a return to independence. Yet even the testimony of two-time armed insurrectionist Wilcox and his fellows in the Home Rule Party placed the majority of their weight behind efforts to shape the imperial relationship into one more favorable to the lāhui than to ending the American occupation. The unlikelihood of such an event within their lifetimes, combined with the immediate need to survive and thrive as individuals and as a lāhui, meant that more immediate matters took precedence in their testimony.[56]

Baker's travels, however, provided him with both broader exposure to the workings of empire and an increased distance from the Hawaiian

[56] CPIPR, *Hawaiian Investigation: Pt 3, Exhibits, Memorials, Petitions, and Letters*, 114–115, 168–169, 170–172, 122–123; US Congress, Senate, CPIPR, *Report of United States Senate, Committee on Pacific Islands and Porto Rico on General Conditions in Hawaii* (Washington, D.C.: Government Printing Office, 1902); 13–14, 541–542.

situation, allowing him to develop and voice a systemic, Oceania-centered critique of empire and the values that drove it. Baker witnessed firsthand the reach of empire, visiting not a single part of Oceania still under Native rule. His unique experiences as both an experienced, well-heeled traveler *and* as a Kānaka put him in a position where he frequently interacted with both colonizers and colonized, allowing him to pick out patterns in imperial thinking as well as patterns in Oceanic culture and perspectives. His conversation with Poro'i proved particularly important in the development of this critique, presenting him with akenui as a model for imperial understandings of desire and lawa as a model for the proper limits needed to control desire.

At times, Baker used these concepts to simply rebut specific colonial logics and discourses. In Tonga, for instance, Baker overheard his fellow tourists comment about the supposed laziness of the Tongan people. Baker reported that he was hurt by such talk about a fellow Oceanic people and recognized it as a general and widely used attack on islanders in general. Channeling his experience at Taravao, he turned to his fellow tourists and berated them:

Between all the red-skinned people I have gone among, the Haole always say these are a lazy people, they are similar to us in all the ways of living, we are a loving, welcoming, and friendly people, and we know this lawa and restful living. Yet, for our failure to pursue after your crazy ideas and chase the dollar until we are laid out with this ake after the dollar and no longer think of resting, you call us a lazy people even though you do not meet with a red-skinned man begging for food like the lazy white man, why is that?[57]

Baker's response may seem surprising considering his own exhortations to his fellow Kānaka and fellow Oceanians to work harder and pursue the dollar. While his own promotion of wealth may have unwittingly promoted colonial/capitalist logics, he perceived a difference in intent between himself and his fellow tourists. Where Baker employed this "bootstrap" narrative as a path for Oceanic peoples to thrive under empire, imperial and colonial actors have typically employed accusations of Native laziness as justification for both the expansion of empire and colonial practices meant to strip Native peoples of land, resources, and power.

In his rebuttal, Baker rejected imperial justifications of empire based on Native laziness and lack of desire, turning them on their head and critiquing imperial and capitalist worldviews as deficient in a basic and

[57] Baker, "Mai Ka Aina Mamao Mai," *Ke Aloha Aina*, November 16, 1907.

destructive inability to understand lawa. The imperial/capitalist celebration of akenui was destructive to the individual, leaving those who sought after the dollar mentally and physically consumed by its pursuit. As Baker had seen in his trips to Europe and America, it also encouraged the rot of wealth inequality and poverty within the imperial core. This inability to understand lawa was not just a culturally subjective failure to live up to the norms of Oceanic cultures, it was an objective danger to those within and in contact with imperial societies and cultures.

In Fiji, Baker built even further upon this akenui-versus-lawa critique in a conversation with an Englishman named Humphrey Berkley, extending the argument to address systematic imperial expansion in Oceania. Berkley had obtained an island from the British and fancied himself a student of Oceanic peoples while claiming the superiority of the European and American way of life. Baker again argued that the heart of the issue was not a contrast between white initiative and Native laziness, but rather one between a Hawaiian/Oceanic sense of lawa and imperial akenui. In the Hawaiian way of thinking, he argued:

Here are the limits of eating, to go until you are satisfied, it is enough, finish and rest, and there is a limit to the meal, and there is a limit for all things ... In our way of living one is to become satisfied, then stop and rest. I think we are an enlightened nation in our way of life, to love, to share the things you have, to be pleasant, not greedy. If one sees a little dog with bones and a big dog with a piece of beef, that [large] one is not satisfied, but, it will fetch the bone of the little dog, this is how it looks at all things, there is no love inside of that one. This is how I see the lahui keokeo [White peoples/nations] ... If you and I look at [Hawaii], and at [Fiji], there are no small [nations] like [Fiji] and [Hawai'i] that have been freed [from empire], Hawaii is in America, Tahiti in France, Rarotonga, Fiji, New Zealand, and Tonga and so forth to Britain, Samoa is in Germany, and many others.[58]

He then moved into specific details of colonization that he had witnessed, with a focus on land dispossession under colonial rule. In Fiji he noted that the British had preserved the rule of the chiefs, but had largely taken the land for themselves and then dispersed it as they saw fit. Furthermore, the system of laws put in place was dictated by and enforced by the British, essentially leaving the chiefs with authority but no power, control over land but only so much land and control as the British were willing to allow them. In Aotearoa, he noted that the British did not allow land sales directly from the Māori lands to the settlers, but rather the government acted as an intermediary buying the land and selling it off to the settler population. If one or two of the heirs to a piece of

[58] Baker, "Mai Ka Aina Mamao Mai," *Ke Aloha Aina*, December 14, 1907.

land sold off their rights, the government considered the entire piece sold, resulting in further losses of Native lands.[59]

Following Poro'i's lead, Baker also intertwined Christian rhetoric and Oceanic value systems, arguing that the Lord had set aside the lands in Oceania, "for the Kanaka,[60] and what can break the kuleana [rights and responsibility] of the land that the Lord has given to every lahui, but here come the people of the empire to scoop up the land of the little people." The term *kuleana* denotes a culturally and even spiritually potent mix of right and responsibility, not simple title or access, buttressing material arguments for the importance of retaining control over the land. It also worked as a rhetorically agile critique, casting land dispossession and colonization as morally deviant according to both Christian and Oceanic value systems.[61]

It is hard to say what effect Baker's critique of empire had on Berkley, on Baker's readership, or even on the thinking of Baker. It certainly had little direct effect on European and American empires in the Pacific, some of which continue until the present day. But Baker's critique lends its voice to similar indigenous and nonindigenous critiques of empire and power, critiques that as a whole have led not just to a change in how people view past and present empires, but also altering and, in some cases, dismantling the empires.

Awareness and critiques of the failings of imperial value systems, however, are still no guarantee of immunity from them. When pushed by Berkley on who were the best among the various peoples Baker had visited, Baker found himself slipping, ever so slightly, back into the capitalist and consumerist mind-set. A nationalist above all else, Baker replied that the Lāhui Hawai'i surpassed all others, as they were a loving and enlightened people and no one had to beg in the streets as in Europe and America. At the same time, however, no one went around without a hat.[62]

When John Baker arrived in Tahiti in 1907, he did so as a man who embraced and defined himself through two very different sets of values: those rooted in the Hawaiian culture of the Kalākaua period and

---

[59] Ibid.

[60] His use of the term *Kanaka* here, and elsewhere to denote Natives, is worth some discussion. Baker, like many others in the era, often used the term not just for Kānaka Hawai'i but for Native peoples across Oceania. While at times confusing, it does help illustrate how Baker and others understood Kānaka Maoli and other Oceanic peoples as one people, as Kānaka, as opposed to the foreigners, the Haole or outsiders.

[61] Baker, "Mai Ka Aina Mamao Mai," *Ke Aloha Aina*, December 14, 1907.

[62] Ibid.

those rooted in capitalism and the pursuit of wealth. Envisioning the Hawaiian future as a combination of the two, he promoted a vision of the individual, male, Kanaka yeoman as the backbone of the lāhui, economically comfortable and somewhat independent while also enmeshed in the cultural ties and connections that held the lāhui together. In many ways, Baker's journey allowed him to promote and expand this vision into a broader call for Native-controlled, capitalist, agricultural development across Oceania.

While Baker never abandoned his efforts to drive his fellow Kānaka Hawai'i – and fellow Oceanians – to embrace agricultural entrepreneurship, his travels did force him to at least acknowledge the potential dangers of replacing Oceanic ethics and values with capitalist ones. By expanding Poro'i's description of capitalism as driven by akenui and lacking an understanding of lawa, Baker developed a powerful critique of empire as both inherently destructive and as a failure of outsiders to conform to the norms of indigenous Oceanic societies. Where the various empires and their proponents tended to justify their actions through supposed failures of Natives to embrace imperially defined modernity, Baker pointed to empire as proof of the inability of the empires and imperial actors to understand as basic and fundamental a concept as *lawa*. The resulting imperial world was not proof of their superiority, but rather proof of the destructive and corrupting power of their culture and their uncontained akenui.

When John Cummins told the US House Committee that the Lāhui Hawai'i intended to make the best of the situation at hand, there were many ways that his comment could have been understood. Some, like Baker, might argue that making the best of the situation would come through working within the logics and institutions of American politics and capitalism. Yet in his travels, even Baker found himself constantly drawn toward another understanding of how to make the best of the situation, using the intellectual resources of Oceania and the ties and connections he made in his travel to critique and attack the very logics that drove and sustained empire. In championing the idea of lawa as a key Oceanic value, perhaps Baker was searching for a way to make the best of the situation not just for himself, but for the people of Hawai'i and for the rest of Oceania as well.

Conclusion

The Return to Kahiki

They came from the North. They came aboard a large, voyaging canoe, guided by the swells, the stars, and the winds, just like those ancient voyagers who had arrived in Hawai'i all those many years ago. This time, however, we know where they came from, why they came, and who they were. Huge crowds greeted them at the shore and a *National Geographic* film crew accompanied them into harbor.

The year was 1975 and the ship was the *Hokule'a*, a double-hulled sailing canoe intended as an archeological experiment on instrument-free navigation. Thor Hyerdahl's *Kon Tiki* experiment had reinvigorated debate over whether the people of Oceania were capable of settlement through purposeful back-and-forth voyages across long distances or whether they had simply drifted aimlessly from one point in the Pacific to the next. For anthropologist Ben Finney, *Hokule'a* was an opportunity to prove that the Austronesians and their descendants were indeed capable of such feats. *Hokule'a*'s navigator, Mau Piailug, came from Satawal, an atoll in the Carolines, one of the few islands where instrument-free navigation remained in practice.

For many Kānaka, including those among the crew, the canoe and the voyage had become a vessel of cultural revitalization, already being celebrated as a major milestone in the growing revitalization of the Hawaiian culture. They had left Hawai'i on May 1, the first Oceanic vessel of its type to leave Hawaiian waters in centuries, headed for distant Kahiki/Tahiti. On May 31, the *Hokule'a* landed at Mataiva, a small atoll in the Tuamoto archipelago. A few days later, they arrived in Papeete Harbor in Tahiti, met by massive crowds eager to greet their distant cousins from the north. The voyage was not just a watershed moment for the

Lāhui Hawai'i, but for lāhui across Oceania eager to turn back the tide of a century of imperial assaults on the knowledge and wisdom of their ancestors.[1]

The voyage marked the start of a broader rebirth of Oceanic voyaging. *Hokule'a* and her repeat journeys back and forth between Hawai'i and the South Pacific led to the development of similar voyaging canoes across Oceania. This was particularly true among the Kānaka Māoli's closest cousins, the Maohi of French Polynesia and the Māori of the Cook Islands and New Zealand. By 1995 a fleet of seven canoes from across Eastern Polynesia departed Nuku Hiva, Marquesas, headed for Hawai'i. Across Oceania, from Guam to Sāmoa, Aotearoa to Hawai'i, voyaging societies have developed, many of them tracing their motivation directly back to the *Hokule'a* and their navigational knowledge back to Mau Pialug and his Kanaka Maoli student Nainoa Thompson.[2]

For many present-day Kānaka, the *Hokule'a* and its voyages still retain a special place as some of the most prominent evidence validating the ingenuity and thus the very humanity of their ancestors. Generations of imperial and settler dominance in Hawai'i had continued the work begun by the mission faction so many years before, attacking the worth of Ka Wā 'Ōiwi Wale to maintain power over Kānaka in the present and future. While never completely successful, such attacks had clearly had a disastrous effect not only on 'Ōiwi culture, but also on Kānaka's collective and individual well-being and sense of self-worth. By the 1970s, Kānaka had begun pushing back against these cultural attacks, largely on the artistic front, a movement often referred to as the Hawaiian Renaissance. *Hokule'a* added to this growing movement, providing concrete proof of the bravery, ingenuity, and na'auao of the people of Ka Wā 'Ōiwi Wale, proof that was hard for anyone with access to the evening news to deny. Thor Hyerdahl and his raft be damned, the people of Oceania were voyagers, not driftwood.

While immigration and travel continued to connect Hawai'i to the rest of Oceania during the twentieth century, the *Hokule'a* voyage brought these connections into a much sharper focus. Future voyages by *Hokule'a* and other vessels continued this work, purposefully presenting Hawai'i

---

[1] Sam Low, *Hawaiki Rising: Hōkūle'a, Nainoa Thompson, and the Hawaiian Renaissance* (Honolulu, HI: Island Heritage Press, 2013), 25–30, 53, 100–101.

[2] Low, *Hawaiki Rising*, 329; Ben Finney, "The Sin at Awarua," *The Contemporary Pacific* 11, no. 1 (1999): 6, 11–12.

and the Lāhui Hawai'i as part of a broader Oceanic Lāhui. These connections proved particularly strong for those who participated in the voyages. Future navigator Nainoa Thompson, overcome by the emotion of leaving Tahiti for the return trip to Hawai'i, noted, "We are family. We are descendants of the same ancestors."[3]

One could argue that the *Hokule'a* and her crew restored and recovered some of the mana that had been stripped away by generations of cultural, spiritual, and political repression. The voyage certainly restored a measure of pride and cultural authority to modern Kānaka. Furthermore, the voyage also had a special quality, connecting pride in the 'Ōiwi past with a pride in broader connections to Oceania at large. The mana they gained or tapped into in that voyage maintained a special quality in part because of its associations with the south, with Kahiki. The same can be seen in other modern pan-Oceanic movements and connections, which find mana in relationships with other Oceanic peoples and in their shared connection to the Oceanic past. The period of isolation had failed to erase the association between Kahiki and mana, a century of imperial rule also proved unequal to the task.

Since the 1970s, the sense of a shared ancestry and shared contemporary issues has also led to numerous intellectual and educational exchanges between Hawai'i and other parts of Oceania. The Punana Leo system of Hawaiian-language immersion preschools, for instance, emerged directly out of contact with and the support of Aotearoa's Māori-immersion Kohanga Reo program. The last thirty years have also seen a broad exchange of ideas between artists and cultural practitioners from Hawai'i and those from other parts of Oceania. Formal exchanges such as at the Pacific Festival of Arts are one part of this, but so are the more informal exchanges such as those carried out by John Baker more than a hundred years ago, organically emerging through travel and exposure. Social media and other forms of technology have sped up this process, allowing cultural exchange, and the sharing of news. It has also allowed for the creation of an online Oceanic community of activists and others increasingly invested in the mutual recognition of a shared ancestry and the creation of stronger pan-Oceanic relationships. Finally, the last thirty years have also seen an increase in academic and intellectual exchanges between Kanaka scholars and others from Oceania, based in part on that very same mix of travel, migration, and social media.

[3] Low, *Hawaiki Rising*, 117.

This book is a product of these late-twentieth- and early-twenty-first-century exchanges in two different but interconnected ways. First, the central themes of this book emerged out of my experiences as a graduate student, studying under, working with, and exchanging ideas with other scholars from across Oceania. Those personal ties, mixed with the clear historical ties within Oceania and the stunning lack of historical writing on those ties, provided much of the early impetus for this project. Second, this book is an explicit attempt to provide a historical context for such modern pan-Oceanic ties. If, as in the Kanaka conception of time, we need to look to the past to understand the present and future, then hopefully the history presented in this book will provide a better understanding of where Hawai'i and Oceania stand at the moment and where they might stand in the future.

More specifically, this book has attempted to provide not just some general context that such relationships existed, but more specifically some context for how Kanaka understandings of themselves and their history intersect with how they understand their relationships with other Oceanic peoples. The Kanaka missionaries in the Marquesas and Micronesia, for instance, were eager to distance themselves and the lāhui from the supposed na'aupō of Ka Wā 'Ōiwi Wale. Foreign mission work provided them the opportunity to proclaim both their religious separation from that past and their embrace of Congregationalism. It afforded proof that they had not only received, but had mastered the na'auao of their American missionary mākua. Yet this foreign mission work also placed them in contact with other Oceanic peoples who they saw as mired in the na'aupō, leading many of them to shape relationships with their Oceanic hosts that echoed the discourses of superiority and paternalism that American missionaries continued to heap on the lāhui at home.

In the case of the diplomatic legation to Sāmoa in 1887, the relationships to both the Hawaiian past and to the Samoans were far less cut and dry. The legation was as interested in shaping a relationship with the Samoans rooted in their shared ancestry as they were in touting Hawai'i's superior advancement in foreign na'auao. On an individual level, the tendency to privilege one viewpoint over another seemed to vary between the primary personnel of the legation, Envoy John E. Bush and Secretary Henry Poor. Bush, like many in Kalākaua's inner circle, seemed to have a strong grasp of and respect for Ka Wā 'Ōiwi Wale and privileged the shared ancestry between the peoples of Hawai'i and Sāmoa in both his rhetoric and his interactions with the Samoan people. Poor, however, tended to hold somewhat negative views of Ka Wā 'Ōiwi Wale and correspondingly low views of Samoan society and, in many cases, Samoans.

Finally, Royal Governor John Tamatoa Baker's tour of Oceania not only allowed him to gain a broader perspective on events at home, but it also allowed him to gain a new perspective on Hawai'i and its place in the world. The closing years of the nineteenth century had pulled Hawai'i closer and closer into the American orbit until, finally, in 1900 it became a territory of the US empire. Baker's personality, deep regard for the Hawaiian past, and status as a Kanaka Hawai'i allowed him to meet and befriend Oceanic peoples throughout his journey. "Aohe Wehena Mai Kakou," Baker argued, nothing separates us, portraying Hawai'i not as a small and abnormal spot within the US empire, but as a part of a broader Oceanic people. In addition, the trip and his engagement with other Oceanic peoples allowed him to develop a broader Oceania-based critique of empire, casting the takeover of Hawai'i and other places not as the failures of Oceanic peoples to adapt to modernity but the failure of the empires to manage their all-consuming greed.

Baker's trip and his writings are also useful in showing that the way Kānaka understood and related to both Ka Wā 'Ōiwi Wale and to other islanders often shifted from situation to situation. When dealing with issues of cultural practices and hospitality, Baker was far more likely to privilege shared Oceanic traits as a way of normalizing Kanaka practices disparaged by the Haole. His personal commitment to capitalist ideologies, however, often led him to view those same Oceanic traits as evidence of a shared economic na'aupō, a lack of capitalist ethics and desire needed to survive in the world. When Poro'i of Taravao directly confronted Baker about the antisocial fallout of such capitalist behavior, Baker was admittedly shaken and continued to reflect on the incident even after his return to Hawai'i. At the same time, however, he continued to preach a gospel of capitalist entrepreneurism whenever possible. Similarly, when trying to convince Samoans of the good intentions of the Hawaiian kingdom, Bush relied largely on a discourse of kinship rooted in the past. When trying to convince them to allow the Hawaiian kingdom to lead the confederacy, however, he relied heavily on a rhetoric of superior Hawaiian advancement through foreign na'auao.

Altogether, the missionaries, the legation, and Baker hold numerous possible lessons for modern-day connections between Oceanic peoples, both about the potential opportunities coming from those connections and the potential dangers. There is, for instance, always the danger of replicating imperial discourses that have proven disastrous to Native peoples across Oceania and elsewhere. This seems especially true when pan-Oceanic relationships are made not to claim connections rooted in a shared past but rather to signal that one side or the other has advanced further according to imperially defined benchmarks of civilization.

The missionaries' efforts to separate themselves from their Oceanic hosts, for instance, sometimes led to disastrous consequences such as the massacre on Tabiteauea. In the case of the legation, Henry Poor's racist and derogatory "Sketch of Samoa" shows the downside of the Hawaiian promotion of their superior na'auao, namely the potential for abuse when they actually start to believe in it. Often these negative views of other islanders as insufficiently na'auao stemmed from a blindness to the ways that foreign na'auao privileged certain groups over others. Baker, for instance, was blinded in the same way that many successful capitalists were, insisting that hard work and "plugging the holes in one's pockets" were the paths to success. In doing so, he not only negated the role of others in his own rise to wealth but also effectively justified the dual inequalities of capitalism and empire through his own bootstraps narrative.

In all three cases, the primarily male actors were also blind to the way that the adaption of non-Oceanic, capitalist gender norms had granted them greater individual power over women. They thus promoted, or at least supported, such norms in one way or another, unable to see how doing so not only strengthened the cultural colonialism of the various foreign empires in the Pacific, but subverted the power and potential of Oceanic women as well. The HBCFM missionaries and Baker both openly promoted such gender norms in the service of Congregationalism and capitalism, respectively. In the case of the missionaries, their blindness to the way these norms potentially affected Oceanic women proved particularly consequential, rendering them unable to understand why their wives periodically ran off with other Oceanic men. In the case of the legation, Bush and Poor maintained a system where high-prestige diplomatic work remained strictly male while women were actively used in informal efforts where their work, though important, was rendered largely invisible.

The potential contemporary implications of these lessons can be seen most prominently with regard to Oceanic migration into Hawai'i, particularly from Chuuk, the Marshall Islands, and Pohnpei. Large-scale migration from these regions following the compact of free association between the United States and the Federated States of Micronesia has resulted in significant ethnic tensions in Hawai'i, with "Micronesians" becoming the latest group to take their turn at the bottom of the ethnic hierarchy of

Hawai'i. While most of the discrimination against these groups has come in the form of relatively standard American anti-immigrant discourses, the low economic status of many Kānaka Maoli has created both a sense of competition for scarce resources as well as a need to create distance to demonstrate superiority over the newcomers. Such discourses rarely include any acknowledgment of either a shared history with these other islanders as descendants of the Austronesian voyagers or as subjects of American imperial expansion and dispossession. Nor do they acknowledge that much of what distinguishes these new migrants culturally is their lack of Americanization, thus reinforcing the settler vision of Hawai'i as first and foremost American rather than Oceanic. Were such issues privileged in public discussions of "Micronesian" migration, they might have an ameliorating effect on the tensions and help develop the potential for collective resistance to the same set of imperial economic and political problems facing both groups.

While the histories of Oceanic connections provide some clear warnings regarding the pitfalls of allowing imperial discourses to shape relationships with other islanders, they also provide equally clear examples of the potential benefits of creating such relationships based on a mutual recognition of a shared past and shared contemporary interests. Bush's efforts to portray the confederacy as an alliance between family members, for instance, created a foundation for political and diplomatic resistance against imperial aggression, albeit too late to meet with any large-scale success. On a less ambitious but far more successful level, Baker could tap into the ability of these relationships to radically rethink not only Hawai'i's relationship with the rest of Oceania but also its relationship with America and other empires. In exploring and celebrating pan-Oceanic connections, for instance, Baker was able to push back against efforts to portray the Lāhui Hawai'i and other colonized peoples as deviants responsible for their own colonization through their inability to conform to European/American norms.

Similarly, all three cases illustrate the need for openness to not just connect and share with other islanders, but also to be open to the potential to learn from other islanders rather than seeing them as passive recipients of Hawaiian na'auao. In the cases of both the HBCFM missionaries and the diplomatic legation to Sāmoa, the underlying logic of the project was a belief that teaching other islanders to be more like Kānaka Hawai'i would further the interests and status of the lāhui Hawai'i and of other islanders. However, Baker's eagerness to create and nurture personal relationships with other islanders left him open not just to finding validation of Kanaka values and practices in the values and practices of other islanders, but also in actively learning from and accepting the critiques of other islanders. Poroʻi's oration on lawa and akenui is the clearest example, but even in small things, like enjoying the ea of a Māori meeting house or sharing the Tongan woman's rebuttal of Baker's fashion advice, Baker learned from other islanders and shared what he learned with his readers at home. Not all foreign naʻauao came from Paris, Connecticut, and London, much of it can be learned from Taravao, Rotorua, and Nukuʻalofa.

Further support for these last two points can also be seen in contemporary Hawaiʻi, and indeed in other parts of contemporary Oceania. Many Kānaka have looked to other parts of Oceania as a way of better understanding traditions from Ka Wā ʻŌiwi Wale that had largely been forgotten. Kānaka eagerness to learn from Mau Piailug, for instance, came in large part from a respect for Mau's navigational knowledge and from an understanding that his skills and knowledge originated from the same set of ancestral voyagers that settled in all of Oceania. Other holders of such Oceanic knowledge have also found receptive students among Kānaka Māoli. Now regarded as the most prominent traditional tattoo artist in Hawaiʻi, Keone Nunes learned the Oceanic method of tattooing in large part from Samoan teachers, studying an art there that had nearly disappeared in Hawaiʻi. In an interview with PBS Hawaiʻi's Leslie Wilcox, Nunes explicitly connected his path with that of Nainoa Thompson and Mau Piailug, describing his teacher, Paulo Suluape, as someone explicitly looking to create pan-Polynesian connections through and for tattooing. Hearing about Nunes's desire to learn to tatau in the traditional tapping method, Suluape called him, "He got excited, because his vision was that he wanted to teach someone from each of the island groups in Polynesia. Because it was our right to do, it was our culture. It was who we were, and who we are now."[4]

One could argue that this willingness to learn traditional Hawaiian knowledge from other Oceanic peoples could be problematic in several ways, not the least of which being the term *traditional*. The anthropological "invention of tradition" arguments of the 1990s, for instance, might easily be reignited over such use of outside knowledge to restore culturally significant arts. This would only be an issue, however, if one ignored

[4] Keone Nunes, interview by Leslie Wilcox, *Long Story Short*, PBS Hawaiʻi, February 18, 2014. http://pbshawaii.org/long-story-short-with-leslie-wilcox-keone-nunes/ (accessed January 21, 217).

the millennia-old transmission of ideas and practices across Oceania. Looking at the history of Hawai'i and indeed the entirety of Oceania, such exchanges of ideas and support, and the occasional war or raiding party, are as long-standing a tradition as any in the region. Nineteenth-century Kānaka Hawai'i participated in these exchanges as well, with varying levels of success, but they provide a bridge between modern recognition of pan-Oceanic ties and the period of migration that brought the first people to Hawai'i so many generations ago.

Glossary

- All terms are in Hawaiian unless otherwise specified.
- In the Hawaiian language, singular and plural are usually marked by articles. In some cases, they are also marked by slight differences in tone and spelling, for instance *Kanaka* is singular, *Kānaka* is plural. In such cases, *Kanaka* and *Kānaka* will be listed together as *Kanaka/Kānaka*.

A

'Ahahui: Organization or group.
'Aiga (Samoan): Family.
'Āi kanaka: Cannibalism.
'Āina: Land.
Ake: (1) Liver. (2) Desire, which in Hawaiian thought was associated with the liver.
Akenui: Great desire.
Akua: God or gods.
Ali'i: Chief.
Ali'i nui: High Chief.
Alofa (Samoan): Love or affection, cognate of Aloha/Aroha.
Aloha: Love or affection, cognate of Aroha/Alofa.
Āloha 'āina: Love for the land, often used for patriotism or a patriot.
Ao: Light, often Ke Ao, the light as a space/time/realm.
Ari'i (Tahitian): Chief, cognate of Ali'i.
Aroha (Te Reo Māori): Love or affection, cognate of Aloha/Alofa.
Auwē: Expression of surprise, grief, or disgust.

'**Awa:** Piper methysticum, a plant whose pounded roots can be made into a calming drink. Cognate of Kawa/kava.

D

Daimonio: Demon.

E

Ea: (1) Air. (2) Breath. (3) Independence and sovereignty.

F

Fa'a Sāmoa (Samoan): Commonly used phrase for the Samoan way.
Fono (Samoan): A council.

H

Ha'alele: (1) To flee or leave. (2) To abandon.
Haka (Te Reo Māori): Māori dance style.
Hale Nauā: Kalākaua's secret society designed to continue the work of the Board of Genealogy.
Hānai: Literally to feed, often used to indicate a relationship formed by adoption or partial adoption. A hānai mother, for instance, is a woman other than a child's biological mother who took on the role of the child's mother on either a full-time or part-time basis.
Hana le'ale'a: Pleasure-seeking activities.
Haole: Foreigner, but after 1850 typically used to describe Caucasians.
Hapa Haole: Part-Haole, typically used to refer to someone who descended from both Kānaka Maoli and Haole ancestors.
Hāule: To tumble or fall, often used by Christians to indicate someone who had sinned or otherwise fallen out of Ke Ao.
Hemahema: Awkward or clumsy.
Hewa: Sin or sinfulness.
Hiolo: Similar to haule, to tumble or fall, often used by Christians to indicate someone who had sinned or otherwise fallen out of Ke Ao.
Hoahānau: Cousin, often used by Christians to describe fellow church members.
Hō'ailona: Signs, often used for supernatural or spiritual signs or omens.
Hoaloha: Close friend, beloved companion.

Hoʻi hope: To turn back or return, backsliding, often used by Christians to indicate someone who had sinned or otherwise fallen out of Ke Ao.

Hoʻomana Pope: Catholic religion, often used in a somewhat derogatory sense similar to *Papist*.

Hoʻoponopono: Conflict resolution practice, often focused on mending relationships and ending conflict rather than assigning blame.

Hula: Dance, especially styles of dance rooted in Oceanic practices.

Huli: To flip, often used by Christians to indicate conversion to Christianity.

I

ʻIli ʻulaʻula: Red skinned, often used by Kānaka to denote themselves and other Oceanic peoples.

Iwi (Te Reo Māori and Hawaiian): Bone/bones. Due to the importance of bones among Māori and Kānaka alike, the term often connoted ties to ancestors or the ancestors. Also used in Te Reo Māori to describe broad kin-based collectives, sometimes referred to as tribes.

K

Kahiki: (1) Tahiti. (2) A term used to denote southern homelands. (3) A term used to denote foreign lands, especially other Oceanic lands.

Kahu: Guardian or caregiver for people, gods, places, or even specific items of importance. Later used for ministers.

Kahuna/Kāhuna: Priest or skilled practitioner.

Kalo: Taro.

Kamaʻaina: A resident or someone who is closely familiar with a region.

Kanaka/Kānaka: Person or man, but commonly used to refer to the indigenous people of Hawaiʻi. See also: Kanaka Māoli, Kanaka ʻOiwi, Kanaka Hawaiʻi.

Kanaka Hawaiʻi: Commonly used to refer to the indigenous people of Hawaiʻi.

Kanaka Māoli: Commonly used to refer to the indigenous people of Hawaiʻi.

Kanaka ʻOiwi: Commonly used to refer to the indigenous people of Hawaiʻi.

Kanikau: Mourning chant.

Kapa: (1) Beaten paper cloth. (2) A blanket, regardless of material used.

Kapu: A religious edict or prohibition, the basis for the Kapu system.

Katolika: Catholic.

Kaukau aliʻi: A subclass within the aliʻi, the chiefly class. Lower than the aliʻi nui and often tasked with meeting the needs and fulfilling the wishes of higher chiefs.

Kāula: Seer or prophet.

Ka Wā ʻŌiwi Wale: The time between the settlement of the Hawaiian Islands and sustained European contact, literally the time that was exclusively native.

Keiki: Child.

Kolea: Golden Plover, a migratory bird that winters in Hawaiʻi.

Kolohe: Naughty or mischievous.

Kuleana: Right and responsibility.

Kuli: (1) Deaf. (2) Stingy, one who is deaf to requests for aid.

Kulipaʻa: Firm/stuck deafness. (1) Absolutely deaf. (2) Very stingy.

Kumulipo: One of several surviving epic genealogies, tracing chiefly lineages as well as recounting creation stories.

Kūpuna: Ancestors.

L

Lāhui: People, tribe, or nation. Not to be confused with Aupuni, a state or government.

Lāhui Hawaiʻi: The Hawaiian people.

Lapaʻau: Traditional medical practices, often focused on a mix of physical and metaphysical elements.

Lapuwale: Vain or worthless.

Lawa: Sufficient.

Leʻaleʻa: Pleasant or enjoyable.

Loʻi kalo: Taro patch.

Loko iʻa: Fish pond.

Luahine: Elderly woman.

Lūʻau: A Hawaiian-style feast or celebration centered around food. Named after the lūʻau, or leaf, of the taro plant that was often served in various ways.

M

Ma hope: After, also used for "in the future."

Maʻi: (1) Sickness. (2) Genitals.

Makaʻāinana: A commoner, literally one who cares for the land.

Makua/Mākua: Parent or elder relative. Cognate of matua.

Mālamalama: Light.

Mālō (Samoan): Victorious side in a conflict.

Ma mua: Before, also used for "in the past."

Mana: Spiritual power or authority.

Marae(Te Reo Māori): Ritual community space at the center of village life.

Matai (Sāmoa): Chiefly title.

Matua (Samoan): Parent or elder relative. Cognate of makua.

Maui nō ka 'oi: Maui is indeed the best, a popular saying among the people of Maui.

Mele: Song.

Moekolohe: Sex outside the boundaries of marriage, literally mischievous sleeping.

Mō'ī: Ruling monarch.

Mo'olelo: Narrative, including fiction, history, and the gray area in between.

N

Na'auao: Enlightenment. In many cases, the connotation is enlightenment through foreign knowledge.

Na'aupō: Ignorance.

Niniu: Dizzy.

O

'Ohana: Family.

Oli: Chant.

'Ōpae 'oeha'a: A form of shellfish in Hawai'i.

P

Pa'a: Firm, steadfast.

Pahu: Drum or box.

Pākeha (Te Reo Māori): Caucasian or white.

Papa (Samoan): Term for any individual title coming from the class of high titles in Sāmoa based on region rather than family: Tui A'ana, Tui Atua, Gatoa'itele, and Tamasoali'i.

Papakū'auhau: Kalākaua's Board of Genealogy.

Pau: Finished, complete, ended.

Piko: The bellybutton, metaphorically the tie to one's ancestors.

Pilialoha: Close friend or friendship.

Piupiu: Māori skirt.

Pō: Darkness, often used as Ka Pō, *the* darkness, as a space/time/realm.

Poi (Hawaiian): A Hawaiian staple dish made of mashed taro corns.

Poi (Te Reo Māori): A type of dance equipment used in haka consisting of pairs of balls on strings.
Pono: Proper or correct.
Pōuli: Deep darkness.
Pounamu *(Te Reo Māori):* New Zealand jade or items made from it.
Pupule: Craziness or insanity.

S

Siapo *(Samoan):* Traditional barkcloth material or tapa, see also *kapa*.

T

Tafa'ifā *(Samoan):* Term used to collectively describe the class of high titles in Sāmoa based on region rather than family: Tui A'ana, Tui Atua, Gatoa'itele, and Tamasoali'i.
Tama'āiga *(Samoan):* Highest level of family-based titles.

U

'Uala: Sweet potato.
'Umeke: Bowl or "calabash," either made of carved wood or a calabash gourd.
'Unihipili: Mourning process that involves talking to and calling upon the dead.
Uwē: Crying or wailing.

W

Wahine/Wāhine: Woman.
Wahi pana: Culturally prominent or famous location.

Bibliography

SPECIAL COLLECTIONS AND ARCHIVES

American Board of Commissioners for Foreign Missions Archives. Houghton Library, Harvard University. Cambridge, MA.

Cabinet Council Minutes. Hawai'i State Archives. Honolulu, HI.

Foreign Office and Executive Collection. Hawai'i State Archives. Honolulu, HI.

Fornander Davis Collection. The Bishop Museum Library and Archives. Honolulu, HI.

The George Robert Carter Collection. Hawai'i State Archives. Honolulu, HI.

Hale Naua Collection. Hawai'i State Archives. Honolulu, HI.

Hawaiian Evangelical Association Archives. Hawaiian Mission Houses Historic Site and Archives, Collections of the Hawaiian Mission Children's Society. Honolulu, HI.

Irwin Papers. I'olani Palace Archive. Honolulu, HI.

Journal of the Legislative Assembly. Hawai'i State Archives. Honolulu, HI.

Journal of the Samoan Embassy. The Bishop Museum Library and Archives. Honolulu, HI.

Kalakaua Scrapbooks. The Bishop Museum Library and Archives. Honolulu, HI.

Kalanianaole Collection. Hawai'i State Archives. Honolulu, HI.

Letters of Henry Augustus Peirce Carter. Hawai'i State Archives. Honolulu, HI.

Letters and Papers of Alexander and Baldwin Families. Hawaiian Mission Houses Historic Site and Archives. Honolulu, HI.

Log of the Kaimiloa. Hawai'i State Archives. Honolulu, HI.

Marquesas Mission Archive. Hawaiian Mission Houses Historic Site and Archives, Collections of the Hawaiian Mission Children's Society. Honolulu, HI.

Micronesian Mission Archive. Hawaiian Mission Houses Historic Site and Archives, Collections of the Hawaiian Mission Children's Society. Honolulu, HI.

Monarchy Collection. The Bishop Museum Library and Archives. Honolulu, HI.

Morning Star Collection. The Bishop Museum Library and Archives. Honolulu, HI.

Photographs Collection. The Bishop Museum Library and Archives. Honolulu, HI.
Photographs Collection. Hawai'i State Archives. Honolulu, HI.
Privy Council Minutes. Hawai'i State Archives. Honolulu, HI.
Reports of the Foreign Minister. Hawai'i State Archives. Honolulu, HI.
Reverend James Kekela Correspondence and Articles 1852–1902. Awaiaulu: Hawaiian Literature Project. Awaiaulu.org.
Sandwich Islands Mission Collection. Hawaiian Mission Houses Historic Site and Archives. Honolulu, HI.

NEWSPAPERS, PERIODICALS, AND ANNUALS

Elele Poakolu, Honolulu, HI, 1880–1881
Hawaiian Gazette/Kukala Pili Aupuni, Honolulu, 1865–1913
Hoku Loa, Honolulu, HI, 1856–1888
Improvement Era, United States, 1897–1970
Ka Hae Hawai'i, Honolulu, HI, 1856–1861
Ka Hoaloha/The Friend, Honolulu, HI, 1845–1954
Ka Hoku o ka Pakipika/Star of the Pacific, Honolulu, HI, 1861–1863
Ka Holomua/The Progressive, Honolulu, HI, 1913–1919
Ka Lama Hawaii, Lahainaluna, Maui, HI, 1834–1841
Ka Nupepa Elele, Honolulu, HI, 1885–1892
Ke Aloha Aina, Honolulu, HI, 1895–1920
Ke Au Okoa, Honolulu, HI, 1865–1873
Ko Hawai'i Pae Aina, Honolulu, HI, 1878–1891
Lahui Hawai'i, Honolulu, HI, 1899–1905
Leo O Ka Lahui, Honolulu, HI, 1889–1896
The Missionary Herald, Boston, 1821–1934
Nupepa Kuokoa, Honolulu, HI, 1861–1927
Ola O Hawai'i, Honolulu, HI, 1916–1919
The Pacific Commercial Advertiser, Honolulu, HI, 1856–1888
Te Pipiwharauroa, Gisborne, New Zealand, 1898–1913

PUBLISHED PRIMARY SOURCES

Aea, Hezekiah. "The History of Ebon, Written by H. Aea, a Hawaiian Missionary Now Living There." *Hawaiian Historical Society Annual Report* 56 (1947): 9–19.
Alexander, James M. *Mission Life in Hawaii; Memoir of Rev. William P. Alexander.* Oakland, CA: Pacific Press Publishing Company, 1888.
Anderson, Rufus. *History of the Sandwich Islands Mission.* Boston: Congregational Publishing Society, 1870.
Armstrong, Richard, and Sheldon Dibble. *Ka Wehewehela, Oia Hoi Ka Hulikanaka.* Oahu, HI: Mea Pai Palapala a na Misionari, 1847.
Baker, Ray Stannard. "Wonderful Hawaii: A World Experimentation Station, Part II, The Land and the Landless." *American Magazine* 73, no. 2 (1911): 201–214.

Bingham, Hiram. *A Residence of Twenty-One Years in the Sandwich Islands.* Canandaigua, NY: H. D. Goodwin, 1855.

Blackman, William Fremont. *The Making of Hawaii; a Study in Social Evolution.* New York: The Macmillan Company, 1899.

Bulu, Joeli. *The Autobiography of a Native Minister in the South Seas.* London: Wesleyan Mission House, 1871.

Coan, Titus. *Life in Hawaii: An Autobiographic Sketch of Mission Life and Labors, 1835–1881.* New York: Anson D. F. Randolph and Company, 1882.

Dibble, Sheldon. *A History of the Sandwich Islands.* Honolulu, HI: T. H., T. G. Thrum, 1909.

A Voice from Abroad, or, Thoughts on Missions, from a Missionary to His Classmates. Lahaina, HI: Press of the Mission Seminary, 1844.

Dole, Sanford B., and Andrew Farrell. *Memoirs of the Hawaiian Revolution.* Honolulu, HI: Advertiser Publishing Company, 1936.

Fifth Legislature of the Territory of Hawaii. *Journal of the Senate of the Fifth Legislature of the Territory of Hawaii: Regular Session, 1909.*

Jewett, Frances Gulick. *Luther Halsey Gulick, Missionary in Hawaii, Micronesia, Japan, and China.* London: E. Stock, 1895.

Kalakaua, David, and Rollin Mallory Daggett. *The Legends and Myths of Hawaii. The Fables and Folk-Lore of a Strange People.* New York: C. L. Webster and Company, 1888.

Kamakau, Samuel Manaiakalani. *Ke Kumu Aupuni: Ka Mo'olelo Hawai'i No Kamehameha Ka Na'i Aupuni a Me Kana Aupuni I Ho'okumu Ai.* Honolulu: Ahahui Olelo Hawai'i, 1996.

Tales and Traditions of the People of Old: Na Mo'olelo O Ka Po'e Kahiko. Honolulu, HI: Bishop Museum Press, 1993.

Ka Po'e Kahiko: The People of Old. Honolulu, HI: Bishop Museum Press, 1992.

Ruling Chiefs of Hawaii. Honolulu, HI: Kamehameha Schools Press, 1992.

Kamehameha V. "Ke Kumukānāwai o ka Makahiki 1864, The Constitution of 1864," trans. by Jason Kāpena Achiu Laekahi 'ōlelo. *Ka Ho'oilina: Journal of Hawaiian Language Sources* 2 (2003): 16–59.

Liholiho, Alexander. *The Journal of Prince Alexander Liholiho; the Voyages Made to the United States, England and France in 1849–1850,* edited by Jacob Adler. Honolulu: University of Hawaii Press, 1967.

Moss, Frederick Joseph. *Through Atolls and Islands in the Great South Sea.* London: S. Low, Marston, Searle, and Rivington, 1889.

Stevenson, Fanny Van de Grift. *The Cruise of the "Janet Nichol" among the South Sea Islands; a Diary.* New York: C. Scribner's Sons, 1914.

Stevenson, Robert Louis. *The Letters of Robert Louis Stevenson,* edited by Ernewst Mehew. New Haven, CT: Yale University Press, 1994.

In the South Seas: Being an Account of Experiences and Observations in the Marquesas, Paumotus and Gilbert Islands in the Course of Two Cruises on the Yacht "Casco" (1888) and the Schooner "Equator" (1889). New York: C. Scribner's Sons, 1896.

Footnote to History: Eight Years of Trouble in Samoa. New York: Cassell, 1892.

Ta'unga, R. G. Crocombe, and Marjorie Tuainekore Crocombe. *The Works of Ta'unga; Records of a Polynesian Traveler in the South Seas, 1833–1896.*

Pacific History Series, no. 2. Canberra: Australian National University Press, 1968.

Thurston, Lorrin A., and Andrew Farrell. *Memoirs of the Hawaiian Revolution.* Honolulu, HI: Advertiser Publishing Co.., 1936.

SECONDARY

Aikau, Hokulani. *A Chosen People, a Promised Land: Mormonism and Race in Hawaiʻi.* Minneapolis: University of Minnesota Press, 2012.

Alexander, Mary Charlotte. *Dr. Baldwin of Lahaina.* Berkeley, CA: Stanford University Press, 1953.

Andrew, John A. *From Revivals to Removal: Jeremiah Evarts, the Cherokee Nation, and the Search for the Soul of America.* Athens, GA: University of Georgia Press, 1992.

———. *Rebuilding the Christian Commonwealth: New England Congregationalists and Foreign Missions, 1800–1830.* Lexington: University Press of Kentucky, 1976.

Armstrong, William. *Around the World with a King.* New York: Frederick A. Stokes, 1904.

Ballantyne, Tony. *Orientalism and Race: Aryanism in the British Empire.* New York: Palgrave, 2002.

Ballara, Angela. *Iwi: The Dynamics of Maori Tribal Organization from. C. 1769 to C. 1945.* Wellington, NZ: Victoria University Press, 1998.

Barman, Jean, and Bruce McIntyre Watson. *Leaving Paradise: Indigenous Hawaiians in the Pacific Northwest, 1787–1898.* Honolulu: University of Hawaiʻi Press, 2006.

Barrere, Dorothy, and Marshall Sahlins. "Tahitians in the Early History of Hawaii: The Journal of Taketa." *Hawaiian Journal of History* 13 (1979): 19–35.

Bausch, Christa. "*Po* and *Ao*, Analysis of an Ideological Conflict in Polynesia." *Journal de la Société des Océanistes* 34, no. 61 (1976): 169–185.

Beamer, Kamana. *No Mākou ka Mana: Liberating the Nation.* Honolulu, HI: Kamehameha Publishing, 2014.

Benham, Maenette Kapeʻahiokalani Padeken. "The Voice 'less' Hawaiian: An Analysis of Educational Policymaking, 1820–1960." *Hawaiian Journal of History* 32 (1998): 121–140.

Bieber, Patricia. "Some Observations on the Hawaiians of the Micronesian Mission." Unpublished paper, University of Hawaiʻi, 1974.

Blouin, Francis X., and William G. Rosenberg. *Archives, Documentation, and Institutions of Social Memory: Essays from the Sawyer Seminar.* Ann Arbor: University of Michigan Press, 2006.

Boutilier, James A., Daniel T. Hughes, and Sharon W. Tiffany, eds. *Mission, Church, and Sect in Oceania.* Ann Arbor: University of Michigan Press, 1978.

Brooks, Jean Ingram. *International Rivalry in the Pacific Islands, 1800–1875.* Berkeley: University of California Press, 1941.

Brown, Marie Alohalani. *Facing the Spears of Change*. Honolulu: University of Hawai'i Press, 2016.

Burton, Antoinette M. *Archive Stories: Facts, Fictions, and the Writing of History*. Durham, NC: Duke University Press, 2005.

Camacho, Keith. *Cultures of Commemoration: The Politics of War, Memory, and History in the Mariana Islands*. Honolulu: University of Hawai'i Press, 2011.

Campbell, I. C. *Worlds Apart: A History of the Pacific Islands*. Christchurch, NZ: Canterbury University Press, 2003.

Island Kingdom: Tonga Ancient and Modern. 2nd ed. Christchurch, NZ: Canterbury University Press, 2001.

"Imperialism, Dynasticism, and Conversion: Tongan Designs on Uvea (Wallis Island, 1835–52)." *The Journal of the Polynesian Society* 92, no. 2 (1983): 155–167.

Chang, David. *The World and All the Things upon It: Native Hawaiian Geographies of Exploration*. Minneapolis: University of Minnesota Press, 2016.

Chapin, Helen Geracimos. *Shaping History: The Role of Newspapers in Hawai'i*. Honolulu: University of Hawai'i Press, 1996.

Chappell, David A. *Double Ghosts: Oceanian Voyagers on Euroamerican Ships*. Armonk, NY: M. E. Sharpe, 1997.

Crocombe, Marjorie Tuainekore. *If I Live: The Life of Ta'unga*. Suva, Fiji: South Pacific Social Sciences Association, 1976.

Ruatoka: A Polynesian in New Guinea History. Sydney: Pacific Publications, 1972.

Crocombe, R. G., and Marjorie Crocombe, eds. *Polynesian Missions in Melanesia: From Samoa, Cook Islands, and Tonga to Papua New Guinea and New Caledonia*. Suva, Fiji: Institute of Pacific Studies, University of the South Pacific, 1982.

Crook, William Pascoe. *An Account of the Marquesas Islands 1797–1799*, edited by Greg Dening et al. Tahiti: Haere Po Editions, 2007.

Curtis, Carolyn. *Builders of Hawaii*. Honolulu, HI: Kamehameha Schools Press, 1966.

Davidson, James W. "Problems of Pacific History." *Journal of Pacific History* 1 (1966): 5–21.

Davis, Eleanor H. *Abraham Fornander: A Biography*. Honolulu: University Press of Hawai'i, 1978.

Daws, Gavan. *A Dream of Islands: Voyages of Self-Discovery in the South Seas: John Williams, Herman Melville, Walter Murray Gibson, Robert Louis Stevenson, Paul Gauguin*. New York: Norton, 1980.

Notes to a Dream of Islands: Voyages of Self-Discovery in the South Seas. New York: W. W. Norton, 1980.

Shoal of Time: A History of the Hawaiian Islands. New York: MacMillan, 1968.

"Writing Local History in Hawaii – A Personal Note." *Hawaii Historical Review* 2, no. 10 (1968): 417–418.

Day, A. Grove. *History Makers of Hawaii: A Biographical Dictionary*. Honolulu, HI: Mutual Publishing of Honolulu, 1984.

Dening, Greg. *Beach Crossings: Voyaging across Times, Cultures, and Self*. Philadelphia: University of Pennsylvania Press, 2004.

The Death of William Gooch: A History's Anthropology. Honolulu: University of Hawai'i Press, 1995.

Mr. Bligh's Bad Language: Passion, Power, and Theatre on the Bounty. Cambridge: Cambridge University Press, 1992.

Islands and Beaches: Discourse on a Silent Land: Marquesas, 1774–1880. Carlton: Melbourne University Press, 1980.

Desha, Stephen. *Kamehameha and His Warrior Kekūhaupi'o.* Honolulu, HI: Kamehameha Press, 2000.

Diamond, Milton. "Sexual Behavior in Pre Contact Hawai'i: A Sexological Ethnography." *Revista Española del Pacífico* 16 (2004): 37–58.

Diaz, Vicente. *Repositioning the Missionary: Rewriting the Histories of Colonialism, Native Catholicism, and Indigeneity in Guam.* Honolulu: University of Hawai'i Press, 2010.

"Moving Islands: Towards an Indigenous Tectonics of Historiography in Guam." Unpublished paper, University of Michigan, 2005.

"'Fight Boys, Til the Last': Islandstyle Football and the Remasculinization of Indigeneity in the Militarized American Pacific Islands." In *Pacific Diasporas*, edited by Paul R. Spickard, 169–194. Honolulu: University of Hawai'i Press, 2002.

"Pious Sites: Chamorro Culture at the Crossroads of Spanish Catholicism and American Liberalism." In *Cultures of United States Imperialism*, edited by Amy Kaplan, 312–339. Durham, NC: Duke University Press, 1992.

Diaz, Vincente, and J. Kehaulani Kauanui. "Native Pacific Cultural Studies on the Edge." *Contemporary Pacific* 13, no. 2 (2001): 315–342.

Dirks, Nicholas B. *Castes of Mind: Colonialism and the Making of Modern India.* Princeton, NJ: Princeton University Press, 2001.

Dow, Derek A. "'Pruned of Its Dangers': The Tohunga Suppression Act of 1907." *Health and History* 3 (2001): 41–64.

Dowd, Gregory Evans. *A Spirited Resistance: The North American Indian Struggle for Unity, 1745–1815.* Baltimore: Johns Hopkins University Press, 1992.

Dwight, Timothy. *The Conquest of Canaan: A Poem in Eleven Books.* Hartford, CT: Elisha Babcock, 1785.

Eastman, Frances. *Pioneer Hawaiian Christians: Batimea Lalana [and] Joel Mahoe.* New York: Friendship Press, 1948.

Egan, Shane, and David V. Burley. "Triangular Men on One Very Long Voyage: The Context and Implications of a Hawaiian-Style Petroglyph Site in the Polynesian Kingdom of Tonga." *The Journal of the Polynesian Society* 118, no. 3 (2009): 209–232.

Eley, Geoff, and Ronald Grigor Suny. *Becoming National: A Reader.* New York: Oxford University Press, 1996.

Elbert, Samuel Elbert, and Noelani Mahoe. *Na Mele o Hawai'i Nei: 101 Hawaiian Songs.* Honolulu: University of Hawai'i Press, 1970.

Ferdon, Edwin N. *Early Observations of Marquesan Culture, 1595–1813.* Tucson: University of Arizona Press, 1993.

Finney, Ben. "The Sin at Awarua." *The Contemporary Pacific* 11, no. 1 (1999): 1–33.

Forbes, David W. *Hawaiian National Bibliography, 1780–1900.* Honolulu: University of Hawai'i Press, 1998.

Garrett, John. *Where Nets Were Cast: Christianity in Oceania since World War II*. Suva, Fiji: Institute of Pacific Studies in Association with World Council of Churches, 1997.

Footsteps in the Sea: Christianity in Oceania to World War II. Suva, Fiji: Institute of Pacific Studies and World Council of Churches, 1992.

To Live among the Stars: Christian Origins in Oceania. Geneva, Switzerland: WCC Publications, 1982.

Gibson, Arrell Morgan, and John S. Whitehead. *Yankees in Paradise: The Pacific Basin Frontier*. Albuquerque: University of New Mexico Press, 1993.

Grimshaw, Patricia. *Paths of Duty: American Missionary Wives in Nineteenth-Century Hawaii*. Honolulu: University of Hawai'i Press, 1989.

Gunson, Niel. "The Tonga-Samoa Connection 1777–1845." *The Journal of Pacific History* 25, no. 2 (1990): 176–187.

Messengers of Grace: Evangelical Missionaries in the South Seas 1797–1860. Melbourne: Oxford University Press, 1978.

"Pomare II of Tahiti and Polynesian Imperialism." *The Journal of Pacific History* 4, no. 1 (1969): 65–82.

Greer, Richard A. "The Royal Tourist – Kalākaua's Letters Home from Tokio to London." *The Hawaiian Journal of History* 5 (1971): 75–109.

Gilson, R. P. *Samoa 1830 to 1900: The Politics of a Multi-Cultural Community*. Melbourne: Oxford University Press, 1970.

Gossler, Claus. "The Social and Economic Fall of the Salmon/Brander Clan of Tahiti." *The Journal of Pacific History* 40, no. 2 (2005): 193–212.

Hand, Mary Kawena, and E. S. Craighill. *The Polynesian Family System in Ka'u, Hawai'i*. Honolulu, HI: Mutual Publishing, 1998.

Handy, Willowdean C. *Forever the Land of Men; an Account of a Visit to the Marquesas Islands*. New York: Dodd, 1965.

Hanlon, David L., and Geoffrey M. White, eds. *Voyaging through the Contemporary Pacific*. Lanham, MD: Rowman and Littlefield Publishers, 2000.

Harris, Paul William. *Nothing but Christ: Rufus Anderson and the Ideology of Protestant Foreign Missions*. New York: Oxford University Press, 2000.

Hau'ofa, Epeli. "Our Sea of Islands." *The Contemporary Pacific* 6 (1994): 148–161.

Tales of the Tikongs. Honolulu: University of Hawai'i Press, 1994.

Hau'ofa, Epeli, Eric Waddell, and Vijay Naidu eds., *A New Oceania: Rediscovering Our Sea of Islands*. Suva, Fiji: School of Social and Economic Development, the University of the South Pacific in Association with Beake House, 1993.

Heffer, Jean, and William Donald Wilson. *The United States and the Pacific: History of a Frontier*. Notre Dame, IN: University of Notre Dame Press, 2002.

Hezel, Francis X. *The First Taint of Civilization: A History of the Caroline and Marshall Islands in Pre-Colonial Days, 1521–1885*. Honolulu: Pacific Islands Studies Program University of Hawai'i Press, 1983.

Horn, Jeremy. "Primacy of the Pacific under the Hawaiian Kingdom." MA thesis. University of Hawai'i, 1951.

Howe, K. R. *Where the Waves Fall: A New South Sea Islands History from First Settlement to Colonial Rule*. Sydney: Allen and Unwin, 1984.

"Pacific Islands History in the 1980s: New Directions or Monograph Myopia?," *Pacific Studies* 3 (1979): 81–89.

Howe, K. R., Robert C. Kiste, and Brij V. Lal, eds. *Tides of History: The Pacific Islands in the Twentieth Century.* Honolulu: University of Hawai'i Press, 1994.

Hulme, Peter, and Tim Youngs. *The Cambridge Companion to Travel Writing.* Cambridge: Cambridge University Press, 2002.

Hutchison, William R. *Errand to the World: American Protestant Thought and Foreign Missions.* Chicago: University of Chicago Press, 1987.

Joesting, Edward. *Hawaii: An Uncommon History.* New York: Norton, 1972.

Kalākaua, David. *The Legends and Myths of Hawai'i.* Honolulu, HI: Mutual Publishing, 1990.

Kamakau, Samuel. *Ruling Chiefs of Hawaii.* Honolulu, HI: Kamehameha Schools Press, 1992.

Kame'eleihiwa, Lilikalā. *Native Land Foreign Desires: Pehea Lā E Pono Ai?* Honolulu, HI: Bishop Museum Press, 1992.

Kamehiro, Stacey. *The Arts of Kingship: Hawaiian Art and National Culture of the Kalākaua Era.* Honolulu: University of Hawai'i Press, 2009.

Kauanui, J. Kēhaulani. *Hawaiian Blood: Colonialism and the Politics of Sovereignty and Indigeneity.* Durham, NC: Duke University Press, 2008.

Kennedy, Paul. *The Samoan Tangle: A Study in Anglo-German-American Relations, 1878–1900.* St. Lucia, Queensland: University of Queensland Press, 1974.

Kent, Harold Winfield, and Robert Louis Stevenson. *Dr. Hyde and Mr. Stevenson; the Life of the Rev. Dr. Charles McEwen Hyde, Including a Discussion of the Open Letter of Robert Louis Stevenson.* Rutland, VT: C. E. Tuttle, 1973.

Kiste, Robert C., and Brij V. Lal. *Pacific Places, Pacific Histories: Essays in Honor of Robert C. Kiste.* Honolulu: University of Hawai'i Press, 2004.

Koppel, Tom. *Kanaka: The Untold Story of Hawaiian Pioneers in British Columbia and the Pacific Northwest.* Vancouver, BC: Whitecap Books, 1995.

Kunimoto, Elizabeth Nakaeda. "A Rhetorical Analysis of the Speaking of King Kalakaua, 1874–1891." PhD thesis. University of Hawai'i, 1965.

Kikuchi, William Pila. "A Legend of Kaimiloa Hawaiians in American Samoa." *Hawaiian Historical Society Review* (1964): 268–269.

King, Michael. *Whina: A Biography of Whina Cooper.* Auckland: Hodder and Stoughton, 1983.

Kling, David W. "The New Divinity and the Origins of the American Board of Commissioners for Foreign Missions." In *North American Foreign Missions, 1810–1914: Theology, Theory, and Practice,* edited by Wilbert R. Shenk, 11–38. Grand Rapids, MI: Eerdmans, 2004.

Krauss, Bob. *Johnny Wilson: First Hawaiian Democrat.* Honolulu: University of Hawai'i Press, 1994.

Kuykendall, Ralph S. *The Hawaiian Kingdom, 1874–1893: The Kalakaua Dynasty.* Honolulu: University of Hawai'i Press, 1967.

———. *The Hawaiian Kingdom, 1854–1874: Twenty Critical Years.* Honolulu: University of Hawai'i Press, 1953.

———. *The Hawaiian Kingdom, 1778–1854: Foundation and Transformation.* Honolulu: University of Hawai'i Press, 1938.

Kuykendall, Ralph S., and A. Grove Day. *Hawaii: A History, from Polynesian Kingdom to American Commonwealth.* New York: Prentice-Hall, 1948.

Latukefu, Sione. *Church and State in Tonga; the Wesleyan Methodist Missionaries and Political Development, 1822–1875.* Honolulu: University Press of Hawaii, 1974.

Little, Jeanette. "…And Wife: Mary Kaaialii Kahelemauna Nawaa, Missionary Wife and Missionary." In *The Covenant Makers: Islander Missionaries in the Pacific,* edited by Doug Munro and Andrew Thornley, 210–234. Suva, Fiji: Pacific Theological College and the Institute of Pacific Studies at the University of the South Pacific, 1996.

Loomis, Albertine. *To All People: A History of the Hawaii Conference of the United Church of Christ.* Honolulu: Hawaii Conference of the United Church of Christ, 1970.

Low, Sam. *Hawaiki Rising: Hōkūle'a, Nainoa Thompson, and the Hawaiian Renaissance.* Honolulu, HI: Island Heritage Press, 2013.

Lucas, Paul Nahoa. "E Ola Mau Kakou I Ka 'Olelo Makuahine: Hawaiian Language Policy and the Courts." *Hawaiian Journal of History* 34 (2000): 1–28.

Lutz, Catherine, and Jane Lou Collins. *Reading National Geographic.* Chicago: University of Chicago Press, 1993.

Lydecker, Robert Colfax. *Roster legislatures of Hawaii, 1841–1918: Constitutions of Monarchy and Republic: Speeches of Sovereigns and President.* Honolulu: Hawaiian Gazette Co., 1918.

Mackrell, Brian. *Hariru Wikitoria! An Illustrated History of the Maori Tour of England, 1863.* Auckland: Oxford University Press, 1985.

Madraiwiwi, Joni. "Muse, Mediator, and Mentor." *The Contemporary Pacific* 22, no. 1 (2010): 104–105.

Matsuda, Matt. *Pacific Worlds: A History of Seas, Peoples, and Cultures.* Cambridge: Cambridge University Press, 2012.

Maude, H. E. "The Raiatean Chief Auna and the Conversion of Hawaii," *Journal of Pacific History* 8 (1973): 188–191.

"Two Letters of Robert Louis Stevenson." *Journal of Pacific History* 2 (1967): 183–88.

Maude, H. E., and Maude, H. C. "Tioba and the Tabiteauean Religious Wars," *Journal of the Polynesian Society* 90, no. 3 (1981): 307–336.

McDougall, Walter A. *Let the Sea Make a Noise–: A History of the North Pacific from Magellan to MacArthur.* New York: Basic Books, 1993.

McGregor, Davianna Pomaika'i. "'Āina Ho'opulapula: Hawaiian Homesteading." *Hawaiian Journal of History* 24 (1990): 1–38.

McRae, Jane. "'E Manu, Tena Koe' 'O Bird, Greetings to You': The Oral Tradition in Newspaper Writing." In *Rere Atu, Taku Manu: Discovering History, Language and Politics in the Maori Language Newspapers,* edited by Jenifer Curnow, Ngapare K. Hopa, and Jane McRae, 42–59. Auckland: Auckland University Press, 2002.

Meleisea, Malama. *The Making of Modern Samoa: Traditional Authority and Colonial Administration in the History of Western Samoa.* Suva, Fiji: Institute of Pacific Studies, 1987.

Menton, Linda K. "A Christian and 'Civilized' Education: The Hawaiian Chiefs' Children's School, 1839–50." *History of Education Quarterly* 32, no. 2 (1992): 213–242.

Merry, Sally Engle. *Colonizing Hawai'i: The Cultural Power of Law*. Princeton, NJ: Princeton University Press, 2000.

Mitchell, John, and Hillary Mitchell. *Te Tau Ihu O Te Waka: A History of Maori of Nelson and Marlborough*. Wellington: Huia Publishers, 2004.

Mookini, Esther. *The Hawaiian Newspapers*. Honolulu, HI: Topgallant Publishing Company, 1974.

Morris, Nancy Jane. "Hawaiian Missionaries Abroad, 1852–1909." PhD thesis. University of Hawai'i, 1987.

Moss, Frederick Joseph. *Through Atolls and Islands in the Great South Sea*. London: S. Low, Marston, Searle, and Rivington, 1889.

Munro, Doug, and Andrew Thornley. *The Covenant Makers: Islander Missionaries in the Pacific*. Suva, Fiji: Pacific Theological College and the Institute of Pacific Studies at the University of the South Pacific, 1996.

Nameu, Myles K. "A Case Study: Hawaiian Missionaries in the Marshall Islands." Honolulu: Hawaiian Mission Children's Museum, 1978.

Neuman, Klaus. "Starting from Trash." In *Remembrance of Pacific Pasts: An Invitation to Remake History*, edited by Robert Borofsky, 62–77. Honolulu: University of Hawai'i Press, 2000.

———. "In Order to Win Their Friendship." *Contemporary Pacific* 6, no. 1 (1994): 111–145.

Nogelmeier, Puakea. "Mai Pa'a I Ka Leo: Historical Voices in Hawaiian Primary Materials, Looking Forward and Listening Back." PhD thesis. University of Hawai'i, 2003.

Nunes, Keone. Interview by Leslie Wilcox, *Long Story Short*. PBS Hawai'i, February 18, 2014.

The Office of Hawaiian Affairs. "The Population of the Hawaiian Islands: 1778–1896." Native Hawaiian Data Book Table 1:1, www.oha.org/databook/databook1996_1998/tab1-01.98.html (accessed October 26, 2010).

———. "The Population of the Territory and State of Hawai'i: 1900–1990." Native Hawaiian Data Book, Table 1:2, www.oha.org/databook/databook1996_1998/tab1-02.98.html (accessed October 26, 1010). Second number includes *hapa* and "full-blooded" Hawaiians.

Osorio, Jonathan Kay Kamakawiwo'ole. *Lāhui Dismembered: A History of the Hawaiian Nation to 1887*. Honolulu: University of Hawai'i Press, 2002.

Parsonson, G. S. *The Conversion of Polynesia Hocken*. Lecture. Hocken Library, University of Otago, 1984.

Paterson, Lachy. *Colonial Discourses. Niupepa Maori, 1855–1863*. Dunedin, NZ: University of Otago Press, 2006.

Petersen, Glenn. "Indigenous Island Empires: Yap and Tonga Considered." *The Journal of Pacific History* 35, no. 1 (2000): 6–27.

Petrie, Hazel. *Chiefs of Industry: Māori Tribal Enterprise in Early Colonial New Zealand*. Auckland: Auckland University Press, 2006.

Pratt, Mary Louise. *Imperial Eyes: Travel Writing and Transculturation*. New York: Routledge, 1992.

Pukui, Mary Kawena, and Samuel Elbert. *Hawaiian Dictionary, Revised and Enlarged Edition*. Honolulu: University of Hawai'i Press, 1986.

Pukui, Mary Kawena, E. W. Haertig, and Catherine A. Lee. *Nana I Ke Kuma* (Look to the source). Honolulu, HI: Hui Hānai, 1972.

Ralston, Caroline. *Grass Huts and Warehouses: Pacific Beach Communities of the Nineteenth Century*. Canberra: Australian National University Press, 1977.

Rogers, Richard Lee. "'A Bright and New Constellation': Millennial Narratives and the Origins of American Foreign Missions." In *North American Foreign Missions, 1810–1914: Theology, Theory, and Practice*, edited by Wilbert R. Shenk, 39–60. Grand Rapids, MI: Eerdmans, 2004.

Sabatier, Ernest. *Astride the Equator: An Account of the Gilbert Islands*, trans. by Ursula Nixon. Melbourne: Oxford University Press, 1977.

Sahlins, Marshall David. *How "Natives" Think: About Captain Cook, for Example*. Chicago: University of Chicago Press, 1995.

Islands of History. Chicago: University of Chicago Press, 1985.

Sandeen, Ernest R. *The Roots of Fundamentalism, British and American Millenarianism 1800–1930*. Chicago: University of Chicago Press, 1970.

Schmitt, Robert C. *Demographic Statistics of Hawaii: 1778–1965*. Honolulu: University of Hawai'i Press, 1968.

Schulz, Joy. "Empire of the Young: Missionary Children in Hawai'i and the Birth of U.S. Colonialism in the Pacific, 1820–1898." PhD thesis. University of Nebraska, 2011.

Silva, Noenoe K. *Aloha Betrayed: Native Hawaiian Resistance to American Colonialism*. Durham, NC: Duke University Press, 2004.

"He Kanawai E Hoopau i na Hula Kuolo Hawai'i: The Political Economy of Banning the Hula." *Hawaiian Journal of History* 34 (2000): 29–49.

Somerville, Alice. "Nau Te Rourou, Nau Te Rakau: The Oceanic, Indigenous, Postcolonial and New Zealand Comparative Contexts of Maori Writing in English." PhD thesis. Cornell University, 2006.

Spurr, David. *The Rhetoric of Empire: Colonial Discourse in Journalism, Travel Writing, and Imperial Administration*. Durham, NC: Duke University Press, 1993.

Spurway, John. "Hiki Mo E Faliki: Why Ma'afu Brought His Floor Mats to Fiji in 1847." *The Journal of Pacific History* 37, no. 1 (2002): 5–23.

Stevenson, Robert Louis. *A Footnote to History: Eight Years of Trouble in Samoa*. New York: Charles Scribner's Sons, 1900.

Talu, Alaima. *Kiribati: Aspects of History*. Tarawa, Kiribati: Published jointly by the Institute of Pacific Studies and Extension Services, University of the South Pacific and the Ministry of Education, Training and Culture, Kiribati Government, 1979.

Tamasese, Tuiatua Tupua. "The Riddle in Samoan History: The Relevance of Language, Names, Honorifics, Genealogy, Ritual and Chant to Historical Analysis." *The Journal of Pacific History* 29, no. 1 (1994): 66–79.

Teaiwa, Teresia. "L(O)Osing the Edge." *The Contemporary Pacific* 13, no. 2 (2001): 343–357.

"Militarism, Tourism and the Native: Articulations in Oceania." PhD thesis. University of California, Santa Cruz, 2001.

Thomas, Nicholas. *Islanders: The Pacific in the Age of Empire*. New Haven, CT: Yale University Press, 2012.

In Oceania: Visions, Artifacts, Histories. Durham, NC: Duke University Press, 1997.

Colonialism's Culture: Anthropology, Travel, and Government. Princeton, NJ: Princeton University Press, 1994.

Thorne, Susan. *Congregational Missions and the Making of an Imperial Culture in Nineteenth-Century England*. Stanford, CA: Stanford University Press, 1999.

Topolinski, John Renken Kahaʻi. "Nancy Sumner, Hawaiian Courtlady." *Hawaiian Journal of History* 15 (1981), 50–58.

United States Congress, Senate, Committee on Pacific Islands and Porto Rico. *Hawaiian Investigation: Pt 3, Exhibits, Memorials, Petitions, and Letters*. Washington, DC: Government Printing Office, 1902.

Valeri, Valerio. *Kingship and Sacrifice: Ritual and Society in Ancient Hawaii*, trans. by Paula Wissing. Chicago: University of Chicago Press, 1985.

Van Dyke, Jon M. *Who Owns the Crown Lands of Hawaiʻi?* Honolulu: University of Hawaiʻi Press, 2008.

Wagner-Wright, Sandra. *The Structure of the Missionary Call to the Sandwich Islands, 1790–1830: Sojourners among Strangers*. San Francisco: Mellen Research University Press, 1990.

Wallace, Anthony F. C., and Sheila C. Steen. *The Death and Rebirth of the Seneca*. New York: Knopf, 1970.

Ward, R. Gerard. *American Activities in the Central Pacific, 1790–1870; a History, Geography, and Ethnography Pertaining to American Involvement and Americans in the Pacific Taken from Contemporary Newspapers Etc.* Ridgewood, NJ: Gregg Press, 1966.

Wexler, Laura. *Tender Violence: Domestic Visions in an Age of U.S. Imperialism* Cultural Studies of the United States. Chapel Hill: University of North Carolina Press, 2000.

Young, Kanalu G. Terry. *Rethinking the Native Hawaiian Past*. New York: Garland Pub., 1998.

Youngs, Tim. *Travel Writing in the Nineteenth Century: Filling the Blank Spaces*. London: Anthem Press, 2006.

Zwiep, Mary. *Pilgrim Path: The First Company of Women Missionaries to Hawaii*. Madison: University of Wisconsin Press, 1991.

Index

CPSIA information can be obtained
at www.ICGtesting.com
Printed in the USA
LVHW011229090222
710593LV00004B/373

9 781316 646991